Charles Lamb:

THE EVOLUTION

OF ELIA

Charles Lamb
1819

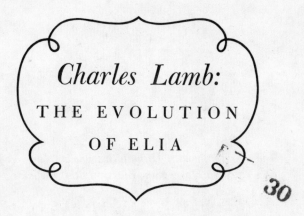

Charles Lamb:
THE EVOLUTION
OF ELIA

30

George L. Barnett

BLOOMINGTON

Indiana University Press

1 9 6 4

Indiana University Humanities Series Number 53
Indiana University, Bloomington, Indiana

EDITOR: Edward D. Seeber
ASSISTANT EDITOR: David H. Dickason
ASSISTANT EDITOR: Hubert C. Heffner

The Indiana University Humanities Series was
founded in 1939 for the publication of occasional
papers and monographs by members of the faculty.

to

M<small>Y</small> M<small>OTHER</small> *and* F<small>ATHER</small>

TABLE OF CONTENTS

ILLUSTRATIONS

Frontispiece: From the water-color drawing by G. F. Joseph (1819)

"Elia": From the original sketch by Daniel Maclise, Victoria and Albert Museum, London

"Dog Days": Portions of MS reproduced with the permission of The Huntington Library, San Marino, California

"Poor Relations": First page of essay reproduced from MS in Victoria and Albert Museum, London

CHRONOLOGY

1775, Feb. 10. Born in London to John and Elizabeth (Field)
Lamb, at No. 2 Crown Office Row, Temple (a law college
where his father was clerk to Samuel Salt); brother, John
("James Elia" in the essays), born 1763; sister, Mary Anne
("Bridget Elia" in the essays), born 1764.

1782–89. Attended Christ's Hospital, the Blue-coat School,
where Coleridge was his schoolfellow, from Oct. 9, 1782 to
Nov. 23, 1789.

1789–91. Probably employed by Joseph Paice, a merchant.

1791–92. Clerk at the South Sea House from Sept. 1, 1791 to
Feb. 8, 1792.

1792, April 5. Began career as clerk in the Accountants' Office
of the East India House.

1794. Living at No. 7 Little Queen St., Holborn, London.

1796, Sept. 22. Mary Lamb, temporarily insane, fatally stabbed
her mother and was placed in a private asylum.

1797. Living with father at No. 45 Chapel St., Pentonville, London. July, visited Coleridge at Nether Stowey, where he
met Wordsworth.

1798. *A Tale of Rosamund Gray* (prose tale) published.
  Blank Verse (in collaboration with Charles Lloyd) published.

1799, April. Lamb's father died, and Charles, assuming responsibility for Mary's safe keeping, brought her to live with him at No. 36 Chapel St., Pentonville, London.

1800, July. Moved to No. 27 Southampton Buildings, Holborn, London.

1801, March. Moved to No. 16 Mitre Court Buildings, Temple, London. Began to contribute to newspapers.

1802. *John Woodvil* (a play) published.

1806, Dec. 10. *Mr. H.* (a farce) failed at Drury Lane Theatre.

1807. *Tales from Shakespear* (for juveniles, in collaboration with Mary) published.

1808. *Adventures of Ulysses* (for children) published. *Specimens of English Dramatic Poets Who Lived About the Time of Shakspeare* published.

1809, March. Moved to No. 34 Southampton Buildings, Holborn, London. May, moved to No. 4 Inner Temple Lane, Temple, London. *Mrs. Leicester's School* (stories for children, in collaboration with Mary) published. *Poetry for Children* (in collaboration with Mary) published.

1811. Contributed essays to Hunt's *Reflector*.

1813. Contributed "Table Talk" paragraphs to Hunt's *Examiner*.

1817, October. Moved to No. 20 Great Russell Street, Covent Garden, London.

1818. *The Works of Charles Lamb. In Two Volumes* published.

1818–20. Contributed to Hunt's *Examiner*.

1820, August, to July, 1825. Contributed essays signed "Elia" to the *London Magazine*.

1821, Oct. 26. John, elder brother, died.

1822. Visited Paris with Mary during summer vacation.

1823. *Elia. Essays which have appeared under that Signature in the London Magazine* published. Adopted Emma Isola, orphan daughter of a Cambridge University official. July, moved to Colebrook Row, Islington, London.

1825, Mar. 29. Retired from the East India House after 33 years of service, on a pension of £450 per annum.

1825–26. Contributed to Hone's *Every-Day Book* and to the

New Monthly Magazine (including a series of "Popular Fallacies").

1827. Contributed to Hone's *Table Book* (including "Extracts from the Garrick Plays"). June, moved to Chase Side, Enfield.

1828. Contributed, until 1834, to the *Spectator,* the *Athenaeum,* and the *Englishman's Magazine. Elia: Second Series* published without authority at Philadelphia.

1830, July. Moved to 34 Southampton Buildings, Holborn, London. November, returned to Enfield. *Album Verses* published.

1833. *The Last Essays of Elia* published.

May, moved to Church St., Edmonton.

July 30, Emma Isola married Edward Moxon (Lamb's publisher).

1834, December 27. Died at age 59, of an infection following a fall while walking. Buried in Edmonton Churchyard.

1847, May 20. Mary Lamb died, aged 82.

Charles Lamb:

THE EVOLUTION

OF ELIA

ΕΛΙΑ
ηλια

Charles Lamb
from the first sketch by Daniel Maclise
for 'FRASER'S MAGAZINE'.

INTRODUCTION

Literary critics readily agree that the familiar essay has suffered a decline in popular favor for some time past, but they
adduce varying reasons for this change in taste. Clifton
Fadiman suggests (*Holiday*, Jan., 1955) that Montaigne's
kind of ego is out of fashion in an era which idolizes the ego
of entertainers such as screen stars as a kind of public util-
ity in preference to the private ego of Montaigne or his
followers. "It is only at the cost of effort" that one may enjoy
the essayist, whereas the enjoyment of public personalities
costs us nothing—intellectually speaking.

David Daiches, editing an essay anthology, characterizes
the familiar essay in the last hundred years as "a thin trickle
indeed when compared with the stream of serious critical
and philosophical discussions in our time" and ventures to
generalize "that ever since the middle of the last century
writers have become increasingly worried, have taken
themselves and their readers ever more seriously, have
more and more lost interest in the light play of ideas . . . ."
He blames too the growth of specialization, with a consequent growth of specialized periodicals addressed to ex-
perts, and attributes the decline of the essay, like that of

conversation, "to the decline of the layman, of the non-specialist inquirer, the intelligent and well-read man of large general curiosity."[1]

Thus, in an age of anxiety, criticism, specialization, and mass-appeal entertainment, the familiar essay finds a limited audience. But before we lament its passing, we should remind ourselves that the name and essays of Montaigne are still known to educated people, after almost four hundred years, although the vogue of the familiar essay, which he originated, has been far from constant during that time. Indeed, while there were some imitators during the two centuries following the publication of his essays, the temper of this period was never conducive to the full flowering of his type of ego; it was not, in fact, until the early nineteenth century—the time of Charles Lamb—that the proper atmosphere obtained. Now again the popularity of this intimate, discursive, and personal type of prose has fallen off, but need this be a permanent eclipse? The evidence indicates otherwise.

Beyond this, to characterize the neglected familiar essay as "a thin trickle" or similarly to indicate its quantitative inferiority implies a rather severely limited definition. The essays of Ernie Pyle had a wide audience when they appeared in the columns of our newspapers during the war years. We read the headlines and feature stories for the facts and the over-all picture, but we read Ernie Pyle for the individual point of view, the intimate glimpse that he invariably gave us of the personal aspects of war that touched the humanist in him—and hence in us. We may choose to call him a columnist and his observations and reflections columns—for academic exercises have attached unpleasant associations to the word *essay*—but he was, in fact, writing the familiar essay. So, too, the work of Bernard De Voto, Christopher Morley, E. B. White, and even

Clifton Fadiman belongs within the category, although we may differentiate it as columns, editorials, articles, or "pieces"—according to its appearance in newspapers, magazines, or as a unified collection in book form. For the familiar essay, like any enduring literary form, is flexible and knows many variations.

We cannot deny the concern of our times with specialization, objective discussion, and socialized recreation. We observe the consequent neglect of generalization, a departure from humanization, and an inability to develop inner resources—above all, a disposition to avoid the effort of reflective thought. But literature transcends public fashion and has its *raison d'être* in its continued nourishment of the individual who possesses the ability to think and the inclination to meditate.

In nonfictional literary writing, the personality of the writer is all-important. Through his written word, we come to know the man, and the more self-revelatory the writing, the more intimate the acquaintance. Our own egoism impels us to look for reflections or contradictions of ourselves in others, and it is this appeal that the essay has always had. "It is myself that I portray," wrote Montaigne, and this pronouncement has served as the keynote of the familiar essayist ever since. In reading the opinions and speculations of an essayist, a reader becomes thoroughly familiar with the writer. This being so, it is clear that the writer must have a strong character if his personality alone is to preserve his essays beyond mere contemporary friendship. Montaigne's personality has met the test; that of Charles Lamb has succeeded for over one hundred years.

Many writers have attempted to delineate the character of Charles Lamb, some with questionable results and others with results that give us the feeling of knowing Lamb better than his own friends did, for the intimate facts of his life were not generally known until after his death. One fact that stands out from the mass of commentary is that the essays *are* Lamb; as one writer expresses it: "Out of his own life the image that governed the essays gradually emerged, and his craftsmanship gave to it an entity that separates it from all the many endeavours of his imitators."[2] It is Lamb's personality as expressed in his essays that has kept them from neglect. That it has done so is testimony to its force and to the interest such a character has for a reader of literature. Speaking of essay-writing in general, an observer makes what seems a particularly applicable statement: "But no kind of writing above mere journalism is more ephemeral. Not only the *Rambler* and the *Idler,* but the *Bee* and the *Citizen of the World,* and even the *Tatler* and the *Spectator,* it is to be feared, now repose undisturbed upon the top shelves; and Hunt's *Indicators* and *Companions* have doubtless joined them there. It is only some remarkable dexterity of style or some unique humor or force of personality that can keep such work from oblivion."[3]

The extent to which Lamb's literary work is still read in our time is evidenced by the tremendous quantity of articles and books which appeared in 1934, the centenary of his death. The authors of most of these were not scholars with critical eyes but ordinary readers whose long familiarity with the essays of Elia led them to express their appreciation in print. Lamb's continued endurance is more graphically illustrated by a quotation from one of the many books deriving from World War II. Robert St. John is describing his experiences as a newspaper correspondent in Patras, Greece, during the German invasion:

We decided that we'd like some dinner too, but the food supply of Patras apparently was reserved for generals and people like that. We couldn't find any anywhere. Then Atherton remem-

bered that once when he was down in Greece before the war he
had stopped in Patras and had met an engineer who lived at
the Cecil Hotel, and so we went to the Cecil. The place had
been badly wrecked by bombs, but we crawled through the
debris and got up to the engineer's quarters.

In some ways going into the engineer's rooms at the Cecil
was just like finding the Monastery of Saint Nicholas on top of
the island of Leukas. As soon as we got inside and shut the door
we were in another world. Outside, most of Patras was in ruins.
There was hardly a building in town with its four walls still
standing. But here in a little room in a bomb-damaged hotel a
man who spoke four or five other languages as fluently as he did
his own was sitting in front of a fireplace listening to soft orches-
tra music on a radio and reading, of all things, one of Lamb's
essays.[4]

Lamb's essays, numbering well over a hundred, are
peculiarly appropriate to all times and all places because
they are devoid of contemporary considerations. They are
as untouched by reference to the momentous political
events shaking Europe in Lamb's day as are the novels of
Jane Austen. Their subject is man and human nature, and
the appeal is to all the senses. Lamb was not a professional
author writing for other authors, but a working man writing for the average reader—of his own day, or today.

This book is concerned with the development of Lamb's
career as a writer and of his essays in particular. What
were the factors in his earlier life which informed and
directed the literary talents of the subsequent Elia? Was
Lamb aware of what his predecessors in the essay had done
and of his position in the tradition? Just what was his place
in that tradition? Was he doing something unique, or was
he adding vitamins to the regular fare by touching old
methods and established features with the spirit of his personality? Some writers have approached these questions,

but more often than not have made only vague generalizations, none the less true for being couched in paragraphs
of praise and admiration, but difficult to reduce to definite
statement. The fact is that in spite of the voluminous bibliography of commentary and criticism on Lamb and his
work, there is much about him that is unknown, doubtful,
and obscure. Much will probably remain so, but the fact
serves as a challenge and an excuse to attempt an explanation of genius. Aside from the discovery of new facts, the
region most deserving of attention in the study of Lamb is
the interpretation of his development as an essayist.

What was the anvil and what the forge that shaped
Lamb into a creative artist whose work was respected by
men of such caliber as Wordsworth and Coleridge? To find
the answer, we must consider his schooling, his vocation,
his friendships, and his reading, all of which influenced his
literary career. Biographical data will necessarily be utilized, but this is not a biography in the sense of a history
of the activities of an individual so much as an analysis and
re-creation of the process of literary creation as exemplified
by the mind of Charles Lamb at work.

In addition to defining Lamb's position in the history of
the essay more clearly than has hitherto been done, this
book explores the development of his essays from their
germinal origins in experience, conversation, and reading—
through their first expressions in talk, letters, and minor
works—to their final form. That the letters of Lamb contain
the germs of many essays has been recognized, but no
writer has gone far beyond the mere statement of this fact
to determine in detail just what part the letters play in
Lamb's development as an essayist and how far the letters
serve as a proving ground for ideas later used in the essays.
A reviewer of the first complete edition of the letters of
Ralph Waldo Emerson commented on their importance to

"investigators of the hidden and devious workings of the creative mind." In this "immense and fascinating territory for exploration," he wrote, "we can follow the long pale rootlets of his thought still farther down into the dark of the Concord years." The letters, he continued, will help make it possible "to trace many of his essays and poems a long way backward toward their inception."[5] It is this same relationship of Lamb's letters to his essays that is here considered. The publication in 1935 of E. V. Lucas' three-volume edition of Lamb's correspondence, containing over one thousand letters,[6] makes it possible to trace many of Lamb's thoughts which were not previously traceable in earlier and incomplete editions.

From this study of the development of the essays through the stages of expression of the thoughts, we are led to the actual composition. Little has been said heretofore about Lamb's writing habits—where and when he wrote and how he worked. This book considers his vocation, his home life, and his friendships for the light they shed on these external matters. From these considerations it is a logical step to follow Lamb in the actual composition of his essays, drawing deductions from the clues he left in his manuscripts: erasures, blots, cancellations, revisions, and alterations. No such extensive examination has ever been made; yet by the use of over twenty extant and representative manuscripts we can read the signs which show us more clearly than anything else Lamb's mind at work. Lastly, an analysis of his prose style indicates the factors influencing its formation; the story of its development and a characterization of its peculiar qualities are necessarily a part of the evolution of Elia.

For the privilege of examining manuscript essays and letters written by Lamb, as well as books from his library, I wish to express my appreciation to the personnel of

Princeton's Firestone Library, now the repository of the Scribner Lamb collection; the Pierpont Morgan Library; the New York Public Library (Manuscript Division and the Henry W. and Albert A. Berg Collection); The Henry E. Huntington Library; the Folger Shakespeare Library; and the Library of the Historical Society of Pennsylvania. For their kindness in supplying photostats, microfilm, and information, I thank the personnel of the Newberry Library, the Library of Congress, the Library of the University of Chicago, the Library of the University of Texas, the Library of Harvard University, the Library of Yale University, The Carl H. Pforzheimer Library, the National Portrait Gallery, the British Museum, the Victoria and Albert Museum, and the Brotherton Library of the University of Leeds. For providing research facilities and a summer faculty research grant, I am indebted to Indiana University. In particular I wish to acknowledge the encouragement of Professor Albert Elsasser of Princeton University, who some years ago guided my initial research on Charles Lamb; the interested suggestions of the late Professor James A. Work of Indiana University; the invaluable criticisms of my wife; and the help of my son, George Jr., and of my daughter, Mary, in the task of reading proof.

Acknowledgment is herewith made to J. M. Dent & Sons, Ltd. for their permission to quote from those of Lamb's letters in which they control the reproduction rights as residuary legatees.

ONE

"A Most Unscientific Head"

LAMB AND THE ESSAY

Perhaps the strongest factor directing Lamb to employ the essay was his own personality. This influence has been generally overlooked in favor of external forces; yet it played a most decisive part in his literary career, not only in the choice of form but in the choice of subject and manner as well. The literary essay is informal by nature, and spontaneity and subjectivity are characteristic of the personal essay in particular. It is "literature of power" rather than "literature of knowledge." Formal organization is at a minimum. It is not a studied treatment but rather "glimpses, suggestions, delightful half-apprehensions, profound thoughts of old philosophers, hints of the innermost reason in things, the full knowledge of which is held in reserve."[1] The personal essayist has a leisurely, discursive habit of mind rather than a logical one, and he does not so much create as comment.

Lamb's fields of interest were circumscribed by his books, his friends, and himself. "I have a most unscientific head," he wrote to Sir Anthony Carlisle, the surgeon, and

9

we find him declining a ticket to an anatomical lecture, for
he had no interest in such matters.[2] Writing of his "totally
un-engineer-like faculties," he termed himself "still less of
an agriculturist than a steam-philosopher, not knowing a
turnip from a potato ground . . . ."[3] "Of politics he knew
nothing; they were out of his line of reading, and thought,"
wrote Daniel Stuart, editor of the *Morning Post*, for which
Lamb had written some paragraphs in the early part of his
career;[4] and Lamb himself testified: "Public affairs—except
as they touch upon me, and so turn into private, I cannot
whip up my mind to feel any interest in . . . . I read histories
of the past, and I live in them . . . ."[5] Edward Moxon, Lamb's
publisher and the husband of his adopted daughter, reported the same deficiency, continuing: "Nor was he a man
of business. He could not pack up a trunk, nor tie up a
parcel. Yet he was methodical, punctual in his appointments, and an excellent paymaster. A debt haunted him."[6]
The following anecdote is revealing: "A friend observing
the absence of this usual adjunct of a business man's attire
[a watch], presented him with a new gold watch which he
accepted and carried for one day only. A colleague asked
Lamb what had become of it. 'Pawned,' was the reply. He
had actually pawned the watch finding it a useless encum-
brance."[7] Time was always a mystery to Lamb, and he frequently omitted to date his letters: "a fig for dates, which
is more than a date is worth," he once punned in a letter to
one of his Quaker friends, Bernard Barton, which he face-
tiously dated in unique completeness "Saturday 25 July A.D.
1829. 11 A.M." There is no evidence that Lamb was anything but informal, even to the point of abruptness at times,
and the spontaneity and egoism of his letters are ample
warrant that these traits were native to him. In short,
Lamb's personality and temperament were admirably
suited to the composition of the familiar essay. The wonder
is that he took so long to discover it.

The fact that Christ's Hospital produced a number of poets, editors, novelists, and critics, including such well-known writers as Coleridge and Leigh Hunt, indicates that the training Lamb received at that school for poor children may have been a directing tendency toward literary expression. Its influence on his prose style is described in a later chapter, but any more direct influence on his writing career, outside of acquainting him with literature, is intangible. There were other, more important influences, as is indicated by Lamb's partiality for a poem which helped to console him in his disappointment at not being able to proceed to the university:

> There need not schools, nor the professor's chair,
>   Though these be good, true wisdom to impart;
> He, who has not enough for these to spare,
>   Of time, or gold, may yet amend his heart,
> And teach his soul, by brooks and rivers fair:
>   Nature is always wise in every part.[8]

Lamb's comparative failures in literary types other than the essay directed him gradually but inexorably toward that medium. His earliest emotional expressions, like those of most youthful writers, took the form of verse. He was known as a poet when a young man and even after he began writing prose. Although one critic has observed that "His poetry is the least poetical thing he has written,"[9] he has left in the midst of his generally mediocre verse two or three poems of a high order of excellence. But Lamb came to realize the limitations of his Muse, and in a manuscript passage not printed in "Witches, and Other Night-Fears" he wrote of the end of a dream: "When I awoke I came to a determination to write prose all the rest of my life."[10] The transition between his poetry and prose was not, however, so sharp as that. Indeed, he wrote poetry at periods throughout his life, but the trend was always towards prose.

The tragic murder of his mother by his temporarily insane sister in 1796 resulted in a voluntary inhibition of his literary life; from that time he had not only to attend to the routine of business and to care for his sister, who was to be subject to periods of insanity for the rest of her life, but also to keep his imagination well in bounds for the sake of his own mental health. He destroyed his early effusions and renounced such "vanities."[11] But there were other forces which drew him from poetry into prose.

For one thing, his early inspiration and enthusiasm, derived largely from Coleridge, changed into a dissatisfaction with his own work as he compared it with that of his master.[12] There were increasing demands on his time, and to write poetry under such circumstances was a task rather than a pleasure, for Lamb's Muse was not obedient to his will but was dependent on seasons and places.[13] Just as he had renounced his love passion,[14] so also when Coleridge included some of Lamb's pieces in the second edition of his *Poems* in 1797, it was for Lamb the "pomp and paraphernalia of parting."[15] He continued to write poetry from time to time, and his preference for the dramatic "above every other form of Poetry"[16] was manifested in his compilation of *Specimens of English Dramatic Poets* of 1808. But the secondary importance his poetical work assumed in his mind is abundantly evident in his letters from the turn of the century to the end of his life. "We have nobody about us that cares for Poetry, and who will rear grapes when he shall be the sole eater?" he asked the Wordsworths in a letter of September 28, 1805.[17] "I wish you Joy of an Amusement which I somehow seem to have done with," he wrote on June 13, 1809, to Charles Lloyd, Sr., a Quaker banker of Birmingham who had just translated the *Odyssey*.[18] To Wordsworth in 1815 he wrote, "I reckon myself a dab at *Prose*—verse I leave to my betters . . . ."[19] Composing his Elian essays in 1822, he referred to poetry as a "harmless occupation,"[20] and to the same correspondent and poet, Bernard Barton, he wrote two years later, "rhymes come with difficulty from me now . . . ."[21] As Leigh Hunt had expressed it only a few years earlier, Lamb "wanted sufficient heat and music to render his poetry as good as his prose."[22]

At least one literary figure was sorry to see Lamb abandon verse, but this regret was probably motivated by selfish considerations, for he was Alaric A. Watts, poetaster, journalist, and editor of *Literary Souvenirs* and other such albums which Lamb grew to detest. Lamb was importuned by Watts in 1824 for some verse, but without much success. In 1821 the latter had written to Blackwood that "Charles Lamb delivers himself with infinite pain and labour of a silly piece of trifling every month in this magazine, under the signature of Elia."[23] Although he was more charitable toward Lamb's prose in one of his "Sketches of Modern Poets," published in the *Literary Souvenir* for 1831 in juxtaposition with similar sketches of Wordsworth, Campbell, and Coleridge, Watts nevertheless expresses the unique idea that his essays were, more or less, the product of a perverse Muse. So far as can be discovered, this contemporary panegyric has never before been reprinted in full:

> Quaint masker! why hide, 'neath a garb so uncouth,
> A well-spring of song, and a day-star of truth?
> Why struggle, to bury a heart-cherished brood
> Of fine fancies and feelings, in crambo so rude?
> Yet thy "faces familiar" are welcome to all,
> And a host of warm wishes arise at their call.
> For what if thy Muse will be sometimes perverse,
> And present us with prose, when she means to give
>   verse?
> For her freak to atone, and her critics to pose,
> She'll as often vouchsafe us a poem in prose;

So sparkling with dew from the fountain sublime,
That we drink in its beauty, and miss not the rhyme.
Henceforth may the plant 'tis thy joy to illume,
For thee ever send forth its mildest perfume;
"Dream Children," revisit thy slumbers, and play
In the light of thy love, till morn melts them away.
For this, may thy fortune be often to list
To thy worthy "Aunt Battle's" opinions of whist;
Thine ears ne'er be pestered again with a jig,
And thy stomach become a depôt for "Roast Pig!"

—A. A. W.

One year later, Lamb was still putting poetry aside: "So much for the nonsense of poetry; now to the serious business of life."[24]

One piece of poetical "nonsense," which yet illustrates Lamb's perfect sympathy, while exemplifying a late effort in this medium, is a hitherto unpublished acrostic on the name Harriet Isola, a type of ingenuity amply represented in his poetry. Little is known of Harriet beyond the fact that she was a sister of Lamb's ward, Emma, whose presence in the household explains this versified invitation, printed here for the first time:

11 Feb. 1833

To H. I. for her Birthday, 14 Feb.

Acrostic

1

Harriet, can you spare a day,
At this busy time to stray
'Round our pleasant Enfield fields,
Reaping all the country yields
In this pleasant time of Spring?
Every bird now prunes his wing,
To prepare himself to sing

2

I will hope on Thursday next—
Sister else will be perplext—
On a fowl you'll with [us] dine.
Like a Lady come, dress'd fine,
And I shall be your Valentine!

Chs Lamb
Enfield 11th feb. 1833[25]

It was, in large measure, the "serious business of life" that turned Charles Lamb to forms of writing other than lyrical poetry. When his early and brief connection with the *Albion* ended in 1801, an association described in "Newspapers Thirty-Five Years Ago," he regretted most that "my revenues have died with it . . . ."[26] About the same time he wrote to his friend Thomas Manning, a private tutor in mathematics at Cambridge, to ask if he were serious about his proposal to collaborate in some series of papers, adding, "I want some occupation, and I more want money . . . Mutton is twelve-pence a pound."[27]

According to a letter written in 1806 by Mary Lamb, Wordsworth—with what seems a peculiar lack of penetration—had advised Lamb to write a novel.[28] Although intrigued by the idea, Lamb recognized that such writing required a more methodical mind than his: "I am the worst hand in the world at a plot," he had admitted to William Godwin, already known as the author of two novels as well as *Political Justice;*[29] and he had confessed to Coleridge in 1798 that he was "unused to composition in which any methodising is required . . . ."[30] Bulwer-Lytton wrote of *Rosamund Gray,* Lamb's excursion into fiction in this same year, that the "victim meets her fate by an accident which seems highly improbable. . . . It argues a want of the intuitive faculty requisite for constructing a well-told tale." He concluded that "Lamb's special genius was as little adapted to romantic narrative as it was to dramatic character and passion . . . ."[31]

In spite of the condemnation given to a published blank verse tragedy, *John Woodvil* (1802), and to a one-night production of a prose farce, *Mr. H.* (1806), Lamb continued to regard the drama as a potential source of supplementary income. "I dont know what to do," he wrote Coleridge in 1809. "Sometimes I think of a drama, but I have no head for play-making, I can do the Dialogue and thats all.—I am quite aground for a Plan, and I must do something for money. Not that I have immediate wants, but I have prospective ones."[32] Even after his success as Elia, when monetary considerations were no longer so important, he returned to the dramatic medium. Failing to find a producer for another prose farce, *The Pawnbroker's Daughter,* in 1825, he began to compose a play based on Crabbe's "Confidant," in spite of his better judgment. "I am doing a tragi-comedy in two acts, and have got on tolerably, but it will be refused, or worse," he wrote Patmore in 1827.[33] That this was *The Wife's Trial,* in blank verse, is confirmed by his more complete description to Mary Shelley: "I am busy with a farce in two acts, the incidents tragicomic. I can do the dialogue *commey fo* [*comme il faut*]: but the damned plot—I believe I must omit it altogether . . . . The characters are three women to one man . . . ."[34]

It appears from an unpublished letter by Lamb that he had hoped to strengthen his chances for success by tailoring *The Wife's Trial* to the talents of a particular actor. This letter, which is inserted in a grangerized edition of Thomas Moore's *Byron,* probably made by Alaric A. Watts, and now in the British Museum, is here printed for the first time:

Dear Sir,

I do not know whether you are in town, but I am desirous of offering to Mr Kemble a two-act drama, not the one you saw, in which I had Mr K's manner of acting in mind in the leading character. Perhaps he may like it. It lies at Mr Hood's, or will lie tomorrow, the author of Whims & Oddities, No 2 Robert Street Adelphi. Perhaps you will trouble yourself with sending for it. I am at Mrs Leishman's, Chase, Enfield, where a line from you would be a favor

Monday, Aug. 20ᵗʰ

Yours truly
Chas Lamb[35]

Although the address portion is missing, the letter, I believe, was written to Robert Jameson, who was connected with *Fraser's Magazine* and had successfully importuned Lamb for some lines for *The Bijou* of 1828, an annual edited by William Fraser.[36] Lamb wrote Jameson on August 30, 1827, saying, "The MS cannot be in better hands, for Mrs. Kemble has always behaved with singular civility towards us. Thank you for your pains."[37] To Thomas Hood the following month he wrote: "Jamieson conveyed the farce from me to Mrs. C. Kemble, *he* will not be in town before the 27th."[38] Kemble was Charles Kemble (1775–1854), an actor and manager of Covent Garden Theatre in 1827, the year to which this new letter can be assigned from internal evidence.[39] In spite of Lamb's effort to write for individual acting talent, his play was not produced and netted him only £20 when printed the following year in *Blackwood's*.

Lamb recognized his limitations even though he did not always conform to them, especially the fact that he could achieve more in a smaller compass; his poems are short, and his criticism is concerned with details and impressions rather than with the larger outlines and structure. Again to Godwin he wrote, "I can vehemently applaud, or perversely stickle, at *parts*; but I cannot grasp at a whole. This infirmity . . . may be seen in my two little compositions, the tale and my play [*John Woodvil*], in both which no reader, however partial, can find any story."[40] Perhaps the best self-analysis made by Lamb is that tucked away in his essay on "Imperfect Sympathies," written at the height of his powers, August 1821:

There is an order of imperfect intellects (under which mine must be content to rank) which in its constitution is essentially anti-Caledonian. The owners of the sort of faculties I allude to, have minds rather suggestive than comprehensive. They have no pretences to much clearness or precision in their ideas, or in their manner of expressing them. Their intellectual wardrobe (to confess fairly) has few whole pieces in it. They are content with fragments and scattered pieces of Truth. She presents no full front to them—a feature or sideface at the most. Hints and glimpses, germs and crude essays at a system, is the utmost they pretend to. They beat up a little game peradventure—and leave it to knottier heads, more robust constitutions, to run it down. The light that lights them is not steady and polar, but mutable and shifting: waxing, and again waning. Their conversation is accordingly. They will throw out a random word in or out of season, and be content to let it pass for what it is worth. They cannot speak always as if they were upon their oath—but must be understood, speaking or writing, with some abatement. They seldom wait to mature a proposition, but e'en bring it to market in the green ear. They delight to impart their defective discoveries as they arise, without waiting for their full development. They are no systematizers, and would but err more by attempting it. Their minds, as I said before, are suggestive merely.

No one who is acquainted with Lamb can fail to recognize his full-length portrait here, with all its shortcomings—and its assets. No one, furthermore, can fail to see that there is only one literary form that such a personality could employ with constant effectiveness. The characteristics here are such as can be expressed only by the essay, and the absolute agreement of the qualities in the author with those requisite for the vehicle resulted in perfection in the type.

With Lamb's personality thus drawing him inexorably

toward the essay in spite of his continued, perverse attempts to achieve success in other media, there wanted only some positive outside direction and encouragement to insure successful endeavor. The encouragement was supplied, in part, by Thomas Manning's comment on his first essay, "The Londoner," published in the *Morning Post* for February 1, 1802: "I like your Londoner very much, there is a deal of happy fancy in it, but it is not strong enough to be seen by the generality of readers. Yet if you would write a volume of Essays in the same stile you might be sure of its succeeding."[41] This eulogy may have prompted Lamb to contribute to Leigh Hunt's *Reflector*, which began publication in 1810. But most of the contributors to this periodical were alumni of Christ's Hospital; so it was only natural for Lamb to be among them. Lamb may have first met Hunt on a visit to Christ's, which the latter entered two years after Lamb had left, but there is no record of such a meeting. The beginning of their close friendship cannot be dated—Lamb says only that "accident" introduced him to Hunt—but they were certainly brought together by the *Reflector*. Through this association, and in other ways, Hunt did more than anyone else to nourish Lamb's abilities in the essay.

We have seen from the foregoing that although the essay was the form of expression best suited to Lamb's temperament, it was far from being the inevitable medium, as is usually uncritically assumed, and was adopted only after others had been tried and as a result of very definite influences. In the same way, the erroneous implication (all but explicitly confirmed by many writers on the essay) given by the customary practice of placing the essays of Elia immediately after those of Goldsmith in anthologies of English literature and in collections of essays, that Lamb's essays burst into full flower without any previous budding or anticipation fails to take into account the development of the essay in the decades between these two authors. Furthermore, critics have neglected to assign to Lamb's contemporaries a proper share of the credit for effecting the shift from the traditional tone of the *Tatler* and *Spectator* to the more subjective one that still persists. Lamb was well aware of his position in the essay tradition and excelled by reason of his use in combination of elements which had all been employed before, the most characteristic of which can be seen in essays of the late eighteenth century. In order to see the extent of the influence of the temper of his age, with its new periodicals, as well as of his own personality on his use of these elements, it is necessary to review briefly the growth of the essay up to the nineteenth century and to indicate its status when Lamb first turned to this form of expression. In no other way can we achieve the perspective necessary to a judicious assessment of his contribution and of his distinctive characteristics.

The history of the essay is cyclic: the influence of early nineteenth-century periodicals on the form resembles that of the early eighteenth-century periodicals; and the essays of that later period were, in many respects, closer to those of the seventeenth century than to those of the eighteenth. Many of the qualities for which Montaigne's *Essais* are noted, qualities which appear in some of the essays of seventeenth-century English writers, are those wherein Lamb and his contemporaries differed from eighteenth-century writers. In addition to the rambling progression, the development of various ideas in any single essay, and the absence of unity and order—characteristics of the familiar essay in general—there is present in the work of Montaigne the infusion of his personality; subjectivity is the distinguishing characteristic of his writing. Frequent quotations and Latin phrases, usually translated, together with allusions and anecdotes in profusion are also evident. His subjects were ordinarily of an abstract nature. For the most part he avoided controversial questions and contemporary events. Although his tone is learned, with little humor, his themes were not homiletic in purpose. In a section of his *Table Talk* entitled "Books with One Idea in Them," which appeared in Hunt's *Examiner* in 1813, Lamb revealed that he had not only read Montaigne but had recognized his importance as well as his characteristic use of personality: "Montaigne is an immense treasure-house of observation, anticipating all the discoveries of succeeding essayists. You cannot dip in him without being struck with the aphorism, that there is nothing new under the sun. All the writers on common life since him have done nothing but echo him. You cannot open him without detecting a Spectator, or starting a Rambler; besides that his own character pervades the whole, and binds it sweetly together."

The essays of Francis Bacon differ in many respects from those of Montaigne: his purpose was to instruct rather than to entertain, and in consequence the approach is impersonal rather than self-revelatory. In contrast to Montaigne's comparative lightness, Bacon is stately and authoritative. His wisdom is contained in closely packed aphorisms, and frequent quotations appeal to Biblical and classical authority. The essay of Bacon is the classic essay. Seventeenth-century writers were primarily concerned with problems of morality, and the tone of the essays was prevailingly didactic. Fuller's essays veer toward the informal by reason of their conversational style and welcome humor, but in subject and handling they are modeled on those of Bacon. Sir Thomas Browne, who was essentially desultory in a Montaignesque way, can be considered as an essayist. His *Religio Medici* contains the personal confidences, the lack

of systematic order, and the emotional as well as the logical appeal—all which suggest the manner of Montaigne. The essays of Cowley, although more orderly, are still closer in their informality, ease, and intimacy to those of Montaigne than are any others of the century. Indeed, Montaigne was the favorite author of Cowley, who followed him in his colloquial style, in his self-analysis—which is, however, more restrained, in the use of anecdotes and quotations, and in his habit of employing his own experience for illustration. He was distinctly more intimate and confidential than his contemporaries, and hence he seems closer to Lamb and his time than does any writer of the intervening period. Lamb had read Cowley in his boyhood, and as early as 1797 we find him expressing his appreciation in a letter to Coleridge of "a poet, very dear to me, the now out of fashion Cowley —favor me with your judgment of him, and tell me if his prose essays, in particular, as well as no inconsiderable part of his verse, be not delicious. I prefer the graceful rambling of his essays, even to the courtly elegance and ease of Addison—abstracting from this the latter's exquisite humour."[42] The last important seventeenth-century essayist, Sir William Temple, Swift's patron, was also a favorite of Lamb. His essays have a Montaignesque digressiveness and variety of subject matter, but his style forms the main connection with the Montaigne tradition, as Lamb realized in praising the "plain natural chit-chat of Temple" in his "Popular Fallacy" entitled "That my Lord Shaftesbury and Sir William Temple are models of the Genteel Style in Writing." The didacticism in Temple's essays is in keeping with his age, but Lamb suggests that Addison and his followers were in his debt for "felicitous antitheses."

With the development of the essay periodical in the latter years of the seventeenth and the early years of the eighteenth centuries, the essay, while still carrying on the

general traditions, underwent certain changes: by reason
of space limitations, it became shorter; the personal element virtually disappeared as the essay in its new dress
became a vehicle for amusement, instruction, and criticism;
its most distinctive function lay in its moderate didacticism
and light satire on the foibles of contemporary society; it
took on new varieties in method and form; and it was directed more to the leisure classes than to the general public.
The importance of Addison and Steele in establishing the
popularity of this new essay in the *Tatler* and *Spectator* is
well known. Its success lay partly in a penetrating insight
into character, partly in the infinite variety, and partly in
the "exquisite humor" which Lamb noticed. The *Tatler* and
Spectator set the standard for the essay and for the essay
periodical for most of the century. The single-sheet journals which carried the imitations of the established type
were, in turn, modeled closely on these two. Their vogue is
shown by the fact that "by 1809 no less than 220 such
periodicals had seen the light in London and other cities of
the British Isles."[43] Judging from the number of editions
published, Montaigne, Cowley, and Temple were widely
read during the eighteenth century, but they had no influence on the essays being written, and the essay showed
no new developments of any importance in form or in
method between the last daily issue of the *Spectator* in
December, 1712, and the last twenty years of the century.

Before we examine the transition from the essay of the
eighteenth century to that of the nineteenth, three familiar
and important figures deserve a word of comment. Dr. Samuel Johnson's papers in the *Rambler* and the *Idler* are
characterized by a heavy moral and melancholy tone,
evolved inevitably from his avowed purpose to "inculcate
wisdom or piety" and hence to correct; they are enhanced
by a ponderous, stately, heavily Latinized, and antithetical

style which earned the name "Johnsonese." Although his papers woefully lacked the characteristic light touch of Addison, he is generally considered as belonging to the Addisonian tradition and, as we shall see, was considered by Lamb to have infused his essays with his personality. On the other hand, his abstract treatment of old subjects in many cases more closely reminds us of the Baconian manner.

James Boswell, better known now perhaps as a writer of self-revelatory journals than as Johnson's biographer, produced a series of autobiographical essays between 1777 and 1783 called the *Hypochondriack*. Those portions written earlier are in the *Spectator* tradition, employing satire with a didactic bent. But in the later part, his digressive tendency, his soul-searching personal confessions without the fictitious mouthpiece employed by the Addisonian imitators reveal Boswell as a transitional figure in the essay. He is not a familiar essayist—he lacks the ease, the intimacy, and the colloquial tone—but some of the traits of the form are discernible.[44]

Goldsmith's early prose shows many features of the Johnsonese style, but he soon abandoned it for a simpler diction and achieved to some degree the charm of a conversational manner. Lamb is reported to have remarked: "Ah! poor Goldy! how I value him; what can be more simple, pure, touching, natural,—than his prose—what can be more descriptive, graceful, original, or impressive than his poetry!"[45] The essays in the *Bee* and in *The Citizen of the World* followed, in the main, the Addisonian tradition in their light ridicule and gentle satire of morals and politics. There is the humor of Beau Tibbs, but there is also the philosophical wisdom shrouding some of the heavier pieces; the tendency is to inform and instruct rather than to suggest and entertain. Yet, there is a touch of personality and

utilization of personal experience in some of the papers, together with hints of humanity in his characterizations,
which, added to the more familiar tone, seem to anticipate
in a slight measure the romantic essayists to come. A reviewer of the collected edition of the *Bee* admitted in 1760
that the style had virtues and the manner was agreeable
but complained that "most of his subjects are already sufficiently worn out, and his observations frequently trite and
common."[46]

Although the Addisonian essay continued to be written,
and the essay periodical to be published, right into the
nineteenth century, it was also wearing out. The novel of
Richardson and Fielding had developed into a body of historical and domestic fiction which gradually superseded
the essay in popularity, and a new class of periodicals with
more varied diet was coming into being. Before looking at
these, however, the continuity of the essay periodical
should be stressed by mentioning a few of the more important ones. The *Connoisseur*, published by Colman and
Thornton between 1754 and 1756, and contributed to by
Cowper, and the *World* of 1753, for which Chesterfield and
Horace Walpole wrote, closely resembled the *Tatler* in that
they were single-essay periodicals with a moralistic bent
aimed at the vices and follies of the day. There was no
innovation in form or manner, and the essays were frequently poor in style and in substance; but it is noteworthy
that they did not follow the Johnsonese style of the *Rambler*—for their purpose was as much to amuse as to instruct.
Other papers imitative of the *Tatler* and *Spectator* manner
were the *Observer* of 1785, the *Microcosm* and the *Devil* of
a year later, and the *Friend* of 1796. Some of the imitators
of Addison and Steele put the single-essay paper to political
uses. But the gradual decline of these imitations, both in
popularity and in number, after Goldsmith, together with

the reactionary development of a familiar and more natural style, indicate that the change from the Addisonian essay to the new, familiar essay had begun. It was not sudden, nor was it brought about by any one writer or influence.

It may be observed here that the familiar letter, containing as it does the qualities of informality, spontaneity, and egoism, which especially mark the work of the early nineteenth-century essayists, helped bring about this change in type. The numerous collections of letters published in the eighteenth century—including those of Horace Walpole, Chesterfield, Lady Mary Montagu, Pope, Swift, Bolingbroke, Cowper, and Gray—manifest the increased use of, and growth of interest in, the familiar letter. The institution of English mail-coaches in 1783 did much to stimulate letter writing. Of course, the letter form was a conventional essay device employed by Addison and Steele and their imitators, but the characteristic self-revelatory mood, the absence of caution and reticence, the sincerity and intimacy were not adopted with the form. These qualities, noticeably absent from the eighteenth-century essay, are observable in letters not written for publication yet collected in print, as well as in letters written with publication specifically in mind. Essayists reading published letters and writing letters themselves could scarcely avoid being impressed by the presence of such contributory qualities in a form of writing so similar to their own.

Just as the essay lost some of its popularity to fiction, so also did the essay periodical bow to a new type of general magazine which was inaugurated as early as 1731 with the publication of the long-lived *Gentleman's Magazine,* referred to by Lamb in 1827 as old-fashioned. Before then, however, these storehouses—for the name was used in that sense—were amazing collections of all sorts of information: politics, news summaries, astronomical data, strange facts, and chronicle matter. They were, naturally, of a more wide-spread interest than the single-essay paper, and the space allotted to literature limited the number of essays. Most of the essays were in the old tradition. The successful *Town and Country Magazine* in 1774 carried a series of essays by "The Observer," and as late as 1802 to 1809 we find the *Gentleman's Magazine* printing a series of such essays under the title "The Projector." Since these magazines were chiefly predatory, compiling their contents in great measure from published sources, contributors were not encouraged by high rates of pay, and the result was a poverty of original, literary essays. Many of the essays, catering to the more general audience, were of a factual nature; such were those in the *Monthly Magazine,* which Lamb was reading in 1796; in the *Literary Magazine*; and in *Blackwood's Magazine.* While there was some entertainment in the pages of these miscellanies, the emphasis was on information. Together with the *Critical Review* and the *Monthly Review,* both of which Lamb read, and other periodicals of a specialized, critical nature, these magazines, like the essay periodicals, continued into the nineteenth century. But long before 1800 they were losing ground to a new type of magazine, more literary, of greater importance in the development of the essay, and the forerunner of the magazines of today.

Although there was a considerable difference between the nature of the eighteenth-century miscellany magazines and that of the newer publications, the transition from one type to the other was gradual, and many periodicals exhibit features characteristic of each. Essays of the Addisonian type appeared in these and even in the new, more literary ones. The *Monthly Mirror,* a better than average periodical offering novels, reviews, and theatrical information, printed in 1796 a series of moralistic essays by "The Censor." In this periodical we find critical reviews alongside literary essays, but critical magazines began to exist about the time Goldsmith was writing essays; the *English Review of Literature* was one of the earliest. Others of later vintage were the *Literary Gazette,* which Lamb disliked because of its harsh comments on his work; the *British Critic* of 1793; the *Edinburgh Review* of 1802; the *British Review,* read by Lamb in 1796; the *Eclectic Review,* a sectarian religious organ of the Dissenters which Lamb was reading in 1828; and the *Anti-Jacobin,* rather political than literary and of minor importance. With the rise of these critical reviews there developed the critical essays, which may be considered an outgrowth of critical features found previously in the essay. In the same way, the increased serialization of novels in the new literary magazine served to absorb the fictional features of the essay. The result of this abstraction of the critical and fictional elements from the periodical essay was a limiting of the nature of the essay and a directing of its form. But the rise of the new magazine had also a more positive influence.

The new magazine differed from its predecessor in many ways. The obsolete "chronicle" matter was gradually eliminated; the prime purpose now was to entertain, and to do this the editors invited papers of a more varied, original, and imaginative nature which they paid for at a comparatively higher rate. By the beginning of the last quarter of the eighteenth century many of the newer periodicals contained chiefly original material; circulation was more general; and the improved appearance, especially in illustrations, was a distinct advance. In the last decade of the century almost forty new magazines were started in London alone, and in the first decade of the nineteenth century about twenty more were initiated. Most of these were short-lived, but the total number of periodicals in existence at a given time grew regularly. During the second decade of the nineteenth century more than thirty magazines were published in London, and during the third decade the total exceeded one hundred.

Of the many transitional magazines such as the *Monthly Repository*, which combined the news features of the old miscellany with the serialized fiction more characteristic of the new type, the *Monthly Magazine*—continued as the *New Monthly Magazine*—is one of the best examples of the change. Beginning like the traditional magazine, it became a more purely literary periodical under the editorship of Thomas Campbell in 1820, and underwent still further improvements in 1824. In that year Lamb expressed his opinion in a letter: "If your club like scandal, Blackwood's is your magazine; if you prefer light articles, and humorous without offense, the New Monthly is very amusing. The best of it is by Horace Smith, the author of the Rejected Addresses. The Old Monthly has more of matter, information, but not so merry. I cannot safely recommend any others, as not knowing them, or knowing them to their disadvantage."[47]

The most important magazine of the early nineteenth century was the *New Monthly's* most serious rival, the *London Magazine*, in which Lamb's Elian essays were published. It devoted more space to literature than any former periodical of the kind had done. The first number appeared in January, 1820, under the editorship of John Scott, former editor of the *Champion*. Scott's death, following his well-known duel with Christie in February, 1821, terminated his connection with the magazine after fourteen issues. Following its sale to Taylor and Hessey, the former served as editor, with Thomas Hood as a subeditor, until September, 1825, when it was sold to Henry Southern, under whom it slowly but inevitably declined for four more years.

The *London* appealed to both literary and commercial readers, and the names of its contributors include most of the important writers of the day: Lamb, De Quincey, Landor, Carlyle, and Hazlitt, to name a few. One of the attractions for contributors was (in addition to the high rate of pay) the privilege of writing pretty much what and how they pleased. Nothing could have been more congenial to Lamb's temperament. It may have been Hazlitt who proposed his friend Lamb as a contributor, but Scott had known Lamb in 1814 as a contributor to his *Champion,* although the association was brief. Lamb had not left a very attractive impression with Scott, and a letter from the latter to Robert Baldwin, the publisher of the *London,* informs us that Scott did not propose Lamb's name, nor was he overeager to secure him: "I should be very glad to have Mr. Lamb as an auxiliary,—but I have no very ready means of procuring him: and indeed I believe he is what is called a very idle man,—who hates trouble, & above all a regular occupation. There are however two or three persons to whom I would reccommend [sic] you to write, enclosing a prospectus, & soliciting their assistance. These I will specify particularly afterwards, & Mr. Lamb may be included."[48]

It is important to notice here that Lamb's friendships with editors and with writers who could introduce him to editors played a great part in promoting his literary life. The essay depended on the periodical press for its existence, and Lamb's essays depended to a large degree on the urgings of editors. Once enlisted as a contributor, Lamb had to be prodded repeatedly to continue sending his monthly essays. The result of this constant prodding and the high pay scale was that Lamb's peak of activity was coterminous with the best years of the *London* and the *New Monthly.* He became sought after as a writer, and we find Leigh Hunt writing from Italy on October 26, 1822, to his brother John, the printer, regarding the organization of their two papers the *Examiner* and the *Liberal*: "Have you made my request to Lamb? . . . Pray ask him to write. (We must pay, of course, in every instance, according to the best pay going,—perhaps a little more would not be amiss.) Lord B. [Byron] admires Hazlitt's writings, and both likes and admires Lamb."[49] With the decline of the *London,* beginning in the same year as his retirement from business, Lamb's interest and productivity waned also. On July 25, 1829, he exclaimed to Bernard Barton, who had been a colleague on the staff of the *London,* "What things are all the Magazines now! I contrive studiously not to see them. The popular New Monthly is perfect trash."

By 1825 the transition from the Addisonian essay to the new, familiar essay, with its more universal appeal, had been completed. This abandonment of old standards and forms is one characteristic of the period, and like the other characteristics, its beginnings are unmistakably discernible in the latter half of the eighteenth century. The infusion of personality, the first signs of the familiar tone and style, and the hints of humanity in the work of Goldsmith anticipate these qualities that are found in full measure in the early nineteenth-century essay. These were definite advances before Lamb began to write prose, and other early appearances of these new qualities can be found by searching the periodicals. A tendency toward the personal element, for example, can be seen in the series of essays called "The Man of the Town" which were appearing in the pretentious and exclusive *European Magazine* for 1782. The romantic tendency to widen the range of subject matter, especially to include the lower classes of society, can be seen in an essay of the August, 1796, number of the *Monthly Mirror,* previously mentioned as a transitional magazine; the title reads: "On the Wretched Situation of the Chimney-Sweepers," and it is signed "Vicus." Its concern with the dangers of the trade shows its humanitarian motivation; the suggestion is made that some mechanical device might be substituted for the sweeps. The style and diction remind us of Lamb in such phrases as "By law, only visible at an early hour" and "If they do not imbibe cruelty with their mother's milk, they are very early brought up to the contemplation and to the practice of inhumanity." There are no verbal parallels with anything in Lamb's famous essay "The Praise of Chimney-Sweepers," but the account of an annual feast instituted through the charity of a Mrs. Montague is worth quoting for comparison with Lamb's account of Jem White's annual bounty:

I remember having been much pleased at the benevolent suggestion of Mrs. Montague, and afterwards put into practice, for the joy and recreation of these deserted orphans, for so *those* may be justly called, who are snatched away in their childhood from the arms of their parents, and the solicitude of their friends.

How must the heart of that charitable lady expand with delight, when she beholds these little groups assembled to partake of her bounty; and once, at least, in a year, with clean faces, enlivened by smiles, and with hands newly scoured, stretched forth in humble, but distant gratitude, to receive the dole that is appointed for their wants, their eyes glistening with the tear of satisfaction, and the sigh of benediction slowly vibrating through their lips.

The sympathetic portrayal of humble life set forth here and in Lamb's essay is vastly different, in both material and treatment, from that pictured by Addison and his imitators. At the same time, it must be admitted that this essay is not entirely free from that tradition, as the last paragraph shows:

Attend this rapturous scene, ye inhuman, and ye senseless accumulators of wealth! Forego your pride, O ye nobles; your stars, O ye vain; and, by mingling with the most degraded objects of creation, learn to know, that from the same original earth ye were, like them, derived; to the same original earth, must, like them descend; and happy will it be for ye, if without early incentives to vice, you have been taught the road to benevolence and virtue!

That Lamb was doing nothing new in writing his sketches of old actors is evident from the appearance in the same number of this periodical of several biographical sketches of actors, including one of Elliston. Furthermore, Lamb's "Imperfect Sympathies" is brought to mind when one glances at the lists of "Antipathies" in this number, including "A lady, a native of France, would faint on seeing boiled lobsters" and "Mr Vaugheim, a great huntsman, in Hanover, would faint, or, if he had sufficient time, would run away, at the sight of a roast pig."

The revolt against convention, another abiding romantic characteristic, also is found in the essay before Lamb. A vivid instance of this is the appearance of a series of refutations, modeled on Browne's *Vulgar Errors*, in the *Connoisseur* for Thursday, February 26, 1756. The preface shows that Lamb's revolt against the convention of proverbs in his *Popular Fallacies*, with his "discovery" of Browne, had been anticipated seventy years before:

The world is indebted to that ingenious inquirer after truth, the famous Sir Thomas Brown [sic], for an excellent treatise, in which he has refuted several idle and ridiculous opinions, that prevailed in his time; to which work he has very properly given the title of Vulgar Errors . . . . I cannot but think, a work, intended as a supplement to the above-mentioned treatise of Vulgar Errors, would be highly acceptable to the public . . . . A work of this nature it is my intention shortly to publish: in the meantime, I shall content myself with laying the following specimen of the performance before my readers.

The Addisonian irony is maintained by slyly hitting at the vices and foibles of society in such refutations as: "That a Maid Cannot be with Child," "That Gaming Depends on Chance," "That Matrimony brings People together," "That the Sabbath is a day of Rest," "That there is any such thing as an old Woman," and "That the Gospel is an object of belief." The continued popularity of such papers is evident in the anonymous publication in the *New Monthly Magazine* of 1835 of "A New Series of Popular Fallacies," in which the "Spirit of Charles Lamb" is addressed.

Another romantic tendency, interest in the past and in the authors of the past, was manifested in the nature of the *Retrospective Review,* which Lamb was reading in 1831 and perhaps earlier. This periodical analyzed and quoted from old books in a contemporary manner of criticism. It is noteworthy that Browne[50] and other seventeenth-century authors are thus brought to the attention of the public. An article in 1820 is devoted to Cotton's translation of the essays of Montaigne; so it is not surprising that Lamb, Hazlitt, and Hunt should have referred to this predecessor in a familiar manner. This periodical had more to do with acquainting these and other writers with early books and authors than is generally known. At the same time, other periodicals included articles on, and extracts from, the literature of the past. For example, as early as 1787–88 the *New Universal Magazine* carried a history of pre-Shakespearian drama; Lamb's *Specimens of English Dramatic Poets who Lived about the Time of Shakspeare* was less of a novelty in 1808 than adherence to fashion.

The appearance in the latter part of the eighteenth century of some of the characteristics differentiating the essays of the new type from those of the old indicates that the temper of the period known as the Romantic had considerable influence on the change. The new style in the essay was achieved not by Lamb or by any other one writer alone, but was one manifestation of this Romantic spirit, which, slowly gathering force in the last part of the eighteenth century, nurtured and directed it.

While the new essay expanded its range of subject matter to include recollection of the past and sympathy for humble life, the early nineteenth-century essayists also continued to use many of the same themes used by their predecessors. The difference in this case lies in the purpose, methods, and handling; in this respect the poetry of the Romantic period has its counterpart in the prose essay. The purpose of the new essays conformed to that of the new periodicals, which abandoned utilitarian instruction and information for amusement and appreciation; the essay abandoned irony and satire for a lighter, less intellectual appeal. The method and handling adopted by the new essayists were those used in other types of literature at the same time—a complete freedom which drew at will from all methods. A familiar, conversational style was more suitable for essays that were to be read for enjoyment, and digressions were a natural concomitant. But it was the personal, subjective manner, more than anything else, which characterized the new essay. Self-analysis and self-revelation are general characteristics of the literature of the early nineteenth century, and this kindly, easy egoism —without the connotation of offensive self-conceit—no less distinguishes the new essay which had developed by the end of the first two decades. There is, too, in the new essays the romantic description of nature and of city life, not found in the work of Addison and his imitators. Lamb, of course, is notable for his concentration on urban scenes, but his delineation of London and its inhabitants is romantic in its sympathy and invested charm, and the handling of nature in the essays of Hunt and Hazlitt is similar to that of the Romantic poets. An external characteristic of the new essay worth mentioning is the generally increased length made possible by greater space given to essayists in the new literary periodicals. While the essays of Hunt are of about the same length as those of his predecessors, and those of Lamb are on the average not very. much longer, Hazlitt's essays are considerably longer, and those of De Quincey are extremely long.

With all these innovations operating as general tendencies of the period, some of the old characteristics continued in vogue. Thus, the character continued to be written as a separate form; and the convention of writing over an assumed signature in the form of a letter to the editor continued to be used by Lamb and his contemporaries. But the characters, now more often incorporated as parts of essays, were usually autobiographical or portrayals of friends and relatives, rather than indistinct manifestations of vices or virtues; and the "letters" partook of the self-revelatory and personal qualities of the genuine familiar letter. In consequence, we can say that while the new essay carried on some of the traditional features, and was a logical development of what went before rather than a distinct, new type, it was differentiated mainly by the romantic treatment and, in its features of familiarity and self-revelation, was a rebirth of the tradition of Montaigne and his seventeenth-century followers.

Of the writers who directed and facilitated the development of the new essay, Leigh Hunt, one of Lamb's closest friends, was largely instrumental. Due credit and praise has been slow to come to Hunt, and his influence is still underestimated. His and Byron's short-lived *Liberal* of 1822, in the words of one scholar, was "the periodical of highest literary quality in the first quarter of the nineteenth century."[51] It was as an editor of papers which fostered the genius of Hazlitt and Lamb in particular, rather than as an essayist himself—although he wrote many fine things—that Hunt was important. Although his early *Reflector* of 1810–11 is a late essay periodical modeled on those of Addison and Steele and their imitator, the *Connoisseur*, it has been described as "the first really successful attempt in the nineteenth century to revive the light periodical essay, after its ponderous mishandling by Johnson in the *Rambler* and *Idler*."[52] The *Examiner*, a Sunday paper begun in 1808, but longer-lived than the *Reflector* and more popular, likewise had the plan of the essay periodical and the manner of the *Tatler* and *Spectator;* and the spirit of Addison and Steele is evident in his *Indicator* of 1819, his *Literary Examiner* of 1823, and his *Companion* of 1828. Yet, in the opening number of "The Round Table," a series of papers inaugurated in the *Examiner* of 1815 in avowed imitation of the eighteenth-century writers, there appeared evidence of Hunt's progressiveness:

A hundred years back, when the mode of living was different from what it is now, taverns and coffee-houses made the persons of the wits familiar to every body. Assumptions of this kind [the use of fictitious names] may have been necessary. *Captain Steele*, for instance, the gay fellow about town, might not always have been listened to with becoming attention, or even gravity, especially if he had been a little too inarticulate overnight;— he therefore put on the wrinkles and privileges of Isaac Bickerstaff . . . . We have not the same occasion for disguise; and, therefore, as we prefer at all times a plain, straight-forward behaviour, and, in fact, choose to be as original as we can in our productions, we have avoided the trouble of adding assumed characters to our real ones; and shall talk, just as we think, walk and take dinner, in our own proper persons.

Hunt was aware that Steele's informality and egoism were kept from full effectiveness by the conventional masking of feeling and speaking through fictitious identities. This discarding of the old conventions of London clubs and invented characters with classical names for the directness of signed pieces was one of the characteristics marking the new familiar essay.

Other old conventions were not discarded by Hunt, and Hazlitt recognized them in saying, in his *Table Talk*, that he "inherits more of the spirit of Steele than any man since his time." The old influence persisted in most of Hunt's work in the *Reflector* and even in his more original *Indicator*. The vast quantity of his work has served to conceal the quality of a few good pieces. Hunt, like Lamb, had that unusual ability of infusing apparently insignificant acts and moods with literary life; in this respect he is closer to his contemporaries than to the essayists of the preceding century. Furthermore, whereas Addison and Steele and their followers had dealt exclusively with city life, Hunt wrote also on rural scenes. His chatty colloquial style furnishes another contrast. But Hunt's personality was only imperfectly conveyed to his readers; it remained for Lamb to utilize pathos and humor, both lacking in Hunt's work, to win the reader's sympathy.

More nearly allied to Lamb in some respects was William Hazlitt, who was more of an individualist than Hunt and less inclined to submit for long to the influence of the old essayists. But he too began in that tradition; his first essay, "On the Love of Life," published in Hunt's "Round Table," has the Addisonian moral earnestness. He contributed abundantly to periodicals during the second decade of the century—especially in the interval between the suspension of the *Reflector* and the appearance of the *London Magazine*, an interval when Lamb was writing comparatively few personal essays. As early as 1815, some of his essays evinced a strong individuality and a tendency toward discursiveness, and his self-revelation helped to estab-

lish this quality in the Romantic essay before Lamb had
perfected his technique. His essay "On Reading Old
Books," published in the *London Magazine* for February,
1821, contains this passage: "The Periodical Essayists I
read long ago. The *Spectator* I liked extremely: but the
Tatler took my fancy most. I read the others soon after,
the *Rambler*, the *Adventurer*, the *World*, the *Connoisseur*.
I was not sorry to get to the end of them, and have no desire
to go regularly through them again." Hazlitt used the essay
as a vehicle of criticism, and his best essays are enthusiastic
and original criticisms of art and literature. A large part of
his work is thus more scholastic and purposeful than by-the-
way and entertaining. It is this which makes comparison
with Lamb's work difficult unless the comparison is limited.
They both occasionally wrote on the same subjects, and
their mutual love of books and of the past provide many
points of comparison in matter. In manner, which is of more
significance to us, Hazlitt is often autobiographical, but the
difference between his self-revelation and Lamb's is that
there is no kindliness and warmth of character beneath
Hazlitt's. He writes in the first person but does so as if he
were answering a factual questionnaire on his likes and dis-
likes. There is a difference in the emotional quality of Hazlitt's essays when compared with those of Lamb—an absence of the appealing wit-melancholy of the latter.
Hazlitt's remarks are frequently caustic, and there is no
humor or archaic diction to soften the blow. In short, he
did not become quite the personal essayist of Lamb's caliber. Like Hunt, he did much to effect the transition from
the eighteenth-century type of essay to the new, but perfection in the form was not habitual with either man—that
remained for Lamb to achieve.

In the first part of this chapter we saw the influences
which directed Lamb into writing his "Londoner" for the

Morning Post in 1802. Projection of this essay against the background which has now been sketched shows that this first essay was largely imitative of the Addisonian type. Aside from the treatment, the subject was by no means new.[53] Similarly, most of Lamb's contributions to the *Reflector* show the influence of the old type in manner and style. Especially in the use of the letter form and the character does he show his affinity to the *Spectator* and *Tatler:* more than half of his fourteen contributions begin "Mr. Reflector" or "Sir."[54] Like the periodical essayists too, Lamb signed his essays with pseudonyms corresponding to the nature of the subjects: "Edax," "Pensilis," "Hospita," "Moriturus," "Innuptus," "Crito," "X.Y.Z.," and "Semel-Damnatus." It is significant that when Lamb later reprinted "A Bachelor's Complaint," he omitted the address and the signature. "The Good Clerk" is a typical seventeenth-century character, introducing an "Account of 'The Complete English Tradesman'"; "The Character of an Undertaker" serves to conclude the essay "On Burial Societies." In addition to affinity in form, some of the essays reflect the same humorous tendency found in some of the *Spectator* papers although Lamb's whimsy is never Addisonian satire.

We must conclude, then, that Lamb, like Hunt and Hazlitt, served his apprenticeship under the Addisonian convention for several years before the originality, the fanciful wit, and the self-revelation of the essays of Elia were manifested in the *London*. This early work of these three influential essayists in particular must be carefully considered to avoid the erroneous conclusion that the familiar essay emerged full blown. The experimental period of 1802–20 was the transition period, and the transition may be observed in such individual essays as Hunt's "A Day by the Fire" in the *Reflector*. The three writers exhibited various rates of progress in breaking with the conventional form. Hunt never completely escaped; Hazlitt's style shows a marked alteration about 1820, and relatively little earlier; Lamb shows hints even in his "Londoner" of 1802 of what was to come, and while it did not come in the familiar essay until Elia was created, it grew to perfection in the critical papers of 1811. "On the Character and Genius of Hogarth" and "On the Tragedies of Shakespeare" are among his best work. His ability to write criticism matured relatively early.

Between the last essays in the *Reflector* and the first Elian essay in the *London Magazine* of 1820, Lamb's work consisted mainly of reviews, criticism, verses, and children's books. There were, to be sure, the essays "Recollections of Christ's Hospital" and "Confessions of a Drunkard" in 1813, but aside from these somewhat transitional papers there was little opportunity to exhibit his technique in the true familiar essay. A plan for Lamb to make up two volumes of essays by reprinting some of the *Reflector* papers and writing new ones was cut off in its infancy by Gifford, editor of the *Quarterly*, whom Lamb damned eternally for his interference. So it came about that all Lamb's most characteristic essays were published between August, 1820, and August, 1825; after 1826 there was comparatively little productivity. Even in these periods, however, Lamb showed occasional traces of the Addisonian tendency as can be seen in "Captain Jackson" and "Barbara S——"; and he utilized the letter form again in his letters to Hone's *Every-Day Book* and *Table Book*.

That Lamb was well aware of the work of his predecessors in the essay has been indicated to some extent, but additional evidence of this is revealed in an eleven-page manuscript review by Lamb of the first volume of Hazlitt's *Table Talk*.[55] So far as is known, this essay has never been published, and extensive quotation cannot be made because of restrictions based on plans for publication sometime in the future. However, portions have been printed and facsimiled in Sotheby's sale catalog for March, 1929, and another section was quoted by Lucas, who saw it in the possession of Mr. Owen D. Young.[56] The date of composition may be placed between April, 1821, the date of publication of Volume I of *Table Talk*, and June, 1822, the date of the appearance of Volume II; the review concerns only the first volume and makes no mention of a second.

Although Lamb's strictures on Hazlitt's complaints of his friends in "On Living to One's-Self" and his praise of him as "one of the ablest prosewriters of the age" are of interest in a consideration of Lamb as a critic, it is Lamb's review of the development of self-revelation in the essay and his evaluation of his predecessors that are of particular interest here. These remarks are introductory to his commentary on the autobiographical nature of Hazlitt's work as an essayist and his avoidance of a "fictitious appellation": "He comes in no imaginary character . . . . He attracts, or repels, by strong realities of individual observation, humour, and feeling." Not only Addison's assumption of a character for a mouthpiece but his predilection for Visions was repugnant to Lamb:

In one particular indeed the followers of Addison were long and grievously misled. For many years after the publication of his celebrated Vision of Mirza, no book of Essays was thought complete without a Vision. It set the world dreaming. Take up any one of the volumes of this description, published in the last century;—you will possibly alight upon two or three successive papers, depicting, with more or less gravity, sober views of life *as it is*—when—pop—you come upon a Vision, which you trembled at beforehand from a glimpse you caught at certain abstractions in Capitals, FAME, RICHES, LONG LIFE, LOSS OF FRIENDS, PUNISHMENT BY EXILE . . . .

Hazlitt, he is thankful, "is no visionary." When we remember that Lamb contributed "A Vision of Horns" to the *London* in January, 1825, we question his sincerity, but in the same month he wrote Miss Sarah Hutchinson, Wordsworth's sister-in-law, "The 'Horns' is in a poor taste, resembling the most laboured papers in the Spectator. I had sign'd it 'Jack Horner:' but Taylor and Hessey said, it would be thought an offensive article, unless I put my known signature to it; and wrung from me my slow consent." Lamb never reprinted this paper.

But it is Lamb's singling out of the autobiographical quality as the charm and unifying factor of Hazlitt's essays that is of most importance. The review opens on this note:

A series of Miscellaneous Essays, however well executed in the parts, if it have not some pervading character to give a unity to it, is ordinarily as tormenting to get through as a set of aphorisms, or a jest-book.—The fathers of Essaywriting in ancient and modern times—Plutarch in a measure, and Montaigne without mercy or measure—imparted their own personal peculiarities to their themes. By this balm are they preserved.

Even the ponderosity of Dr. Johnson, in Lamb's opinion, serves as a desirable cohesive force:

The Author of the Rambler in a less direct way has attained the same effect. Without professing egotism, his work is as essentially egotistical as theirs. He deals out opinion, which he would have you take for argument, and is perpetually obtruding his own particular views of life for universal truths. This is the charm which binds us to his writings, and not any steady conviction we have of the solidity of his thinking. Possibly some of those Papers, which are generally understood to be failures in the Rambler—its ponderous levities for instance and unwieldly efforts at being sprightly—may detract less from the general effect, than is [if] something better in kind, but less in keeping, had been substituted in place of them.

In view of Lamb's earlier quoted comment on Goldsmith's prose as "simple, pure, touching, natural," his juxtaposition of him with Johnson is of interest:

If the Author had taken his friend Goldsmith into partnership, and they had furnished their quotas for alternate days, the world had been the gainer by the arrangement, but what a heterogeneous mass the work itself would have presented!

Here Lamb indulged in a bit of fancy which he later cancelled, perhaps as too light for a serious review; but it is still legible:

The bird of Athens pairing with the light Tom Tit—the graceful palfrey helping the heavy one to drag along his cumbersome wain—might be no inappropriate emblems of so perverse a cooperation.

Passing on to a consideration of Addison and Steele, Lamb points out the varying effectiveness of fictitious names:

Another class of Essayists, equally impressed with the advantages of this sort of appeal to the reader, but more dextrous at shifting off the invidiousness of a perpetual self-reference, substituted for themselves an *ideal character;* which left them a still fuller license in the delivery of their peculiar humours and opinions, under the masqued battery of a fictitious appellation.

Steele's Isaac Bickerstaff was a successful fictitious appellation, but the Spectator was not, because like so many of Bickerstaff's imitators, he lacked a personality of his own to color and give a pervading unity to his essays. Lamb had used numerous fictitious appellations as he worked in his imitative period, as we have seen. Elia was successful, because after he had served his apprenticeship he learned how necessary it was to give it individual coloring. It was not simply a nom de plume, nor merely an effective way of avoiding "the invidiousness of a perpetual self-reference."

Having carefully analyzed the reason for the success and failure of his predecessors, he profited therefrom and succeeded by a calculated effort.

We have seen now that Lamb was fully aware of his predecessors' work in the essay and thoroughly familiar with their methods and characteristics. Specifically, he realized the importance of self-revelation and the value of creating a personality for a fictitious appellation if there was to be unity. Lamb's pre-eminence in these achievements was not a haphazard one but a purposeful, studied use, albeit aided by the subjective tendency of the time and his own eminently suited temperament.

"I hate concealment and love to give a faithful journal of what passes within me," wrote Lamb to Coleridge in 1796,[57] and after his first, experimental period, more than any other writer he adopted Montaigne's habit of letting his personality flavor almost everything he wrote. Lamb was not unique in this practice of self-revelation; we have observed it in Cowley, Browne, Goldsmith, and in both of his chief contemporaries—Hazlitt and Hunt. But none of these writers revealed himself to such a degree as did Lamb. Many essayists before Lamb had used the first person, but that alone is barren. Lamb's egoism suggests more than Lamb's person; it awakens in the reader reflections of kindred feelings and affections. Moreover, the partial connotation of selfishness or conceit in the word *egoism* is avoided by the admixture of the humble, the sympathetic, and the solitary. Anyone could write "I," but not many could combine it with a character like Elia's. "C'est le caractère de Lamb lui-même qui nous attire," wrote a French biographer with unusual insight, continuing, "teignant de ses couleurs l'objet mis sous nos yeux et c'est la réflexion de ce caractère dans l'objet qui arrête notre esprit . . . . Il est toujours agréable de sentir l'homme sous l'écrivain."[58]

From our survey of the essay before Lamb, we have seen

that its history was continuous from the time of Bacon and that the essays of Elia incorporated many features of their predecessors. They were not, as has too often been stated or implied, a sudden and new creation, but the logical result-ant of several forces. Lamb's acquaintance with earlier essays and his realization of their virtues and defects pro-vided a conscious direction to his innate skill. His personal temperament, defined above, was not only suited to the use of the essay as a form of expression but was also such as enabled him to improve and enhance the qualities his un-erring judgment recommended to itself. The social nature of the eighteenth century had not been conducive to the development of the true familiar essay, which depicts an individual. But the subjective temperament of the Roman-tic period, encouraging the writer to express his feelings, had manifested itself on the essay before Lamb began to write; so it would be improper to say that Lamb invented the familiar essay of his time or that he was a nineteenth-century Montaigne in uniqueness. That this new familiar essay was the result of progressive, logical development is emphasized by the fact that the early essays of Lamb and his important contemporaries were largely imitative of the older type; that the development of this new essay was not Lamb's personal achievement is brought home when we recognize that Hazlitt and Hunt both made use of subjec-tive and personal elements, albeit not to such a degree, nor with such success, as did Lamb.

Wherein, then, lies the secret of Lamb's reputation and continued popularity? His perfection of the type and his pre-eminence in the form were the result not of his inven-tion of the qualities and elements of the new essay, but of his judicious combination of them, and of his use with self-revelation of the pathos, the sentiment, and the humor which sprang from his own emotional life. He was not unique in his choice of subjects but rather in his shaping of them. Like the seventeenth-century essayists, Lamb, as well as Hunt and Hazlitt, used the convention of the character. But whereas in the *Reflector* he usually treated the character as an individual essay, in certain of the Elia essays he used it for variety as part of an essay subordinate to the main theme. Furthermore, Lamb's characters were not hypothetical but real people—often his friends such as the famous Mrs. Battle, and sometimes, as in "The Convalescent," himself. His sympathetic understanding permitted him to humanize his characters into personalities with individuality and fundamental characteristics of deep interest to a reader. Beyond these considerations, he was in tune with his age. In his imaginative response to the past, in his sympathy for the humble, and in his utilization of the subjective approach, he is at one with the Romantic Movement.

T W O

"But Where Shall I Get Another Subject?"

ORIGINS

By means of the biographical data about Lamb, which are now in little danger of being radically modified, and of his correspondence, which is now in a more nearly complete form than ever before, it is possible to trace many of the ideas in his essays backward toward their inception. In this manner we are able to see how the essays developed in a perceptive, creative mind. The origins of the ideas are to be found in Lamb's experience, friendships, reading, and in suggestions of editors and fellow writers. First, let us look at the part played by experience in the evolution of Elia.

Nostalgia for the past, in which, incidentally, Lamb shows his kinship with the Romantic Movement, was a product of Lamb's environment. His early home in the Temple with its ancient surroundings helped to mold his taste for the medieval; Christ's Hospital, likewise, had a tradition in name and appearance; and the South Sea House, with its quaint old bachelors, breathed reminis-

cence. Love for the past was nurtured by his reading of
the old authors; it was manifested by his use of it in "Oxford in the Vacation," "Old China," "Blakesmoor in
H——shire," "Mackery End in Hertfordshire," and "The
Gentle Giantess." Reminiscence of his own past is the core
of "The South Sea House," "Christ's Hospital Five and
Thirty Years Ago," "The Old Benchers of the Inner Temple," "The Praise of Chimney-Sweepers," and "A Complaint of the Decay of Beggars."

"From Coleridge and Wordsworth," writes a critic, "he
learned of the glory of childhood and the place of memory
in poetry."[1] Whether learned from them or others, certainly
the qualities of childhood often combined with the past to
attract him. Another commentator points out, "That searching back towards childhood appeared already in the autobiographical elements in his story *Rosamund Gray:* it
recurs frequently in the essays."[2] "Christ's Hospital Five
and Thirty Years Ago" may well have been inspired by his
attendance as a guest at the dinner of the Society of Blues
on February 11, 1817, where he was apparently shown the
record of another dinner at the Nag's Head Tavern on St.
Matthew's Day in 1790 attended by the visitors and Senior
Scholars: "Samuel Taylor Coleridge, Robert Allen, and
Chas. Valentine Le Grice all of the Grammar Schl."[3] That
this appeal of childhood to the essayist was not limited to
his personal experience but was universal in extent is evident from "Barbara S——." The basic incident here came
not from his own but from the early life of Fanny Kelly,
the talented actress to whom Lamb once proposed.

Generally speaking, however, Lamb's peculiar ability lay
in the personal note. When he was submitting short contributions to the *Morning Post* in 1802, he complained that
"Most of them are rejected; all, almost, that are *personal,*
where my forte lies."[4] Stuart, the editor, explained the rejec-

tions by saying, "his drollery was vapid, when given in short paragraphs fit for a newspaper."[5] Usually Lamb's essay-characters were modeled after real people. In this connection, we must not overlook his own family for the prototypes they furnished his writing. His sister, Mary, figures prominently as Bridget Elia, his cousin, in "Mackery End in Hertfordshire," "Mrs. Battle's Opinions on Whist," and "Old China." John Lamb, his brother, is sketched at full length as his cousin James in "My Relations" and is introduced as uncle to his "Dream-Children." Practically all we know of his father, John, we may read in "The Old Benchers of the Inner Temple," where he is presented as Lovel. More extensively used than any other relative is Sarah Lamb, his Aunt Hetty, who figures in "Christ's Hospital Five and Thirty Years Ago," "A Dissertation upon Roast Pig," "Witches and Other Night-Fears," "My Relations," and "Poor Relations."

We are not concerned here, however, with tracing the autobiographical elements in Lamb's essays; in the main they are obvious to anyone familiar with his life. It is Lamb's creative method applied to actual experience rather than reminiscence that is of paramount interest. His amusing "Amicus Redivivus" (Dec., 1823) is particularly revealing in this connection. When George Dyer, that most eccentric, lovable, and near-sighted character, walked out of Lamb's Islington house into the New River one Sunday in early November, 1823, his rescue gave Lamb an opportunity to memorialize his friend in an essay. Twenty-three years before, Lamb had written to Coleridge, "If I could but calculate the precise date of his death, I would write a novel on purpose to make George the hero. I could hit him off to a hair."[6] He never wrote the novel, but he had described Dyer in "Oxford in the Vacation." Now, a week after Dyer's involuntary immersion, he related the incident in a letter to Mrs. Hazlitt:

What I now tell you is literally true. Yesterday week George Dyer called upon us, at one o'clock (*bright noon day*) on his way to dine with Mrs. Barbauld at Newington. He sat with Mary about half an hour, and took leave. The maid saw him go out from her kitchen window; but suddenly losing sight of him, ran up in a fright to Mary. G. D., instead of keeping the slip that leads to the gate, had deliberately, staff in hand, in broad open day, marched into the New River. He had not his spectacles on, and you know his absence. Who helped him out, they can hardly tell; but between 'em they got him out, drenched thro' and thro'. A mob collected by that time and accompanied him in. "Send for the Doctor!" they said; and a one-eyed fellow, dirty and drunk, was fetched from the Public House at the end, where it seems he lurks, for the sake of picking up water practice, having formerly had a medal from the Humane Society for some rescue. By his advice, the patient was put between blankets; and when I came home at four to dinner, I found G. D. a-bed, and raving, light-headed with the brandy-and-water which the doctor had administered. He sung, laughed, whimpered, screamed, babbled of guardian angels, would get up and go home; but we kept him there by force; and by next morning he departed sobered, and seems to have received no injury.[7]

These are the facts, and they are, in the main, confirmed by the account of Bryan Waller Procter ("Barry Cornwall"), who arrived on the scene about fifteen minutes after Dyer was rescued.[8] A comparison with the essay shows notable differences. The one-eyed doctor has become Monoculus, and a long paragraph of delicate humor is derived from his character. Almost the whole latter half of the essay is concerned with classical allusions and with admonitions to Dyer. The details of the first half of the essay, though elaborated, are much the same. But the most interesting feature is the characteristic introduction of Lamb himself, contrary to the facts, as the chief figure, next to Dyer. Although Procter believed that the maid had "assisted at the rescue,"[9] she is unmentioned. It is Lamb who sees Dyer walk into the river, and it is he who effects the rescue: "How I found my feet, I know not. Consciousness was quite gone. Some spirit, not my own, whirled me to the spot. I remember nothing but the silvery apparition of a good white head emerging; nigh which a staff (the hand unseen that wielded it) pointed upwards, as feeling for the skies. In a moment (if time was in that time) he was on my shoulders, and I—freighted with a load more precious than his who bore Anchises." This personal element working in the essays—especially in those stemming from experience—is perhaps the most characteristic feature in Lamb's excellence, and "Amicus Redivivus" is an excellent example. Lamb was, indeed, so convincing that Procter's own two accounts differ in details, and in one he credits Lamb with going for a surgeon and administering "a formidable dose of Cognac and water to the sufferer . . . ."[10]

Throughout his essays we find that Lamb has not hesitated to adopt for his own the incidents and anecdotes of others. In "Imperfect Sympathies" he tells the story of his trip in a coach with three Quakers who wrangled over the meal check. While reading the essay, we have no reason to doubt that it was an autobiographical experience, but in a letter to Bernard Barton, a Quaker friend, written two years after this essay was published, Lamb confessed that he was not a participant but that the story was told him by Sir Anthony Carlisle.[11] On the other hand, "The Convalescent" (July, 1825) is based on an actual period of illness in the summer of 1825. The point is that in the finished literary product the autobiographical quality is everywhere convincing.

Not all this personal or adopted experience is used to furnish the main themes; much, and perhaps most, of it is found in phrases and sentences with a subordinate purpose. A comparison of some of these with factual statements from the letters and elsewhere is of interest and value: "I have played at serious whist with Mr. Liston," wrote Lamb of an actor friend in "Barbara S——"; in one of Mary's letters to Mrs. Hazlitt we read of a whist party at Godwin's, where "We finished there at twelve o'clock (Charles and Liston brimfull of gin and water and snuff) . . . ."[12] This is only one of many epistolary references substantiating Lamb's "partiality for the production of the juniper berry," as he put it in his "Autobiographical Sketch." In "Old China" he recalled the pleasure "in the first dish of peas," and in "Grace before Meat," while regretting that vegetables generally have lost their "gust" with him, he adds, "Only I stick to asparagus, which still seems to inspire gentle thoughts"; writing to Dorothy Wordsworth, the poet's sister, from Covent Garden, Lamb had spoken of now being situated "where we are morally sure of the earliest peas and 'sparagus."[13]

Lamb's statement in "A Chapter on Ears" that "I have no ear . . . for music . . . I have received a great deal more pain than pleasure from this so cried-up faculty" has generally been received as an exaggeration. De Quincey's testimony that Lamb "had an insensibility to music more absolute than can have been shared by any human creature, or perhaps than was ever before acknowledged so candidly" is discounted by Edmund Blunden: "Lamb's 'no ear' was one of his pretences, to which De Quincey has fallen a victim. There are many intimations in his Works that he had a passion for *some* music; but he was not going to be bullied into the fashionable worship of prescribed composers."[14] Was it merely pretense? Shortly before the composition of this essay, Lamb had complained to Mrs. Wordsworth of being kept awake at nights by singing in a public house close to his bedroom.[15] In the essay itself he writes of being bored at a musical, but "a draught of true

Lutheran beer . . . at once reconciles me to the rationalities
of a purer faith"; the reality of his boredom is proved by a
reminiscence of Edmund Ollier, son of the publisher of
Lamb's *Works*, prefaced to an edition of *Elia:* "Once at a
musical party at Leigh Hunt's, being oppressed with what
to him was nothing better than a prolonged noise . . . he
said—'If one only had a pot of porter, one might get through
this.' It was procured for him and he weathered the Mozar-
tian storm."[16] The music for which Lamb had a "passion,"
as Blunden puts it, seems rather limited. Hunt testified,
"He would put up with no anthems but Kent's and with no
songs but Water Parted from the Sea." Lamb's friends included William Ayrton, music critic, and Vincent Novello,
organist at the chapel of the Portuguese Embassy; but his
friendship with them no more suggests a love of music than
his friendships with Manning and Rickman suggest a love
of mathematics and statistics. It was Novello's daughter
Clara, "the most musically gifted of the Novello children
. . . one of the greatest singers of her generation,"[17] who
wrote in her *Reminiscences:* "my father made me sing to
him one day; but he [Lamb] stopped me, saying, 'Clara,
don't make that d——d noise!' for which, I think, I loved
him as much as for all the rest."[18]

Occasionally the letters give the lie to his essay statements. In "Tom Pry" he writes of letter seals, "I carry a
rich gold one, which was my grandfather's, always about
me"; but in a letter to Barton he writes, "I never had a seal
too of my own."[19] Of course, some of the discrepancies between the essays and the letters resulted from a change in
opinion and are not deliberate misrepresentations for literary purposes. "I want no more wealth than I possess. A
more contented being than myself, as to money matters,
exists not," he wrote in "The Last Peach," published one
month after he had been retired from the East India House
on an annual pension of £450; some sixteen years earlier

he had exclaimed to Coleridge, "I must do something for money. Not that I have immediate wants, but I have prospective ones. O money money how blindly thou hast been worshipped, and how stupidly abused! Thou art health, and liberty, and strength and he that has thee may rattle his pockets at the Devil!"[20] Again, after disparaging Hastings and the seaside in "The Old Margate Hoy," he confided to Barton, "I abused Hastings, but learned its value. There are spots, inland bays, etc., which realise the notions of Juan Fernandez."[21]

The important thing is not whether these personal elements—used for a major theme or a minor embellishment— are strictly autobiographical; it is that they exist in the essays and help to create the impression the reader forms of their author. This admixture of the personal element differentiates the essays from commonplace journalism and from the work of his contemporaries. Because emotions are basic in all experience, essays that reflect their author are universal in appeal; and we respond to Lamb's emotions and personality as representative of the universal. The subjective modification of the content of his letter to Mrs. Hazlitt about George Dyer's near-drowning raised reportorial fact to literature.

Lamb's friendships—with their attendant conversation and correspondence—were of equal, if not of greater, importance than experience in furnishing ideas for essays. Did anyone ever have more good friends than Lamb? Certainly any biography of him is largely an account of his friendships; his essays are full of references to, and sketches of, his friends and acquaintances. Evidence of the high caliber of his mind and the attractive nature of his personality lies in the fact that he was surrounded by men of importance in widely varied fields of activity: literature, of course; but also music; mathematics; travel and adventure; law; art; politics; journalism; and merchandising. In most cases it was some oddity in their personality that attracted Lamb. "I have never made an acquaintance . . . that lasted; or a friendship that answered; with any that had not some tincture of the absurd in their characters," he wrote in "All Fool's Day"; the simple naïveté of Dyer, which we have already witnessed, the egotism of Wordsworth, and Coleridge's inability to bring a project to a conclusion serve to illustrate the truth of this remark. These friends stimulated Lamb's genius to such an extent that without them we should not have the essays of Elia. Let us see how they helped to evoke his rare qualities and contribute to his evolution.

The most important and most lasting of Lamb's friend-ships was that with Samuel Taylor Coleridge, whom he came to know as a fellow scholar at Christ's Hospital. It was Coleridge's book-borrowing habits that inspired the writing of "The Two Races of Men." His influence on Lamb's creative work can hardly be overestimated. Their friendly meetings at the Salutation and Cat over "egg-hot" in the autumn and winter of 1794–95, where Coleridge's conversation was so brilliant that the host of the tavern gave him free hospitality in return for his presence, was an auspicious beginning. Coleridge's strengthening letters to his friend after the tragedy of 1796 were so full of religious consolation that Lamb departed from his customary prac-tice of destroying letters to preserve these few. They not only helped him through the crisis but persuaded him not to abandon his interest and efforts in literature. Coleridge even went so far as to include some of Lamb's poems in his 1796 volume. He recommended him to the editor of the *Morning Post,* for which Lamb wrote "The Londoner" and some short dramatic reviews. "He has lugged me to the brink of engaging to a newspaper, and has suggested to me for a first plan the forgery of a supposed manuscript of Burton the anatomist of melancholy," wrote Lamb to

Thomas Manning[22] in reference to his "Curious Fragments," as he entitled the imitation. Coleridge generally encouraged Lamb's poetical abilities and introduced him to metaphysics and George Wither, whom Lamb later discussed in a critical essay, as well as to Jeremy Taylor and other authors.[23] "To you I owe much under God," acknowledged Lamb.[24] The debt was not one-sided, for Lamb introduced Coleridge to books and gave him the benefit of his very frank criticism of his poetry. For the most part, Coleridge valued this criticism; he quoted Lamb in letters to his friends. Wordsworth and Southey also received from Lamb letters full of the minutiae of criticism. Coleridge's interest in Lamb's work as an essayist in later years is indicated by a letter to Hessey, the publisher of the *London*, in 1825: "I am *delighted* with the 'Superannuated Man.' I have read it a dozen times at least: It is worthy of Charles Lamb in his happiest Carolo-lambian Hour. And that is saying a great deal."

One of the most valuable services Coleridge rendered Lamb was to introduce him to such men as Godwin, Southey, Wordsworth, Hazlitt, and the Lloyds. Godwin and his publishing ventures provided the motive force for the *Tales from Shakespear* and the various children's books written by Charles and Mary. It was Southey, Coleridge's brother-in-law, who in 1808 interested a publisher in Lamb's *Specimens of English Dramatic Poets*. Writing to Edward Moxon on February 2, 1836, he stated that "Lamb, Lloyd, and White were inseparable in 1798." White is the James White whose collaboration with Lamb on the *Falstaff Letters* has been guessed though never proved, and of whom Lamb wrote in "The Praise of Chimney-Sweepers," where he is immortalized, "He carried away with him half the fun of the world when he died—of my world at least." It might be noted that the well-known sense of humor of Samuel Le Grice, whom Lamb knew at Christ's, must have stimulated and nurtured the fanciful wit in the essays of Elia, but Bryan W. Procter, who did not come to know Lamb until 1817, overlooked him in distinguishing White as a lover of fun; in his *Memoir* of 1866 we read, "Lamb's earliest friends and confidants, with one exception, were singularly void of wit and the love of jesting."[25] The exception is not named in the printed book, but in the original manuscript, preserved at the Huntington Library, Procter's marginal note names the exception as "Jem White."

Wit and a love of the pun in particular was one of the bases of Lamb's close friendship and extensive correspondence with Thomas Manning, a mathematician whom Lamb first met in 1799 on a visit to his friend Charles Lloyd, the younger, then a student at Cambridge University. Crabb Robinson's Diary for June 10, 1824, gives us Lamb's opinion of Manning: "On my walk with Lamb, he spoke with enthusiasm of Manning, declaring that he is the most wonderful man he ever knew, more extraordinary than Wordsworth or Coleridge. Yet he does nothing. He has travelled even in China, and has been by land from India through Thibet, yet, as far as is known, he has written nothing. Lamb says his criticisms are of the very first quality." This respect for opinion was mutual, but of equal importance was Manning's sense of humor, which made him a fit target for some of the most amusing "matter-of-lie" letters that Lamb wrote. This love for the whimsical in Manning must have helped to develop in Lamb that mixture of fact and fancy which we see later in full force in the essays. There is, too, to Manning's credit the earliest recorded recognition of Lamb as an essayist, expressed in a previously quoted passage from a letter of 1802. Another point of kinship lay in their love of good food; Lamb's letters to Manning contain many expressions of appreciation for gifts of delicacies. Writing to Lamb on May 30, 1819, after settling

in Lamb's beloved Hertfordshire on his return from the
Far East, Manning describes the pleasures of rural life: "I
say if you come to the grosser delights, what can be more
delightful than killing a pig? . . . What benefits accrue from
the death of that stubborn ill-manner'd animal! & yet what
a noise a' makes at the time. One would think to hear him
one was doing a mischief instead of a service!"[26] Writing
to Barton a few months after the publication of his famous
"Dissertation upon Roast Pig," Lamb acknowledged his indebtedness: "The idea of the discovery of roasting pigs, I
also borrowed from my friend Manning . . . ."[27]

Perhaps the most important way in which his friends influenced his essays was through their conversation. At one
time Lamb and his sister held open house every Thursday
evening—later changed to every Wednesday. His correspondence is interlaced with brief, often undated, invitations. One of the most frequent recipients of these little
notelets was Thomas Allsop, a well-to-do silk merchant
whom Lamb met in 1820. A love of good food and an
admiration for Coleridge bound them together. Two previously unpublished letters to Allsop will illustrate the type
of invitation he and others habitually received. One is dated
only "Sat*" but is clearly postmarked "Jan. 27, 1821":

Dr. Sir, can you come this Eveng? I expect Liston.

C. L.

The second letter, which is—uncharacteristically—dated,
follows:

Dear Sir, I have been much out of order lately, and we shall not
be in Town till Xmas day. Let us see you on *Wednesd* *Even*
the 27th. We think of not going to Coleridge's till after the
holydays.—

Yours Truly

Tuesd 19 Dec '20   CL[28]

It was at these conversation-parties that ideas filled the air, whence Lamb snatched them to store up for future use. Then too, these gatherings often listened to Lamb speak for the first time what proved to be—without his necessarily knowing it himself—rough drafts of some of his essays-to-be. The nature of these *conversazioni* is described in many places, perhaps nowhere better than in Procter's biography:

When you went to Lamb's rooms on the Wednesday evenings (his "at Home,") you generally found the card table spread out, Lamb himself one of the players. On the corner of the table was a snuff-box; and the game was enlivened by sundry brief ejaculations and pungent questions, which kept alive the wits of the party present. It was not "silent whist!" . . . The supper of cold meat, on these occasions, was always on the side table; not very formal, as may be imagined; and every one might rise, when it suited him, and cut a slice or take a glass of porter, without reflecting on the abstinence of the rest of the company. Lamb would, perhaps, call out and bid the hungry guest help himself without ceremony . . . .[29]

William Hazlitt adds to the picture in his essay "On the Conversation of Authors," written for the *London Magazine* of September, 1820: "An utterly uninformed person might have supposed this a scene of vulgar confusion and uproar. While the most critical question was pending, while the most difficult problem in philosophy was solving, P[hillips] cried out, 'That's game,' and M[artin] B[urney] muttered a quotation over the last remains of a veal-pie at a side table . . . ."

The habitués of these parties were not all famous men, nor were they associated by profession—indeed some of them did not have professions. Yet they were all thinkers—some eccentric, some original—but all devoted to the intellect. "I never, in all my life, heard so much unpretending good sense talked, as at Charles Lamb's social parties," wrote Procter, pointing out that the chief beauty of these evenings was that everyone was on the same level and had an equal chance to speak and to be heard.[30] Occasionally there was friction, as when Lamb's brother, who sometimes attended the parties, and Hazlitt came to blows over whether Holbein's coloring was as good as that of Vandyke, but even then Hazlitt's black eye did not seriously affect the spirits of the company: "I do not mind a blow, Sir," explained Hazlitt; "nothing affects me but an Abstract Idea!"[31]

Not all the conversations were carried on under Lamb's hospitable roof. Sarah (Mrs. James) Burney, the original of the titular figure in "Mrs. Battle's Opinions on Whist," and her husband, the admiral who had circumnavigated the globe with Cook, held whist parties at their home in James Street; to them came regularly Hunt, Hazlitt, Southey, Robinson, Ayrton, Rickman, Molesworth Phillips, and, of course, the Lambs. As was previously noted, the marriage of the Burneys' daughter, Sarah, to her cousin John Payne furnished Lamb with the subject of "The Wedding." John was the nephew of Thomas Payne, the father of Mrs. James Burney. He succeeded him about 1825 in the book-selling partnership with Henry Foss, a name combination which had provoked Lamb's reply to an account of De Quincey's complaints of ill health that he should have employed Payne and Fuss as his publishers. In a hitherto unpublished letter, postmarked April 14, 1832, to John Payne—the only one he is known to have written to him—Lamb expressed his sorrow for the death of Payne's mother-in-law and recalled his own association with the family. The letter is addressed to "John Payne, Esq., 26 James St., Buckingham Gate":

My dear Payne,

I learned the melancholy event first from a Newspaper. It came over us very sadly indeed, not knowing there was any reason for apprehending it. Half of the pleasantness of the better half of my life was from the Society in James' Street. It lasted longer than such friendships are used to do. Mary sends her very kindest love to *Sally*—tis her old appelation, and returns forcibly on this occasion. Twill not be a great while before we shall be in London, when we shall make it a point of religion to see you. God bless you all.

C. Lamb[32]

There were also irregular gatherings at Godwin's and Leigh Hunt's, the latter described by a contemporary as follows: "Lamb's gentle humor, Hunt's passion, and Curran's volubility, Hazlitt's sharpness and point, and Godwin's great head full of cold brains, all coming into contact and conflict, and agreeing in nothing but their common hatred of everything that has been more successful than their own works, made one of the most curious and amusing *olla podrida* I ever met."[33]

When the *London Magazine* passed into the hands of Taylor and Hessey in 1821, a custom of monthly dinners for the contributors was inaugurated. Thomas Hood, the subeditor, is our informant here:

On the right hand then of the editor sits Elia, of the pleasant smile, and the quick eyes . . . . Next to him, shining verdantly out from the grave-coloured suits of the literati, like a patch of turnips amidst stubble and fallow, behold our Jack i' the Green—John Clare . . . . Elia—much more of house Lamb than of grass Lamb—avowedly caring little or nothing for pastoral; cottons, nevertheless, very kindly to the Northamptonshire poet, and still more to his ale, pledging him again and again as "Clarissimus," and "Princely Clare," and sometimes so lustily as to make the latter cast an anxious glance into his tankard . . . . But besides the tankard, the two "drouthie neebors" discuss poetry in general, and Montgomery's "Common Lot" in particular, Lamb insisting on the beauty of the tangental sharp turn at "O! she was fair!" thinking, mayhap, of his own Alice W——, and Clare swearing "Dal!" (a clarified d——n) "Dal! if it isn't like a dead man preaching out of his coffin!"[34]

The difference in the conversation of Lamb's friends is evident from the various reports. We hear of the "strenuous talk of Hazlitt, who never descended to fine words,"[35] and Hazlitt's essay "On the Conversation of Authors" shows us Captain Burney, "who had you at an advantage by never understanding you," Rickman, "who asserted some incredible matter of fact as a likely paradox, and settled all controversies by an *ipse dixit*, a *fiat* of his will," and Mrs. Reynolds, "who being of a quiet turn, loved to hear a noisy debate." Procter speaks also of the "unaffected quiet conversation of Manning," of "the vivacious excursive talk of Leigh Hunt," and of the "monologues of Coleridge," the last recalling Lamb's reply when Coleridge once asked him if he had ever heard him preach: "I never heard you do anything else," said Lamb. Lamb hated long talkers as much as they hated his habit of interrupting their grave discussions with a light jest. Talfourd's talk was "too egotistical to be generally popular—still his admirable law stories, though somewhat too frequently told, are highly interesting, and show the man of great social talent," wrote Thomas Powell, who singled out Hunt's conversation for special praise: "It is a perpetual flow of mental champagne, sparkling with anecdotes, refined jokes, witticisms, repartees, the peculiarities of celebrated men, celebrated streets, celebrated houses, celebrated mountains, celebrated mice; in short it is a brilliant group of heterogenous recollections presided over by a genial appreciation . . . We have now an anecdote of Byron—then of Shelley—illustrated by some well known passage in their works, the origin of which is developed— all this lively stream is given in a peculiar crisp voice which makes the '*tout ensemble*' perfect."[36] Hazlitt also testified to Hunt's conversational powers, in his "On the Conversation of Authors," speaking of his pleasantry and ability to tell stories, mimic actors and acquaintances, and laugh at other people's jokes as well as at his own.

Given this extreme variety in personality among his
friends, it is noteworthy that when Lamb was host, he made
the effort to adapt himself to each, just as in his letters he
adopted a different attitude to each of his many correspondents. B. W. Procter details his thoughtfulness toward his
guests: "It was curious to observe the gradations in Lamb's
manner to all his various guests; although it was courteous
to all. With Hazlitt he talked at [as] though they met the
subject in discussion on equal terms; with Leigh Hunt he
exchanged repartees; to Wordsworth he was almost respectful; with Coleridge he was sometimes jocose, sometimes deferring; with Martin Burney fraternally familiar;
with Manning affectionate; with Godwin merely courteous; or if friendly, then in a minor degree."[37] Perhaps this
variety of conversation explains in part why Lamb was not
Boswellized. It seems unfortunate to us that no one bothered to give more than general impressions of his talk when
writing about the man; yet one of his contemporaries prays,
"Heaven preserve us from a Boswell in his case!—for he
would infallibly dissipate the charm and the fragrance
. . . ."[38] Another writer dwells on this quality: "the racy
freshness, that was like an atmosphere of country air about
it, was better than all; the perfect simplicity, absence of all
conceit, childlike enjoyment of his own wit, and the sweetness and benevolence that played about the rugged face,
gave to it a charm in no way inferior to the poetical enjoyment derived from the more popular conversation of his
friend [Coleridge]."[39]

From the numerous and scattered references to Lamb's
conversation, we may draw certain conclusions: He habitually kept in the background, especially when politics or
abstract ideas were being discussed, unless something was
said that gave him an opportunity to stammer out a pun or
to make a real contribution. He loved to discuss persons

and books, but he never talked unless he understood the
subject. Apparently his speech impediment, although not
severe, limited his utterances to short sentences, which,
because of the necessity of compressing the thought, were
the more effective. The observer just quoted contrasted
Lamb's speech with that of Coleridge in this respect: "It
was not one uninterrupted flow, but a periodical production of sentences, short, telling, full of wit, philosophy, at
times slightly caustic, though that is too strong a word for
satire which was of the most good-natured kind."[40] Lamb's
habit of mind resulted in odd associations and transitions.
His innate honesty and sincerity, avoiding the hypocrisy
and affectation he detested, led him to make statements which often shocked and startled the company because of their oddity or lack of regard for convention and
even, sometimes, of politeness. Once "sitting next some
chattering woman at dinner; observing he didn't attend to
her, 'You don't seem (said the lady) to be at all the better
for what I have been saying to you.' 'No, Ma'am (he answered), 'but this gentleman at the other side of me must,
for it all came in at one ear and went out at the other.' "[41]
Talfourd, Lamb's friend and first biographer, reveals this
frank honesty in the only recorded remark of Lamb's childhood: "when a very little boy, walking with his sister in a
churchyard, he suddenly asked her, 'Mary, where do the
naughty people lie?' " This early reflection on the eulogistic
nature of churchyard inscriptions was manifested years
later in *Rosamund Gray*, where we read: "I said jestingly,
where be all the *bad* people buried?" Hazlitt's tribute to
Lamb's conversation in his essay "On the Conversation of
Authors" is one of the highest; he calls him "the most delightful, the most provoking, the most witty and sensible of
men. He always made the best pun, and the best remark
in the course of the evening. His serious conversation, like

his serious writing, is his best. No one ever stammered out such fine, piquant, deep, eloquent things in half a dozen half-sentences as he does. His jests scald like tears: and he probes a question with a play upon words. What a keen, laughing, hair-brained vein of home-felt truth! What choice venom!"

On the other hand, Patmore wrote that Lamb's conversation was distinguished only when it was tête-à-tête by his own fireside with one or two friends; in a large company he did not shine or say anything deserving of note. The Rev. J. F. Russell found that Lamb required to be drawn into conversation, and wrote that he spoke by fits and starts but with loud, rich tones which, with the deep pathos that came into his voice when he read, gave to poetry a great weight. De Quincey confirmed this tribute to his ability to read aloud: "Of all our poets Lamb only and Wordsworth read well."[42]

With Coleridge, Hazlitt, and Lamb brought together so frequently in conversation, it is not surprising that they should have exchanged ideas that were later developed into literary form, sometimes with two writers using the same theme at the same or at different times. Ideas were common property, and it is not possible to ascertain the originator in many cases, but the authors themselves were aware of their mutual dependence and influence. Hazlitt, in his essay "On the Conversation of Authors," wrote of Lamb that "He has furnished many a text for C[oleridge] to preach upon." Coleridge, for his part, maintained in a letter of 1816: "Almost all the *Sparkles* and *originalities* of his [Hazlitt's] Essays are, however, echoes from Poor Charles Lamb—and in his last libel the image of the Angel without hands or feet, was stolen from a letter of my own to Charles Lamb, which had been quoted to him."[43] In his *Table Talk* for August 6, 1832, Coleridge further suggested that one "compare Charles Lamb's exquisite criticisms on Shakespeare with Hazlitt's round and round imitations of them." Hazlitt frankly acknowledges, in his essay "On the Conversation of Authors," his indebtedness to Lamb for his idea in "Of Persons One Would Wish to Have Seen"; Lamb, he says, "was for making out a list of persons famous in history that one would wish to see again," and he urged Lamb to write an essay on the subject, but since he would not, he supposed he must do it: "I am," he continues, "sometimes, I suspect, a better reporter of the ideas of other people than of my own." Both writers developed the subject of Guy Fawkes from a conversation on the same occasion. Lamb's reference in his opening lines to Hazlitt's observations, published in the *Examiner* a few months earlier, establishes the order of writing, although the last portion of Lamb's *London Magazine* article was a slightly altered reprint of a *Reflector* essay of 1811 which he had entitled "On the Probable Effects of the Gunpowder Treason in this Country if the Conspirators had accomplished their Object." Hazlitt seemed unaware of this when he wrote in "Elia and Geoffrey Crayon," "we believe he never heartily forgave a certain writer who took the subject of Guy Faux [sic] out of his hands."

In several instances there are similarities between Lamb's essays and ones by Hazlitt that appeared in print earlier. Lamb's "The Two Races of Men" (*London,* Dec., 1820), shows similarities to Hazlitt's "On the Conversation of Authors," published in the same magazine in September of the same year. Lamb's "Detached Thoughts on Books and Reading" (*London,* July, 1822) shows similarities to Hazlitt's "On Reading Old Books" (*London,* Feb., 1821). Some of Lamb's comments in "A Quakers' Meeting" (*London,* Apr., 1821), in "Imperfect Sympathies" (*London,* Aug., 1821), and in "Grace before Meat" (*London,* Nov., 1821) are anticipated by Hazlitt's remarks on the character of Quakers in his "Tendency of Sects" (*Examiner,* Sept. 10, 1815). These similarities are not such as to indicate plagiarism but rather the natural result of utilizing the same ideas derived from conversations at which both were present.[44] After reading Lamb's "New Year's Eve" in the *London* for January, 1821, Hazlitt wrote to the editor, John Scott, to inquire whether he would keep his own essay, "The Past and Future," which he had submitted: "You see Lamb argues the same view of the subject. That 'young master' will anticipate all my discoveries, if I don't mind."[45] Scott apparently agreed with him, for he returned the manuscript, and "The Past and Future" was first published in Hazlitt's *Table Talk* in June, 1821. In Volume II of *Table Talk,* published in June, 1822, the essay "On the Fear of Death" shows even closer resemblances to Lamb's "New Year's Eve." A comparison of two passages will illustrate the closeness:

Not childhood alone, but the young man till thirty, never feels practically that he is mortal. He knows it indeed, and, if need were, he could preach a homily on the fragility of life; but he brings it not home to himself, any more than in a hot June we can appropriate to our imagination the freezing days of December. But now, shall I confess a truth?—I feel these audits but too powerfully. I begin to count the probabilities of my duration, and to grudge at the expenditure of moments and shortest periods, like miser's farthings. [Lamb]

No young man ever thinks he shall die. He may believe that others will, or assent to the doctrine that "all men are mortal" as an abstract proposition, but he is far enough from bringing it home to himself individually. Youth, buoyant activity, and animal spirits, hold absolute antipathy with old age as well as with death; nor have we, in the hey-day of life, any more than in the thoughtlessness of childhood, the remotest conception . . . . [Hazlitt]

Hazlitt's first line here recalls his opening statement in "On the Feeling of Immortality in Youth" (1827): "No young man believes he shall ever die. It was a saying of my brother's, and a fine one."

"New Year's Eve," like other essays employing ideas worked on by both Lamb and Hazlitt, derived from conversation, although Hazlitt was not present at the one recorded. Talfourd, describing his first meeting with Lamb in 1815, wrote, "We discoursed then of life and death, and our anticipation of a world beyond the grave . . . which he so finely indicated in his "New Year's Eve" years afterwards."[46]

Two other essays illustrating the importance of conversation as a medium for the first expression, as well as the genesis, of an idea are "Grace before Meat" and "On the Total Defect of the Quality of Imagination observable in the Works of Modern British Artists." The former grew out of a discussion of the temptation scene in *Paradise Regained*. "With what discrimination," wrote Hazlitt in "On the Conversation of Authors," "he hinted a defect in what he admired most—as in saying that the display of the sumptuous banquet in *Paradise Regained* was not in true keeping, as the simplest fare was all that was necessary to tempt the extremity of hunger." The second essay named was first expressed in a conversation with Thomas Hood, who writes of accompanying him on walks where Lamb calculated distances, not by miles, but by pints. This, incidentally, is not a unique, but a widespread method, ranging from German signposts giving the number of minutes, to the Turkistan use of pots of tea, Holland canal travellers' use of pipes they smoke, and the Burmese use of a word meaning "to sit" equivalent to miles—as measures of distances when one walks. On a walk measured by ale and beer, Hood says: "He once delivered to me orally the substance of the 'Essay on the Defect of Imagination in Modern Artists,' subsequently printed in the *Athenaeum*. But besides the criticism, there were snatches of old poems, golden lines and sentences culled from rare books, and anecdotes of men of note. Marry, it was like going a ramble with gentle Izaak Walton, minus the fishing."[47] Although a reasonable doubt may be nourished about the accuracy of such anecdotes touching on the similarity of Lamb's conversation and his essays, the evidence indicates that some of his ideas not only derived from conversation but also found their first crude expression therein.

Lamb's extensive reading—which provided him with a multitude of quotations and helped to form his stylistic characteristics—stimulated ideas for several personal essays as well as furnished subjects for numerous pieces of criticism. In "Ritson versus John Scott the Quaker" he writes of "this rainy season, which really damps a gentleman's wings for any original flight, and obliges him to ransack his shelves, and miscellaneous reading, to furnish an occasional or make-shift paper." Reading was Lamb's chief delight in life, and his tendency to throw away all modern books and retain "even the trash he liked when a boy,"[48] together with his habit of buying from bookstalls whenever his purse would allow it, made his library the subject of many comments. Crabb Robinson, the diarist, thought it "the finest collection of shabby books I ever saw. Such a number of first-rate works of genius, but filthy copies, which a delicate man would really hesitate touching, is, I think, nowhere to be found."[49] Hunt confirmed Lamb's "handsome contempt for appearance," while Bernard Barton's daughter Lucy remembered that the price tags of the secondhand dealers were never removed. Lamb's habit of lending his "midnight darlings" to friends such as Coleridge, who considered that his own marginalia "spoiled a book in order to leave a relic," and to Wordsworth, who, according to De Quincey,

habitually cut apart the pages with a butter knife not free
from butter, contributed to their bad condition. Certainly
his employment of a cobbler as his bookbinder added to
their individuality. Like Wordsworth's library, Lamb's was
for use rather than for show; yet he loved the volumes for
themselves. When someone asked how he could tell one
book from another, he replied, "How does a shepherd know
his sheep?"[50] Throughout his life he read intensively as well
as extensively. A reported interview with Lamb in 1831
includes the following colloquy:

"Do you spend much time in reading?" we inquired.
"Yes, the mornings invariably; and sometimes the evenings
too."
"You approve, then, of varied and extensive reading?"
"Decidedly. If a man's mind be well disciplined, he can
scarcely read too much. I mean, of course, that his reading
should be close, careful, meditative."[51]

Lamb told Southey that his *Rosamund Gray* was inspired
by reading a ballad: "In good truth, nothing else but the
first words of that foolish ballad put me upon scribbling my
'Rosamund.'"[52] As for the essays, it seems probable that his
reading of an essay by William Hay, written in 1754 but
included in Dodsley's *Fugitive Pieces* of 1794, furnished the
impulse for his "On the Danger of Confounding Moral with
Personal Deformity."[53] We know that Lamb composed his
essay "On the Poetical Works of George Wither" by arranging his marginal notes in a copy of selections of Wither's
poems sent to him by the publisher, John Gutch; the notes
were Lamb's own comments on Wither together with his
comments on the criticisms Dr. John Nott wrote in of
Lamb's first notes. Very likely Lamb's essay on "Detached
Thoughts on Books and Reading" and his *Popular Fallacy*
"That my Lord Shaftesbury and Sir William Temple are

models of the Genteel Style in Writing" owe their titles, if not their inception, to Shenstone; among that writer's essays are "Detached Thoughts" on Books, on Writing and Books, on Books and Writers, and on Men and Manners; and in one place is the sentence: "The writer who gives us the best idea of what may be called the genteel in style and manner of writing, is, in my opinion, my Lord Shaftesbury."

R. W. Babcock, supporting his thesis that the criticism of Shakespeare by Lamb, Coleridge, and Hazlitt is more a reflection of eighteenth-century criticism than original effort, submits that Lamb's comparison of Middleton's *The Witch* with *Macbeth* was not "quite original" and suggests looking at it alongside an article by Edmund Malone entitled "Conjectures concerning the date of the tragedy of Macbeth," published in *Walker's Hibernian Magazine* for October, 1786.[54] A close comparison of Lamb's editorial note to his selection from *The Witch* in his *Specimens of English Dramatic Poets* (1808) with Malone's article does reveal some similarities in thoughts and words: Malone admits the possibility of Shakespeare's indebtedness to Middleton for some hints of the Witches, which favors "the supposition, that Middleton's piece preceded that of Shakspeare . . . . But nothing that hath yet been produced of Shakspeare's plagiarism, can deprive him of one tittle of his almost prescriptive right to all the honours of a great and unequalled original." To prove this contention, he has "made these remarks, in order to evince, how essentially different the gay witches of Middleton are from the awful sisters of Macbeth." Speaking of their "incantations at the cauldron," Malone defined the differences:

Shakspeare hath the admirable art not only of applying his borrowed parts with propriety, but of embellishing and improving them. He adds to them a grace and dignity, which, at least, are his own. In the tragedy of Macbeth, his spirits, though simi-

lar in name to those of Middleton (particularly the presiding
deity hath in each the Grecian name of Hecate), yet they differ
from Middleton's in almost every essential attribute of conduct
and character. Middleton's faeries are light, frisky beings, who
wreak their malice on small culprits, and revenge little mis-
chiefs. Shakspeare's are brought on the stage for purposes of
higher account. They are to be the instruments of dire events—
revolutions that were worthy the councils of the gods. This
great object was of sufficient importance to excuse the interposition of supernatural beings. Hence, what Middleton invented
to amuse, Shakspeare's more daring genius improved into instruments of terror. This he hath accomplished with wonderful
propriety; and we admire that skill and power which, on so
slight a basis, could erect such a stupendous fabric.

Lamb begins his note thus:

   Though some resemblance may be traced between the
charms in Macbeth, and the incantations in this play, which is
supposed to have preceded it, this coincidence will not detract
much from the originality of Shakspeare. His witches are distinguished from the witches of Middleton by essential differences. These [Middleton's] are creatures to whom man or
woman, plotting some dire mischief, might resort for occasional
consultation. Those [Shakespeare's] originate deeds of blood,
and begin bad impulses to men . . . . These witches can hurt
the body, those have power over the soul . . . . The names, and
some of the properties, which the other author has given to his
hags, excite smiles. The Weird Sisters are serious things.[55]

Lamb may have read Malone's article in the original periodical or, perhaps, reprinted in another place, any time
before 1808. But we need not assume that he had it before
him as he wrote. Malone had made other comparisons, such
as the difference in the ingredients in the cauldron, which
are not found in Lamb's note. And Lamb's criticism contains other "essential differences," such as the fact that

whereas Middleton's Hecate has a son, "the hags of Shak-speare have neither child of their own, nor seem to be descended from any parent. They are foul anomalies, of whom we know not whence they are sprung, nor whether they have beginning or ending. As they are without human passions, so they seem to be without human relations." None of this is in Malone. Here is another case where the retention of some ideas from his reading apparently served as the genesis of a piece of criticism, into which some of the original phrasing was, probably unconsciously, incorporated. One may agree that "this coincidence will not detract much from the originality of"—Charles Lamb.

Some of Lamb's subjects were suggested, directly or in-directly, by editors, fellow essayists, and their writings. In an undated letter to Charles Ollier, the publisher, Lamb wrote, "It is enough once for all to assure you, that I never could succeed in anything proposed to me to do, & I wont strive against my poor obstinate grain—"[56] Thus, when Taylor, on one occasion, suggested an essay on Midsum-mers Day, Lamb refused and suggested that Leigh Hunt could do it well.[57] However, Wainewright, writing in the *London* one month later about the pictures at the Royal Academy, was led by his observations on Stephanoff's "Poor Relations" to suggest the topic for an essay to "our Elia"; Lamb's "Poor Relations" appeared about two years later. Then, on May 3, 1823, he wrote Barton, "Poor Relations is tolerable—but where shall I get another subject . . . ?"[58] Writing to Hessey of the *London* on February 17, 1825, about his "Reflections in the Pillory," he commented, "You see I am driven to shifts, when I take suggested subjects."[59] One month earlier his parody on De Quincey's *Letters to a Young Man whose Education has been Neglected* (1823) opened with: "Dear Sir,—I send you a bantering Epistle to an Old Gentleman whose Education is supposed to have been Neglected. Of course, it was *suggested* by some Letters of your admirable Opium-Eater; the discontinuance of which has caused so much regret to myself in common with most of your readers." Horace Smith's essay entitled "Death —Posthumous Memorials—Children," in the *London* for March, 1821, is a commentary on Lamb's "New Year's Eve"; regretting the apparent pessimism, he observes that Elia has always "delighted in antithetical presentments," meaning his two views of Christ's Hospital and his two attitudes toward tobacco, and therefore hopes he will "chant a palinode." It seems likely that this was the impetus for Lamb's "Rejoicing on the New Year's Coming of Age" (*London*, Jan., 1823). In the same essay, Smith's reference to Elia's bachelor state and the value of children in overcoming depression may well have been the inspiration for "Dream-Children."

THREE

"Being So Akin"

Of more importance than conversation in the expression of ideas, and one stage closer to the finished product, are Lamb's letters, of which more than one thousand have been preserved. We have seen how informal gatherings stimulated ideas which otherwise might never have been provoked into being. Some of these were used by Lamb and by others in the formation of prose pieces which often were composed years after the inception of the idea. We have seen further how these conversations enabled Lamb and others to try the effect of their wit and wisdom on their friends and to give the first rough form to their thoughts. However rough these first shapes may have been, this process was a valuable preliminary to paper and ink and may be regarded, in many cases, as equivalent to the first draft.

Just as the presence and mental stimulation of many friends were necessary for productive conversation, so also Lamb's many correspondents gave him an excellent opportunity of expressing his thoughts on paper. Following the custom of the times, he seldom prepaid the postage on his letters; and he felt obliged to make them worth their cost to the recipients—a much larger sum than that required today and determined by the number of sheets. The result was careful and interesting writing, dealing not only with the usual epistolary personal feeling and experience, but also with opinions on people and customs and criticisms on literature.

Because of the distractions at his East India House office, where Lamb wrote most of his letters, he often expressed an aversion to correspondence.[1] At the same time, writing to Barton, shortly before his retirement, he showed that he cared enough about his letters to spend considerable time in correction and revision: "I am sadly given to blot, and modern blotting-paper gives no redress; it only smears, and makes it worse, as for example [*here is a smear*]. The only remedy is scratching out, which gives it a Clerkish look."[2] His letters are full of blots and corrections. He "never could come into the custom of envelopes . . ." he acknowledged to Southey; " 'tis a modern foppery."[3] He usually wrote on faintly ruled India House paper; folded his letters unevenly, as he freely admitted to Mrs. Williams;[4] and, after his retirement, used "wafers of the coarsest bran" instead of sealing wax, which he rarely possessed.[5] Except for letters from Manning and Coleridge, he seldom kept those he received.[6] Yet his high regard for this form of writing is evident in his copying into his commonplace books letters of such writers as Ascham, Cowper, and Cobbett. There is similar evidence that he sometimes regarded his own letters rather highly. Not altogether facetious is his remark to Barton: "When my Epistles come to be weighed with Pliny's, however superior to the Roman in delicate irony, judicious reflexions, etc., his gilt post will bribe over the judges to him."[7]

The experience thus provided by the letters in phrasing and style generally was important, but it is the letters as a proving ground for ideas that were later developed into, or utilized in, his essays that we are particularly concerned with. A great number of the letters contain, or are as a whole, sketches and essays little different from those he published. Many of these were forgotten after being dispatched to the addressee. Ideas in many others were retained for future use after this first trial. It is not unrecognized that the germs of some of Lamb's essays are to be found in his letters, but no one has heretofore examined the extent of this germination.[8] Some editors have indicated a parallel here and there between essays and letters, but Lamb's development of his epistolary ideas and re-use of his phrasing are here thoroughly investigated for the first time. A comparison of the letters with the essays is startlingly revealing for the light it throws on the way Lamb's mind worked, and hence on the process of literary creation.

Of course, the letters with which the essays are compared are bona fide correspondence and do not include the many essays printed in the form of letters to the editor of a periodical or letters to a hypothetical personage. These were established forms, stemming from the eighteenth century, and were employed partly because the author of a letter, even of a merely ostensible one, would be considered freed from the restrictions regarded as governing a more literary form. The "Letter of Elia to Robert Southey, Esquire" is Lamb's only essay addressed to an actual named individual other than editors, and when it was included in the *Last Essays*, only the concluding portion, the less personal part, was printed under the title "Tombs in the Abbey." That Lamb's "Death-Bed" was purposely written as a private letter with the knowledge that it would be shown to people to interest them in aiding the family of Randal Norris, a long-time friend of the Lambs, is evident from letters written shortly after January 20, 1827, when this letter was sent to Crabb Robinson. The letter form was retained when it was revised on February 10 for publication in Hone's *Table Book* on April 7,[9] but a number of artistic alterations were made, in addition to inserting blanks and substitute names for figures and true names. The changes include transposition of words, phrases, and sentences; changes of one word—a more precise or more literary—for another; a few additions of words for clarity and smoothness; and many deletions for compactness and force. Certainly, Lamb must have had his letter again in his hands while making his revisions, and the changes are interesting as serving to fit the letter for the general public as distinguished from a select group of friends.

These two essays were consciously revised from letters. In other instances where parallels of thought or phrase occur, it is the subconscious that is responsible for the retention. There is no evidence that Lamb kept copies of any letters he wrote; to have done so would have been inconsistent with his character as we know it. Moreover, there is his statement, quoted below, that he did not keep his own letters. Consequently, such parallels must be considered the result, not of revision, but of his ability to retain ideas and phrases, even over a period of years, in that "deep well of unconscious cerebration."

When Walter Wilson published his *Memoirs of the Life and Times of Daniel Defoe* in the latter part of 1829,[10] he included Lamb's "Estimate of De Foe's Secondary Novels," written shortly before for the occasion. He also included a large part of a letter containing comments on Defoe's writing, which Lamb had sent him on December 16, 1822. In both papers Lamb had commented on the illusion of truth given by Defoe's repetition and by his use of emphatic phrases such as "I say." In both he had labelled the style "homely" and had italicized the word to indicate its "heartiest sense." In the letter he wrote, "Robinson Crusoe is delightful to all ranks and classes, but it is easy to see that it is written in phraseology peculiarly adapted to the lower conditions of readers: hence it is an especial favorite with seafaring men, poor boys, servant maids &c. His novels are capital kitchen-reading . . . ." In the more formal paper we read: "While all ages and descriptions of people hang delighted over the 'Adventures of Robinson Crusoe' . . . which made an ingenious critic observe, that his works, in this kind, were excellent reading for the kitchen. And, in truth, the heroes and heroines of De Foe, can never again hope to be popular with a much higher class of readers, than that of the servant-maid or the sailor. Crusoe keeps its rank only by tough prescription." Lamb himself was surprised by the similarity and wrote to Wilson, characteristically mistaking the time interval: "The two papers of mine will puzzle the reader, being so akin. Odd that, never keeping a scrap of my own letters, with some fifteen years' interval I should nearly have said the same things. But I shall always feel happy in having my name go down any how with De Foe's, and that of his historiographer."[11] Probably conversation helped to keep his ideas alive; we know of one discussion of Defoe in the seven-year interval. Thomas Moore's Diary for April 4, 1823, contains the entry: "A good deal of talk with Lamb about DeFoe's works, which he praised warmly, particularly 'Colonel Jack,' of which he mentioned some striking passages."[12]

    If Lamb had been in a position to compare other essays and letters, he would undoubtedly have been even more surprised. "On the Ambiguities Arising from Proper Names" (Jan.–Mar., 1811) consists entirely of an anecdote told in a letter to Wordsworth five years earlier.[13] The development of the story is the same, and there are some verbal parallels.

The two versions present a good example of the difference between a composition written for the eyes of an individual and one written for the public. The essay shows more careful structure and more literary diction. Parentheses made necessary in the letter by secondary and explanatory thoughts are avoided in the essay by foresight; on the other hand, one or two elaborations were added to the essay which would have been superfluous for William Wordsworth. Undoubtedly, the act of writing out the story, though five years previous to the act of writing the essay, aided Lamb in remembering it and in expressing it in such enjoyable form.

Lamb's letter to John Bates Dibdin, a clerk in another office, of January 11, 1825,[14] asking him to thank his father for his volume of poems, was probably written at the same time as his "Review of Comic Tales, Etc. By C. Dibdin the Younger," published in the *New Times* on January 27, 1825. The one quotation in this short critical piece was also singled out for special praise in the letter as a "capital simile." The essay's phrase "redolent of Swift and Gay" recalls the letter's "He should have lived with Gay and his set." The letter continues: "The Chessiad is so clever that I relish'd it in spite of my total ignorance of the game," and the essay: "To a lover of Chess, who at the same time can relish the Rape of the Lock, the poem which forms the distinguishing feature of this volume cannot fail to impart pleasure." Just as the letter singled out the "Chessiad" for special mention, so the essay is confined to this one poem. Here also, as in the other cases, we find the literary touch: Lamb's "total ignorance of the game" of chess becomes "We confess we are more at home in Hoyle than in Phillidor . . . ."

In a letter of December 1, 1824, Lamb jocularly warned Bernard Barton from temptation and the consequent fate of the "unfortunate Fauntleroy," who had recently been hanged for crime. Since Barton as a banker handled quan-

tities of money, he must be especially on his watch against
an "unguarded hour."[15] Four months later, in April, 1825,
Lamb published in the *London* an essay called "The Last
Peach." The title was taken from the section of the essay
telling of himself as a child plucking a forbidden fruit, but
the first and last portions of the essay are derived from the
thought in this letter. Lamb has personalized the essay by
speaking of himself as a banker who experienced "feelings
of self-mistrust" produced by "the apprehension of that unfortunate man." From his interest in a contemporary scandal heightened by the play of his humorous fancy, Lamb
formulated a paragraph for a letter; into this crystallization
of thoughts, together with a real or imagined experience
from childhood, Elia has injected his personality and
evolved an essay fraught with elements of the past, of
pathos, of humor, and of humanity.

Some of the essays have parallels in two or more letters.
"The Gentle Giantess," a character in the seventeenth-century manner, was published in the *London* for December,
1822. On January 8, 1821, Lamb had described the subject
to Dorothy Wordsworth:

> Ask any body you meet, who is the biggest woman in Cam-
> bridge—and I'll hold you a wager they'll say Mrs. Smith.
>
> She broke down two benches in Trinity Gardens, one on the
> confines of St. John's, which occasioned a litigation between the
> societies as to repairing it. In warm weather she retires into an
> ice-cellar (literally!) and dates the returns of the years from a
> hot Thursday some 20 years back. She sits in a room with oppo-
> site doors and windows, to let in a thorough draught, which
> gives her slenderer friends toothaches. She is to be seen in the
> market every morning at 10, cheapening fowls, which I observe
> the Cambridge Poulterers are not sufficiently careful to stump.[16]

All these features of character except the last have a place
in the essay, which is considerably longer as the result of

artistic elaboration and of addition of details. Mrs. Smith
of Cambridge has become the widow Blacket of Oxford.
Lamb's unconcern about matters of time has resulted in
setting back the "hot Thursday" five additional years. The
benches, resolved into one, are located at Maudlin, "or
rather, situated between the frontiers of that and ******'s
college . . . ." The characteristic personal touch of the Elian
essays is added by Lamb's assuming the toothache, slightly
altered, for himself: "I owe a painful face-ache, which op-
presses me at this moment, to a cold caught, sitting by her,
one day in last July, at this receipt of coolness."

A portion of an unpublished letter written by Lamb to
his fellow clerks Dodwell and Chambers on August 26,
1819, takes us back further to the time when Lamb, on vacation in Cambridge, first saw Mrs. Smith. Her method of
locomotion, described in the essay, is here defined with the
word "waddle." The idea of concealing her name is indicated by the use of "Clementina"—"for delicacy" after
"Mrs. Smith" has already been written. She "presses with a
dreadful weight upon the wood," according to this letter,
anticipating the "pressing and breaking of" the bench in the
essay. The letter, like the essay, speaks of only one bench,
which, however, "divides Trinity from St. John's walks," as
it does in his letter to Miss Wordsworth. Her reading and
literary conversation with "the resident fellows" are other
features common to both this letter and the essay. In addition to these aspects that are not mentioned in the letter to
Miss Wordsworth, there is her custom of escaping hot
weather by retreating into "grottoes and underground
lurking places" in the earlier letter, which is similar to the
"ice-cellar" of the other two accounts. The essay, we observe, drew from both "first drafts," selecting those elements that seemed most appealing at that later time.[17]

Lamb's enthusiasm for London is expressed in at least

four letters in late 1800 and early 1801, previous to his literary eulogy in the *Morning Post* for February 1, 1802. The
presentation in both the letters and the essay of the same
ideas results in some close parallels. Lamb writes in "The
Londoner" of his general aversion to rural scenes: "This
aversion was never interrupted or suspended, except for a
few years in the younger part of my life, during a period
in which I had set my affections upon a charming young
woman. Every man while the passion is upon him, is for a
time at least addicted to groves and meadows and purling
streams." In a letter to Wordsworth of January 30, 1801, he
had written: "I have no passion (or have had none since I
was in love, and then it was the spurious engendering of
poetry & books) to groves and vallies."[18] Again, in the essay:
"A mob of happy faces crowding up at the pit door of
Drurylane Theatre, just at the hour of six, gives me ten
thousand sincerer pleasures, than I could ever receive from
all the flocks of silly sheep that ever whitened the plains of
Arcadia or Epsom Downs." A corresponding passage in a
letter to Robert Lloyd, brother of Charles, postmarked February 7, 1801, reads: "A mob of men is better than a flock
of sheep—and a crowd of happy faces justling into the
playhouse at the hour of six is a more beautiful spectacle to
man than the shepherd driving his 'silly' sheep to fold."[19]
In the same letter he wrote of "the pavements of the motley
Strand crowded with to and fro passengers"; in the essay
he spoke of rushing "out into her crowded Strand." Also in
this letter he exclaims over "the shops all brilliant, and
stuffed with obliging customers and obliged tradesmen,"
which parallels "The obliging customer, and the obliged
tradesman" of the essay. Two letters to Manning likewise
remark on this feature, together with many others used in
the essay.[20] It looks as if Lamb was beginning to write his
essay at this time, but in the absence of definite evidence,

the assumption must be that he wrote his essays shortly
before the date of publication. At any rate, such laudatory
passages on London helped him to formulate his impressions so that the final literary expression was the more
nearly perfect.

After the publication in September, 1822, of his most
famous essay, "A Dissertation upon Roast Pig," Lamb was
obliged at various times in the next few years to write many
"thank-you" notes to people who sent him presents of pigs.
Invariably these expressed in flowing terms his gustatory
appreciation of roast pork. This same sort of appreciation is
found also in several letters antedating the essay. As early
as February of 1805 we find such sentiments in a letter to
Manning, who, as we have noted, is credited with giving
Lamb the idea for the basic incident in his essay.[21] The
letter to Coleridge of March 9, 1822, was so full of praise
for pig as one commodity he could not bring himself to part
with that Coleridge referred to it as Lamb's *epistola por-
cina*.[22] Here Lamb relates in full the illustrative anecdote
of his childhood regret at giving away a plum-cake to a
beggar. There are slight differences between this version
and that in the essay: for example, in the letter the incident
occurred in his way "home through the Borough," whereas
in the essay it was in his way "to school (it was over London
bridge)." However, most of the details are the same, there
are some verbal parallels, and the development is similar.
The association of this incident with his appreciation of
roast pig was made when this letter was composed, and it is
all but certain that had it never been written, the essay
would not have been so delightfully enriched with this
human and personal paragraph. In the analysis of his feelings about including pig among the many delicacies he
freely imparts unto his friends, Lamb's letter approximates
more closely than any other in these parallels the honest

sentiment and the intimate, yet literary, style of the essays. The composition of "Distant Correspondents" was a direct consequence of the correspondence of Charles and Mary Lamb with Coleridge and Sarah Stoddart in Malta, with Barron Field in Australia, and with Manning in China. To the last of these, Lamb once expressed his lack of time and space consciousness, evident throughout his life: "Nothing puzzles me more than time and space, and yet nothing puzzles me less, for I never think about them."[23] As early as 1804, Mary commented to Sarah Stoddart, later Hazlitt's wife, on the difficulty of writing abroad: "I sit writing here, and thinking almost you will see it to morrow; and what a long, long time it will be before you receive this."[24] Undoubtedly, she and Charles discussed the confusion of tenses involved in writing a letter that would not be read for weeks or months, for other letters at intervals after this contain much the same idea.[25] Writing to Lamb from Canton, China, on November 20, 1807, Thomas Manning said: "How strange & unsocial it seems to be at such a distance. I can't ask whether Mary has received her letter. I sent it last spring! I am sure it is not arrived yet, but it ought to be long before this reaches England; & it would be two years before I could get an answer to the question!!"[26] In a letter to Manning of December 26, 1815, Lamb comments: "A correspondence with the uttermost parts of the earth necessarily involves in it some heat of fancy, it sets the brain a going . . . ."[27] The recurrence of these thoughts shows that the idea remained in Lamb's mind over a period of years. It culminated in a letter dated August 31, 1817, to Barron Field in Australia, his lawyer friend who became Judge of the Supreme Court of New South Wales. Here, as in the essay, there are conjectures about the legendary thievery of Australia, the status of poetry there, and the different chronology.[28] The relationship of this letter to the essay is magnified by the fact that the essay, published in March, 1822, bore the subtitle: "In a Letter to B. F. Esq. at Sydney, New South Wales."

The essential differences between Lamb's epistolary and literary styles are well illustrated in the essay and letter just referred to; they are equally well evidenced in a comparison of "The Superannuated Man" (May, 1825) with letters that preceded it. When Lamb retired on Tuesday, March 29, 1825, after thirty-three years of service as an accountant in the East India House, he expressed his sentiments in several letters. One of April 6, 1825, to Wordsworth, written in a more formal manner than he used toward most of his other correspondents, has "It was like passing from life into Eternity . . . . Now, when all is holyday, there are no holydays."[29] In the essay we read, "It was like passing out of Time into Eternity . . . . Having all holidays, I am as though I had none." And in a letter of April 18, 1825, to Wordsworth's sister-in-law, Sarah Hutchinson: "All being holydays, I feel as if I had none . . . ."[30] On December 23, 1822, he had written with characteristic informality to Barton: "better than anything short of *all one's time to one's self* . . . TIME! in other words, LIFE."[31] Having achieved this desideratum with retirement, he wrote again to Barton on April 6, 1825: "I will live another 50 years; or, if I live but 10, they will be thirty, reckoning the quantity of real time in them, *i. e.* the time that is a man's own."[32] The fusion of these ideas, using even the same figures, is found in the essay: "For *that* is the only true Time, which a man can properly call his own, that which he has all to himself . . . . My ten next years, if I stretch so far, will be as long as any preceding thirty." This same hypothesis was expressed in the letter to Wordsworth just quoted: "Every year to be as long as three, i. e. to have three times as much real time, time that is my own, in it!" These three letters, each slanted toward the personality of the recipient, were written in the month before the publication of the essay, or at about the time Lamb was composing it. There are other verbal parallels in them, and the "incomprehensibleness" and "shock" of his "emancipation" are expressed in all; but of more importance is the way in which the comparisons show Lamb's personality as a whole revealed in the essay, unhampered by the modifying restrictions imposed on a letter to an individual.[33]

Some of the ideas in this essay were expressed even earlier than the dates of these letters. The essay sentence "I had grown to my desk, as it were; and the wood had entered into my soul" was anticipated partly in a letter to Barton of September 11, 1822, where he wrote, "I have almost grown to the wood,"[34] and partly in a letter of July 19, 1824, to W. Marter, a former colleague at the India House, where he wrote, "the desk enters into my soul."[35] An undated letter to Barton, probably written a year before his "gaol delivery,"[36] contains a close parallel: "If we are to go 3 times a day to church, why has Sunday slipped into the notion of a *Holli*day? A Holyday I grant it. The puritans, I have read in Southey's Book, knew the distinction. They made people observe Sunday rigorously, would not let a nursery maid walk out in the fields with children for recreation on that day. But *then*—they gave the people a holliday from all sorts of work every second Tuesday." The third paragraph of the essay begins: "It is true I had my Sundays to myself; but Sundays, admirable as the institution of them is for purposes of worship, are for that very reason the very worst adapted for days of unbending and recreation." A footnote to this in the *London,* omitted from the collected *Last Essays,* reads: "Our ancestors, the noble old Puritans of Cromwell's day, could distinguish between a day of religious rest and a day of recreation; and while

they exacted a rigorous abstinence from all amusements
(even to the walking out of nursery maids with their little
charges in the fields) upon the Sabbath; in the lieu of the
superstitious observance of the Saint's day, which they
abrogated, they humanely gave to the apprentices, and
poorer sort of people, every alternate Thursday for a day
of entire sport and recreation."

Several letters contain not so much verbal parallels as
brief, unpolished expressions of thoughts which were later
expanded into essays. These pregnant observations stimulated the growth of ramifications in Lamb's mind, and the
act of crystallizing vagrant ideas kept them tangible so that
they did not perish for want of expression. For example,
when thanking John Payne Collier, the Shakespearian
critic, for sending him his *Poetical Decameron* in 1820,[37]
Lamb quoted and commented on the character of the ass,
which had been quoted by Collier from an older book. "The
Ass," an article printed in Hone's *Every-Day Book* for
October 5, 1825, uses this as a point of departure.

The value of Lamb's correspondence to preliminary
expression of ideas is evident in other essays. As early as
October 31, 1799, just returned from a "few red-letter days"
in Hertfordshire, Lamb wrote to Southey of "an old house
with a tapestry bed-room . . . an old marble hall with Hogarth's prints and the Roman Caesars in marble hung
round."[38] Here we have the first tabulation of the elements
that twenty-five years later were compounded into
"Blakesmoor in H——shire." The scenes were too fresh in
1799 to be cast into the enchantment of an essay—"there
are feelings which refuse to be translated, sulky aborigines,
which will not be naturalized in another soil"—and, too,
Lamb had not yet evolved as an essayist. Manning's residence in Hertfordshire led Lamb on May 28, 1819, to
express ideas developed two years later into "Mackery End

in Hertfordshire": "How are my cousins, the Gladmans of Wheathamstead, and farmer Bruton? Mrs. Bruton is a glorious woman. Hail Mackeray end—"[39]

One of the few parallels heretofore definitely noted by commentators on Lamb is that between the correspondence and "The Two Races of Men" (Dec., 1820), which was the outgrowth of his experiences with book borrowers. As early as June 7, 1809, we find him complaining to Coleridge: "I fetch'd away my books which you had at the Courier Office and found all but a 3rd Vol. of the Old Plays . . . . Pray, if you can remember what you did with it, or where you took it out with you a walking perhaps, send me word . . . ."[40] At a later time he wrote half-seriously of chaining his library to the shelves—"More Bodleiano."[41] An undated letter to Coleridge contains many close similarities to the essay.[42]

Besides his criticism of Defoe and Dibdin's *Tales,* discussed above, other of Lamb's critical reviews are antedated by letters with hints of ideas or quotations used in the literary work. Usually the letters contain the same poems or selections for commendation as the reviews. An example is his "Review of Moxon's Sonnets," published in the *Athenaeum* for April 13, 1833. One of the two sonnets quoted is "To the Nightingale"; in an undated, laudatory letter to Moxon, he picked the same poem for special mention.[43] Another example concerns his review of Wordsworth's *Excursion* in the *Quarterly Review* for October, 1814. Lamb's letter of August 9, 1814, to Wordsworth is a review in miniature, containing in condensed form many of the ideas in the essay as well as identical passages selected for commendation;[44] "Tales of the Churchyard," the story of Margaret, the mountain scenery, and the coolness of a country church are all commented on in both places.

Criticism of the theater found expression, likewise, in

the correspondence before being developed into essay form. On June 26, 1801, Lamb wrote to Robert Lloyd: "Cooke in 'Richard the Third' is a perfect caricature. He gives you the *monster* Richard, but not the *man* Richard."[45] His dramatic criticism entitled "G. F. Cooke in 'Richard the Third,'" printed in the *Morning Post* for January 8, 1802, contains the thought: "This Actor presents us with a very original and very forcible portrait (if not of the *man* Richard, whom Shakspeare drew, yet) of the *monster Richard*, as he exists in the *popular idea* . . . ." This same objection to Cooke's interpretation is thoroughly developed, without verbal parallel, in what is his best-known critical essay, "On the Tragedies of Shakspeare," printed in the *Reflector* of 1811.

Lamb's criticism of art also has its foreshadowings in the letters. Writing to Barton on June 11, 1827, he discussed the weaknesses of two paintings by the contemporary artist, John Martin.[46] These analyses formed the origin of his detailed analysis of modern art, written in October, 1831, and first published in full in 1833 as "On the Total Defects of the Quality of Imagination, observable in the Works of Modern British Artists,"[47] wherein both these paintings are criticized much more fully. The discussion of *Don Quixote* in the last part had been expressed in a letter of 1825 to Robert Southey.[48]

In addition to this retention of ideas, and sometimes phrasing, that were later developed into the fundamental themes of essays, there are numerous close parallels of thought and words in incidental passages or secondary themes. Sometimes there is little time lapse between the letter and the essay: the description of his fellow-essayist Thomas Griffiths Wainewright, who wrote under the pseudonym "Janus Weathercock," as "the light, and warm-as-light hearted, Janus of the London" in the "Letter of Elia

to Robert Southey" (Oct., 1823) was anticipated by a
phrase in a letter to Barton of September 2, 1823: "their
best stay, kind light hearted Wainwright [sic]—their
Janus."[49] Wainewright, incidentally, was later convicted
on a charge of forgery and transported to Van Diemen's
Land; he was also suspected of being a poisoner. In "Grace
before Meat" (Nov., 1821), we read, "I shrink instinctively
from one who professes to like minced veal." And "Those
unctuous morsels of deer's flesh were not made to be received with dispassionate services." The manuscript shows
that Lamb first wrote "juices."[50] This was the word he had
used in a letter of 1817 to Charles Chambers, a Christ's
Hospital schoolmate who became a naval surgeon: "I es-
teem you for disrelishing minced veal . . . . I love you for
your noble attachment to the fat unctuous juices of deer's
flesh . . . ."[51] Obviously, he had retained the word in context,
but on careful consideration he substituted a more accurate
term.

Some of the closest verbal parallels of subordinate
thoughts were written five, ten, or even more years apart.
"New Year's Eve" (Jan., 1821) contains this passage: "Any
alteration, on this earth of mine, in diet or in lodging, puzzles and discomposes me. My household gods plant a terrible fixed foot, and are not rooted up without blood." To
Dorothy Wordsworth on November 21, 1817, Lamb had
written: "Here we are, transplanted from our native soil
. . . . We never can strike root so deep in any other ground.
This, where we are, is a light bit of gardener's mold, and if
they take us up from it, it will cost no blood and groans like
mandrakes pull'd up."[52] Not only this change to Russell
Street, Covent Garden, but also the earlier one to No. 4
Inner Temple Lane had elicited the comment on his household gods in a letter of 1809 to Coleridge and one of 1810
to Robert Lloyd.[53] The letter of March 28, 1809, to Man-

ning, fearing and anticipating this earlier move, is particularly vivid in specifying the alterations that discomposed him.[54] "Mackery End in Hertfordshire" (July, 1821) commented on how "words written in lemon come out upon exposure to a friendly warmth," and on September 23, 1816, Lamb had written to Wordsworth that "it scarce strikes the pupil with any consciousness of the letters being there, like letters writ in lemon."[55] "The Two Races of Men" (Dec., 1820) refers to his suffering from Coleridge's theory "that 'the title to property in a book . . . is in exact ratio to the claimant's powers of understanding and appreciating the same.'" Lamb's belief in this dictum was manifested on June 2 of the same year, when he gave Wordsworth a copy of the 1671 edition of *Paradise Regained,* inscribed "C. Lamb to the best Knower of Milton, and therefore the worthiest occupant of this pleasant Edition." But as early as August 13, 1814, he offered the use of his books to Coleridge, free from "a foolish scruple of some Book-proprietor, as if books did not belong with the highest propriety to those that understand 'em best."[56] In "The Wedding" (June, 1825), written on the occasion of the marriage in April, 1821, of Admiral Burney's daughter Sarah to her cousin John Payne, a bookseller, he confesses, "I cannot divest me of an unseasonable disposition to levity upon the most awful occasions." Ten years before, writing to Southey, he possessed the same disposition: "I am going to stand godfather; I don't like the business; I cannot muster up decorum for these occasions; I shall certainly disgrace the font. I was at Hazlitt's marriage, and had like to have been turned out several times during the ceremony. Any thing awful makes me laugh."[57] Another personal confession is in "New Year's Eve" (Jan., 1821): "I am naturally, beforehand, shy of novelties; new books, new faces, new years . . . ." As early as October 30, 1809, he had written

Coleridge: "I am out of the world of readers. I hate all that do read, for they read nothing but reviews and new books. I gather myself up unto the old things."[58] Even earlier, on September 13, 1804, he had confessed to Robert Lloyd, "I am naturally shy of new faces";[59] and an undated letter contains the sentence: "The fact is, I am foolish shy of new faces."[60] Personal also is his introspective discovery of "no sort of disposition . . . to bewail my celibacy" in "Mackery End," which substantiates his feeling seventeen years earlier as expressed to Robert Lloyd: "All these new nuptials do not make me unquiet in the perpetual prospect of celibacy."[61] Some of the words used in "New Pieces at the Lyceum" (Aug. 8 & 9, 1819) to describe "poor Holcroft's last Comedy, which positively died from the opposite excess; it was choked up with men, and perished from a redundancy of male population" carried over from a letter of December 5, 1806, to Manning: " 'The Vindictive Man' was damned about a fortnight since. It died in part of its own weakness, and in part for being choked up with bad actors."[62] The description of Admiral Burney, who prided himself upon having planted the first pun in Otaheite, as "a merry Captain" in "Barron Field's Poems" (Jan. 16 & 17, 1820) recalls the same phrase in a letter of February 19, 1803, to Manning, where it is "a merry *natural* captain, who pleases himself vastly with once having made a Pun at Otaheite in the O. language."[63] In "Odes and Addresses to Great People" (Apr. 12, 1825), he disagrees with "those critics who condemn Cowley for excess of wit"; the same phrase in reference to George Dyer's demonstration "that Cowley was ruined by excess of wit" in a letter to Coleridge twenty-five years before establishes the fact that Dyer was one of the critics Lamb had in mind.[64]

The comparison of these passages shows that nearness of parallel is not in direct proportion to nearness of time. Here is another tribute to Lamb's memory, which could retain ideas over a long period and even re-use, albeit unconsciously, the very phrases he had first used to express them. Some of these ideas he must have been fond of repeating, even after his essay was published—as, for example, he told Mary Shelley about Burney's Otaheite pun.[65] Thus, they were kept alive rather than being merely revived. The difference in the expressions of the same thought is the difference between writing for the eyes of a single friend and for the eyes of the average magazine reader.

As one would expect, there are many more parallels of thought than of words, and these, too, have varying degrees of time between them: "On the Custom of Hissing at Theatres" (Apr.–Sept., 1811) contains the sentence, "A culprit in the pillory (bate the eggs) meets with no severer exprobation [than an author whose play is hissed]." Writing to Manning on February 26, 1808, Lamb had said, "I suppose you know my farce was damned. The noise still rings in my ears. Was you ever in the pillory?—being damned is something like that."[66] In "Detached Thoughts on Books and Reading" (July, 1822) Lamb blasts the "wretched Malone" for whitewashing "the painted effigy of old Shakespeare." "By ———, if I had been a justice of peace for Warwickshire, I would have clapt both commentator and sexton fast in the stocks, for a pair of meddling sacrilegious varlets." A letter to John Britton of 1818, not included in Lucas' edition, has the line: "I did not know the extent of Malone's atrocity; had I been churchwarden of Stratford I would have set the knave in stocks."[67] In the same essay, Lamb wrote, "I have no repugnances . . . . I can read anything which I call a *book* . . . . I bless my stars for a taste so catholic, so unexcluding." Writing to Wordsworth on August 9, 1815, he said, "What any man can write, surely I may read."[68] The inclusion in this essay of "the works of Hume, Gibbon, Robertson" as *"books which are no books"* was anticipated as early as March 1, 1800, in a letter to Manning: "None of the Damned philosophical Humeian indifference, so cold, and unnatural, and inhuman! None of the damned Gibbonian fine writing, so fine and composite. None of Mr. Robertson's periods with three members."[69] That Lamb's antipathies toward these three authors were constant is proved by Thomas Moore's recording in his Diary for March 27, 1832, that Lamb excluded them from his library.[70] On the subject of authors, Lamb wrote in "Imperfect Sympathies" (Aug., 1821), "In my early life I had a passionate fondness for the poetry of Burns . . . ." Years before, on December 10, 1796, he had expressed this fondness to Coleridge in the words, "Burns was the god of my idolatry."[71] In the same essay, Lamb praised the singing of the tenor John Braham, comparing it with Kemble's acting; as early as February 26, 1808, he had admired his singing in a letter to Manning, even making the same comparison.[72] In a footnote to "Oxford in the Vacation" (Oct., 1820) Lamb confesses, "There is something to me repugnant . . . in the written hand. The text never seems determinate. Print settles it." On April 28, 1815, he had written to Wordsworth, "All things read raw to me in MS.—to compare magna parvis, I cannot endure my own writings in that state."[73] Earlier the same month, April 7, 1815, he had complained that having to work overtime until nine or eleven at night kept him from having "a holyday now once in ten times, where I used to keep all red letter days, and some fine days besides which I used to dub Nature's holydays."[74] In this essay he regrets the abolition of some holidays—"the red-letter days."

"Distant Correspondents" (Mar., 1822) contains the thought: "Formerly, I thought that death was wearing out,—I stood ramparted about with so many healthy friends. The departure of J. W., two springs back corrected my delusion." This is literally true, for James White died on March 13, 1820; John Lamb, on October 26, 1821; and Admiral Burney, on November 17, 1821. Writing to John Rickman, whom Lamb had called "a perfect man," on November 20, 1821, shortly after the last of these three deaths had intensified his thinking, he says: "I have been used to death lately. Poor Jim White's departure last year first broke the spell. I had been so fortunate as to have lost no friend in that way for many long years, and began to think people did not die. But they have since gone off thickly. My brother's death . . . ."[75]

Further parallels of thoughts show the tenacity of Lamb's mind for ideas and the value of the correspondence in crystallizing them for better retention. "We love our friend because he is like ourselves," wrote Lamb to Robert Lloyd[76] probably a quarter of a century before the line in "Many Friends" (Jan., 1825): "to a just friendship, something like a proportion in stature as well as mind is desirable." Another letter, probably of 1815, to Wordsworth, contains the accurate self-analysis: "I reckon myself a dab at *Prose*— verse I leave to my betters . . . ."[77] This anticipates his acknowledgment in "Witches, and Other Night-Fears" (Oct., 1821) "when I feel that idle vein returning upon me, I presently subside into my proper element of prose . . . ." "The Latin Poems of Vincent Bourne" (Sept., 1831) contains a protest against albums, which, compared to his previous epistolary outbursts on the subject,[78] is mild indeed: "We are no friend to Albums. We early set our face against them . . . . seriously we deprecate with all our powers the unfeminine practice." Writing of his aunt in a letter of February 5, 1797, to Coleridge, Lamb told how she used to bring him fag at school "when I only despised her for it";[79] regret for his attitude no doubt led him to avoid his characteristic self-reference when, in "Modern Gallantry" (Nov.,

1822), he condemned the hypothetical man who was "the disparager and despiser of his no less female aunt . . . ." The love for "the life contemplative," expressed so intensely in "The Superannuated Man" (May, 1825), is found in a letter of February 10, 1825, to Barton, as well as in two undated letters, to Manning and to Matilda Betham, an author and miniature-painter.[80]

Anecdotes in the essays characteristically appear first in the correspondence if they appear at all. Thus, the story of the Quaker moved by the spirit in "A Quaker's Meeting" (Apr., 1821) had been written to Coleridge over twenty years before.[81] The incident of the petition of the beggar lady, omitted from "A Complaint of the Decay of Beggars" (June, 1822) in the collected edition, had been told more than a dozen years earlier in a letter to Manning.[82] In both these examples, the versions in the essays are more elaborated and more carefully developed.

Occasionally the comparison of parallel passages will help to identify people and places, usually disguised in the essays. Speaking of roasted hare in "Thoughts on Presents of Game" (Nov., 1833), Lamb wrote, "In *our* way it eats so 'crips,' as Mrs. Minikin says." The use of the same word in a letter to Henry Dodwell, an India House colleague, of October 7, 1827, with the parenthetical explanation "(That's the Cook's word)" and the following sentence, "You'll excuse me, I have been only speaking to Becky about the dinner tomorrow,"[83] serves to "establish the fact," as Lucas points out, "that Mrs. Minikin was Becky's name when she was exalted into print."[84] Another case involves "The Old and the New Schoolmaster" (May, 1821), in which Lamb expressed his sense of gratitude for the "occasional communion" with superior minds but "would not be domesticated all my days with a person of very superior capacity to my own . . . the habit of too constant intercourse with

spirits above you, instead of raising you, keeps you down."
Some years previous to this he had written to Wordsworth
that while he holds "the personal presence" of him and
Coleridge, "potent spirits at a rate as high as any," yet if he
lived with them, "I should in a very little time lose my own
identity, and be dragged along in the current of other people's thoughts, hampered in a net."[85] We may be certain
that Lamb had Coleridge and Wordsworth in mind when
he wrote his essay. Another instance of identification,
though not involving the letters here, is the sentence in the
Popular Fallacy "That You Must Love Me and Love My
Dog" (Feb., 1826): "Cannot we like Sempronia, without
sitting down to chess with her eternal brother?" Lucas says,
"Probably Lamb was inventing."[86] But in 1815 Mary Lamb
had printed an essay "On Needle-Work" in the *British
Lady's Magazine,* over this same signature. It would seem
that Lamb had his sister and himself in mind. While the
association of letters with the essays in this manner does
not always result in clear-cut identification, it often dissi-
pates some of the literary disguise. Compare, for example,
the advice at the beginning of "Blakesmoor in H——shire"
(Sept., 1824) to go alone on a week-day to some country
church if you would "know the beauty of holiness" with
the three descriptions in the correspondence of the small
country church near Hastings which Lamb came to love
during a visit one year before the composition of the essay.
The letter to Barton (July 10, 1823) and the one to Thomas
Hood (Aug. 10, 1824) were written previous to the essay,
while the one to John Bates Dibdin was penned on June 30,
1826.[87] There is no doubt that Lamb had in mind his own
experience in this little church.

The frequent necessity of curtailing his expression in
order to avoid unwieldly length left many things unsaid.
These subordinate ideas, limited to sentences or a para-

graph, in the essays themselves remained in Lamb's mind
for further cerebration and often appeared later in their
own right as complete essays. Thus, the first expressions of
the main themes, as well as incidental ones, of several essays
are to be found in other essays previously written. These
first expressions served to fix the thought in the author's
mind, which worked over it and examined its potentialities,
perhaps largely unconsciously, until the play of wit, imagination, and serious thought had formed it into a piece of
literature. Let us see, first, how the main themes of some
essays were expressed in undeveloped form in earlier
works.

The short *Table Talk* essay "The New Acting," published
in the *Examiner* in 1813, was, as Lucas notes, "a kind of
trial sketch for the papers on 'The Old Actors,' which Lamb
contributed to the *London Magazine* nine years later."[88]
In the same way, as has been pointed out earlier, an article
in the *Reflector* of 1811 was practically reprinted to form
the last part of "Guy Faux," published in 1823. If "A Sylvan
Surprise," published in the *Examiner* in 1813, was written
by Lamb, as is generally conjectured, it would be a predecessor in the same way to "The Praise of Chimney-Sweepers" (May, 1822); in connection with this essay, it has been
suggested that the stimulation for writing it may have been
provided in the description of the chimney sweeps in Barry
Cornwall's essay "On May Day" (*London*, May, 1820)[89]—
it is significant that Lamb's essay bears the subtitle "A May-
Day Effusion." The latter part of another *Table Talk* essay,
"Playhouse Memoranda," "becomes a first sketch for the
Elia essay 'My First Play,' 1821 . . . ,"[90] while the allusion
to the Gothic heads of old Round Church was previously
used in Lamb's story "First Going to Church" in *Mrs. Leicester's School*. The main idea in "On the Inconveniences
Resulting from Being Hanged" (Jan.–Mar., 1811) was later

used in Lamb's farce, *The Pawnbroker's Daughter* (1825).[91]
"On the Genius and Character of Hogarth" (Apr.–Sept.,
1811) contains a passage amplified into the section of "Table
Talk by the Late Elia" printed in the *Athenaeum* for May
31, 1834. Lamb's story of "The Witch Aunt," written under
the name Maria Howe for *Mrs. Leicester's School,* contained the expression of his nervous terror of darkness
and solitude—derived from poring over the illustrations
in Stackhouse's *Story of the Bible*—and the reference
to his Aunt Hetty which are found thirteen years later
in "Witches, and Other Night-Fears." The reflection on
puns in "Distant Correspondents" (Mar., 1822) provoked
more thought on this favorite subject, and a few years
later he expressed himself more fully in the *Popular
Fallacy* "That the Worst Puns are the Best" (Jan., 1826).
The paragraph in "Distant Correspondents" concerning
the wish of Lord Camelford to be buried in Geneva
substantiates the attribution by some editors to Lamb of
"The Choice of a Grave," published in "The Miscellany"
of the *London* for January, 1823. A passage in the essay
"On the Tragedies of Shakespeare" (Oct.–Dec., 1811)
may have stimulated the writing of the *Popular Fallacy*
"That Great Wit is Allied to Madness" (May, 1826). The
expression of pleasure in gifts of game in another *Fallacy,*
"That We Must Not Look a Gift Horse in the Mouth"
(Apr., 1826), engendered the essay entitled "Thoughts
on Presents of Game" (Nov. 30, 1833). Incidentally, this
Fallacy speaks of "our friend Mitis," whom Lucas cannot
identify; it can at least be pointed out that the name
occurs again in "A Vision of Horns," where he is described
as "the little cheesemonger in St. ****'s Passage." The
theme of "Many Friends" (Jan. 8, 1825) was first fully expressed in a letter of February 18, 1818, to Mrs. Wordsworth, although it is found to a lesser degree as early as

September 24, 1802, and May 10, 1806, in letters to Manning;[92] the writing of the essay did not exhaust the ideas, and some of them were elaborated in the *Popular Fallacy* "That Home is Home Though It Is Never So Homely" (Mar., 1826), and another *Fallacy*, "That You Must Love Me and Love My Dog" (Feb., 1826), contains the theme of endless visitors. "The Fable for Twelfth Day" (Jan. 6, 1802) was the ultimate origin of three essays. It was first expanded into "Rejoicings Upon the New Year's Coming of Age" in 1823. Then, two passages in this "Rejoicings" were expanded in 1825 to make the "Remarkable Correspondent," the protest of the Twenty-ninth of February; and another passage, containing the grievance of August Twelfth against April Twenty-Third, later became "The Twelfth of August, or A Humble Petition of an Unfortunate Day."

Less important and less extensive are passages which have been elaborated into subordinate sections, rather than into the main themes, of later essays. The analysis of Don Quixote's character in "On Some of the Old Actors" is more thorough in the later essay on "Barrenness of the Imaginative Faculty." Another example is a passage in "Amicus Redivivus" telling of exploring New River, which is slightly more amplified in "Newspapers Thirty-Five Years Ago."

This study of the development of ideas from their origin in experience, friendships, and reading, through first expressions, oral and written, throws significant light on the origin and composition of Lamb's essays in particular and on the process of literary creation in general. The act of expression in conversation and in his correspondence helped him to retain ideas, sometimes for years, until they emerged as full-fledged essays. It is not possible to trace the development of all his essays through his letters, but the discovery in the correspondence of early expressions of so many essays reveals the value of his letters as a laboratory in which Lamb experimented with perfecting the communication of his thoughts on paper. The appearance there of the first trials of so many suggests that if we possessed every letter that Lamb wrote, we would be able to see this practice operating to an even greater extent.

FOUR

"An Author by Fits"

OFFICE AND HOME

Thomas Hood, poet, editor, and miscellaneous writer, wrote the following sonnet as an introduction to one of the numbers of his *Reminiscences* in the *Comic Annual* for 1833:

Time was, I sat upon a lofty stool,
At lofty desk, and with a clerkly pen
Began each morning, at the stroke of ten,
To write in Bell and Co.'s commercial school;
In Warnford Court, a shady nook and cool,
The favourite retreat of merchant men;
Yet would my quill turn vagrant even then,
And take stray dips in the castalian pool.
Now double entry—now a flowery trope—
Mingling poetic honey with trade wax—
Blogg, Brothers—Milton—Grote and Prescott—Pope—
Bristles—and Hogg—Glyn Mills and Halifax—
Rogers—and Towgood—Hemp—the Bard of Hope—
Barilla—Byron—Tallow—Burns—and Flax!

The general thought of these lines applies so well to Charles Lamb that they serve here as an introduction to the influence of the external factors of business and private life on

Lamb the craftsman. How was his writing affected by his business career? When did he find time for his literary work? Where did he write? What was his own attitude toward his literary creations? These questions have never been thoroughly explored, but they can be answered by reference to Lamb's own correspondence and external testimony. It is important that they be answered, for Lamb served the East India House—the Philistines, as he called his masters—for thirty-three years, during which time not only most, but the best of his essays were written.

The East India House, founded at the end of the sixteenth century, was a famous company incorporated to exploit trade with India and the Far East. The building, now replaced by other structures, was located in Leadenhall Street. The Accountant's Office, where Lamb worked, was a large room divided, as are some modern offices, into compartments, called "compounds," each accommodating six clerks. Once being asked for the meaning of the term, Lamb quipped that it was "a collection of simples." It was in such a compound that Thomas De Quincey found Lamb at work one winter day of 1804–5, when he carried a letter of introduction to him: "I walked . . . into one of the two open doorways of the railing, and stood closely by the high stool of him who occupied the first place within the little aisle. I touched his arm, by way of recalling him from his lofty Leadenhall speculations to this sublunary world; and, presenting my letter, asked if that gentleman (pointing to the address) were really a citizen of the present room; for I had been repeatedly misled, by the directions given me, into wrong rooms. The gentleman smiled; it was a smile not to be forgotten. This was Lamb."[1] De Quincey continues by describing Lamb's gracious acknowledgment of the introduction and his invitation to dine with him and Mary that very night.

When, in April, 1792, at the age of seventeen, Lamb was appointed to the Accounts Department of the East India House, he found that his schooling was of little value to his work. He was in the same position as a young man of today who has had a college preparatory course in high school but is obliged to become a bookkeeper in industry. Furthermore, his temperament was not congenial to mathematics, the one thing most needful to him. According to Talfourd, the neat handwriting of his later years was acquired at the India House, but it did not come at once. A fellow clerk in the office, one Ogilvie, is reported to have said, "He was neither a neat nor an accurate accountant: he made frequent errors, which he was in the habit of wiping out with his little finger."[2] And a modern historian of the establishment testifies, on questionable authority, that "there was little reason to suppose that he was a particularly good clerk, and nothing to connect him with India, trade, or shipping."[3] However, from all accounts he was faithful to his job, and the record of periodical raises proves his competence, if not his excellence, as an accountant. Granted that he regarded his position solely as a means of livelihood, he gave value received.

The nature of Lamb's duties is defined by William Foster.

At the period of Lamb's service the Company was still a vast trading concern. Tea and indigo, drugs and piecegoods, poured in a great stream into its warehouses, and were disposed of periodically at the auctions held in the Sale Room of the East India House. The accounts relating to this multifarious business passed through the department of which Lamb was a member. Hence his references to auditing warehousekeepers' accounts: to "doing" the deposits on cotton wool; to making out warrants; to the "indigo appendix"; and to a tea sale which he had just attended, in which the entry of notes, deposits, etc., had fallen, as usual, mostly to his share.[4]

We know from Lamb's letters that his office hours were from ten to four. He dined at four-thirty (at four on Sundays), had tea at about six, and usually cold mutton or some other supper at nine. On occasion he had to return to the office for evening work. His protests against such overtime are loud and shrill: "If I can but begin my own day at 4 o'clock in the afternoon," he wrote Wordsworth on August 9, 1815, "I shall think myself to have Eden days of peace and liberty to what I have had."[5] But even when he left the office at four, he complained of the work which "takes all the golden part of the day away, a solid lump from ten to four."[6] Writing again to Wordsworth on March 20, 1822, he used much the same words: "Thirty years have I served the Philistines, and my neck is not subdued to the yoke. You don't know how wearisome it is to breathe the air of four pent walls without relief day after day, all the golden hours of the day between 10 and 4 without ease or interposition."[7]

Lamb admitted in "The Superannuated Man" that "besides Sundays," which he protested were least suitable for recreation, "I had a day at Easter, and a day at Christmas, with a full week in the summer . . . ." From passages in the correspondence it appears that his annual holiday was actually one month, rather than one week, but it is hard to say whether he received the same amount of free time each year. It seems to have depended very often on the pressure of work. However, it is easy to understand how his vacations were "spent in restless pursuit of pleasure, and a wearisome anxiety to find out how to make the most of them . . . . Before I had a taste of it [the promised rest], it was vanished." "My theory is to enjoy life," he wrote Wordsworth in the letter just quoted, "but the practice is against it."

In spite of his protests, the good fellowship in the office

must have done much to relieve the monotony. Lamb was "Charley" to his fellow workers, and when Charley's ill-fated play *Mr. H.* was produced in Drury Lane Theatre, a large number of his co-workers came to lend their applause. Then too, there was an annual feast which is mentioned with enthusiasm more than once in Lamb's letters. Competition for appointments to the firm was severe, for the age of admission to a clerkship was low, an employee was assured of a good income for a moderate amount of work, and the retiring allowance was handsome. All classes of society were represented by the clerks, but the majority belonged to the well-to-do bracket. Foster reports that according to tradition the inclination of this majority to affect the powdered hair and top boots of the "man about town" led to an order prescribing conservative dress, and that "the majority of the clerks restricted themselves to sober black."[8] Lamb's habitual black, customarily interpreted as one of his characteristic whimsies manifesting a love for the quaint, was, therefore, simply conformance to office practice.

That the India House atmosphere, if not the work, was congenial to Lamb's temperament, and may have influenced its development—and hence his essays—is strongly suggested by Foster's discovery among the workers of such Lambian qualities as kindliness, geniality, and reserve. "Almost invariably," he writes, the testimonials supporting the application for employment "declared the disposition of the candidate to be 'mild and docile,' as though ferocity in a subordinate was the one thing dreaded by the Directors."[9] Phrases used to describe John Stuart Mill, clerk at the India House from 1823 to 1858, remind us of Lamb: "kindliness of heart . . . regarded with affection . . . fondness for walking." Thomas Love Peacock, novelist and one-time Chief Examiner of the India House, was analyzed by Sir

Edward Strachey as "A kindly, genial, laughter-loving man, rather fond of good eating and drinking, or at least of talk-ing-as if he were so," and Foster adds, "an ardent champion of old institutions and old customs; deeply versed in clas-sical literature and always ready to exalt it at the expense of modern writers."[10]

Humor in the form of horseplay was rampant in Lamb's office. While the milder wit in the essays has no direct asso-ciation with this, yet Lamb's sense of humor was kept in trim by the pranksters in the Accountant's Room. Crabb Robinson tells how in 1811 he once found Lamb half blinded from some ink thrown into his face by his fellow-worker Wadd. Foster tells how practical jokers transferred a colleague's horse, on which he had ridden to work, to some obscure livery stable, while within the office rulers were sometimes flung into the air to descend on a hapless head in some other compound. He continues: "Sport in all its forms had many devotees; and some of the clerks kept dogs in their official rooms. A certain individual went further still, for he brought his pistols with him, and re-lieved the tedium of his duties by using a mantelpiece at the end of the room as a target. This speedily produced a complaint to the Secretary from one of the clerks seated near the said mantelpiece; whereupon the marksman was given a commission in a cavalry regiment and sent to India."[11] If report be true, Lamb acquired some degree of impertinence from this roughhouse atmosphere. When his superior once asked him, "What are you about, Mr. Lamb?" he replied, "About forty." Another time his late arrival prompted the comment, "How late you come, Mr. Lamb!" "Yes," he replied, "but you should see how early I go!"[12]

Judging from a three-and-one-half-page, folio manu-script by Lamb that has recently come to light, Lamb did not conceal his whimsicality from his colleagues. Entitled

"Rules and directions to be observed by Mr Chambers at the end of June 1823 (applicable to any month when I am absent) concerning deposits, voucher, Error Ledger, and other circumstances of Mr Lamb's department of the Journal system . . . ," this humorous skit was undoubtedly designed solely for their amusement, with no thought of publication. "Love your enemies, hate your friends," he advises, "stir your tea with a finger instead of a tea-spoon, put butter in your brandy & water, anoint yourself with steel shavings instead of brimstone and treacle, nib your pen at the feather end, write off the tea notes endways, subtract by multiplication, sign your name in the appearance book backwards (to make the directors laugh) . . . ." Perhaps the humor of this farrago of nonsense was enhanced by the mutual recognition of personal shortcomings, habits, and errors that had become common office gossip. Whatever interpretation we put on it, however, it is further evidence of the leisurely atmosphere, the congeniality, and the good humor that prevailed in the establishment where Lamb spent so much of his life.[13]

From the vantage point of retirement, Lamb expressed his opinions of his former colleagues in a letter of October 7, 1827, to one of them, Henry Dodwell. The text in the Lucas edition gives only blanks for the many names, with the editor's note: "Too late to be able to supply the names for the blanks: all old East India Company colleagues." The original letter contains the names, with the exception of a cross to designate himself:

I am afraid now you and + are gone, there's scarce an officer in the Civil Service quite comes up to my notion of a gentleman. Dowley certainly does not, nor his friend Bland. Cole bobs. Kershaw *curtsies*. White bows like the son of a citizen; Field like a village apothecary; Chambers like the Squire's younger Brother; Rice like a crocodile on his hind legs; Huddy never bows at all— at least to me. Smith sputters and stutters. Wadd halters and

smatters. Rouse is a coal-heaver. Wolf wants my clothing. Cabel
simmers, but never boils over. Dupuy is a Butterfirkin, salt butter. Collet, a pepper-box, cayenne. For A. E. & O., I can answer
that they have not the slightest pretensions to anything but rus-
ticity. Marry, the remaining vowels had something of civility
about them.[14]

John Chambers, brother of the naval surgeon, and Dodwell
are both mentioned in "The Superannuated Man," and
Lamb wrote letters to these, as well as to White; Crabb
Robinson records in his Diary for July 13, 1816, that he took
tea at Lamb's and "White of the India House was there."
In an undated letter to John Chambers, Lamb commented
on Dodwell's slowness at work and his use of office hours
to read the *Times*.[15] In the *East-India Register* for 1803 a
Henry Dodwell is listed as an ensign in the Third Regiment
of the Royal East-India Volunteers, and in the same work
for 1810 the list of clerks in the Accountant-General's Department includes C. Lamb, John Mathie, H. Dodwell, H.
Rouse, and H. Wadd. In a letter of December 16, 1822, to
Wilson, Lamb referred to Wadd as "a sad shuffler," meaning slow in arranging notes of sales.[16] In the *Register* for
1803 appears the name "Samuel Wolfe," listed as a captain
in the First Regiment of the Brigade of Royal East-India
Volunteers. Henry Rouse is listed as an ensign in the same
regiment. The letter to Chambers just mentioned refers to
two more of these men: "Cabel has taken an unaccountable
fancy into his head that he is Fuller, member for Sussex.
He imitates his blunt way of speaking . . . . Dowley danced
a Quadrille at Court on the Queen's birthday with Lady
Thynne, Lady Desbrow, and Lady Louisa Manners." Rice
was probably the Vincent Rice of Islington who witnessed
Lamb's will. Peter Solomon Dupuy, who rose to be Second
Clerk, had translated an obscure French novel in 1795, and
Lamb had helped to polish his translation. William Collet,
next in rank to Dupuy, stayed on after Lamb to die on the

very day his retirement and annual pension of £550 were
to have begun.

Lamb seems not to have valued the literary abilities of
his colleagues in any higher light than he did their pretensions to gentility: "There is not as much metaphysics
in 36 of the people here as there is in the first page of
Locke's treatise on the Human understanding, or as much
poetry as in any ten lines of the Pleasures of Hope or the
more natural Beggars' Petition," he wrote to Wordsworth
on April 26, 1816. "I never entangle myself in any of their
speculations."[17] When one of his colleagues was about to
publish some poems, Lamb wrote to John Chambers: "Bye
is about publishing a volume of poems . . . chiefly amatory,
others of them stupid, the greater part very far below
mediocrity; but they discover much tender feeling; they
are most like Petrarch of any foreign Poet, or what we
might have supposed Petrarch would have written if Petrarch had been born a fool!"[18]

Many employees of the India House had been professional writers on India: Orme, Bruce, Auber, and Kay dealt
with the history; Halhed, Wilkins, and Wilson with Ori-
ental learning; Dalyrymple with nautical matters; and Edward Thornton with geography and history. Thomas Run-
dall edited the early voyages. Moffat James Horne described personal experiences in the East in *The Adventures of Naufragus*. William T. Thornton wrote on Indian
affairs and social science while producing three volumes
of poetry as well. Antiquarian research occupied the time
of Thomas Fisher, whose activities earned him a place in
the *Dictionary of National Biography*. Horace Grant was
the author of several educational manuals. Macvey Napier
published the correspondence of his father, who had been
an editor of the *Edinburgh Review*.

Better known of the nonliterary authors in the employ
of the India House are James Mill and his son, John Stuart

Mill. The former published his *History of India* in 1818, one year before being appointed to the Examiner's Department. John Stuart Mill was appointed to the Examiner's Department on May 21, 1823, at the age of seventeen. Like others in the office he found leisure to write letters and compose articles for the *London Review*. Writing to Carlyle on June 30, 1837, he says, "I have very little to do here at present. I have worked off my arrear of business at this office, and the work does not now come in nearly as fast as I can do it. It is the way of my work to go in that sort of manner—in fits—and I like that well enough, as it gives me intervals of leisure. I am using this interval to get on with my book . . . ."[19]

The "great boast and ornament of the India House" was John Hoole, who had retired in 1785 after working his way up from the Accountant's Office to succeed George Old-mixon, an Italian scholar, as Auditor of Indian Accounts. Influenced by Oldmixon, Hoole unsuccessfully attempted playwriting and acting. But his translations of Tasso, Ariosto, and Metastasio were very popular, and Sir Walter Scott conceived the ambition to master Italian after reading some of Hoole's work. But Lamb's criticism, in a letter to Coleridge of February 5, 1797, is disparaging: "Fairfax I have been in quest of a long time. Johnson in his life of Waller gives a most delicious specimen of him, & adds, in the true manner of that delicate critic, as well as amiable man, 'it may be presumed that this old version will not be much read after the elegant translation of my friend, Mr. Hoole.' I endeavour'd—I wish'd to gain some idea of Tasso from this Mr. Hoole, the great boast and ornament of the India House, but soon desisted. I found him more vapid than smallest small beer sun-vinegared."[20] Lamb's criticism has never been reversed; Macaulay chose Hoole as a typical imitator of Pope's versification without Pope's genius.

The position of Thomas Love Peacock in literature is

well known. It is said that he owed his appointment in 1819 to Peter Auber, Secretary of the Company and author of *The Rise and Progress of British Power in India;* Auber realized the value "of a clear and brilliant style in the conduct of the company's correspondence."[21] Peacock replaced James Mill as head of the Examiner's Department in 1836, when the latter died.

Of lesser importance, but serving to define completely the frequently mentioned literary tradition of the India House, are Walter Wilson and James Cobb. The former is known as a friend of Lamb and author of *Memoirs of the Life and Times of Daniel De Foe,* with which Lamb helped. The latter was Secretary from 1814–18 and author of no less than twenty-four plays, many of them popular at the time. His play *The Humourist* was produced by Sheridan at Drury Lane in 1785.

In view of this large quantity of writing, both literary and nonliterary, produced by India House employees, from the lowest to the highest, are we justified in bemoaning Lamb's servitude as some critics have, who assume that he would have been more prolific and even greater if he had not been chained to a mercantile desk? The literary tradition of the establishment was not hampered by its commercial activities. Lamb gained invaluable knowledge of character there from association with representatives of various classes of society. He received a comfortable income and a liberal retirement allowance at the age of fifty. His work was hardly slave labor, and for six hours a day he gained a security which literature alone would not have afforded him. Except for periods when work was pressing, his time was his own after four in the afternoon. Besides this, there were frequent opportunities for writing letters or literary work during actual office hours. De Quincey realized the therapeutic value of the routine for Lamb:

Clerks of the India House are as blind to their own advantages as the blindest of ploughmen. Lamb was summoned, it is true, through the larger and more genial section of his life, to the drudgery of a copying clerk—making confidential entries into mighty folios, on the subject of calicoes and muslins. By this means, whether he would or not, he became gradually the author of a great "serial" work, in a frightful number of volumes, on as dry a department of literature as the children of the great desert could have suggested . . . . Such a labour of Sisyphus . . . seems a bad employment for a man of genius in his meridian energies. And yet, perhaps not. Perhaps the collective wisdom of Europe could not have devised for Lamb a more favourable condition of toil than this very India House clerkship.[22]

For a man of Lamb's unsteady temperament the regularity of office work was the best thing possible. His holidays and evenings with his friends were the more valuable for their relationship to his desk work. After retirement, his leisure was not so precious, and his literary productivity began to decline immediately. Rather than speculate on how much more he would have done had he not been employed, we might well speculate on how much more he would have done had he continued to be employed! In spite of his occasional protests against task-work and his ecstasy over his escape, Lamb himself realized his good fortune. When Bernard Barton contemplated leaving his job to devote himself full-time to writing, Lamb's advice, on January 9, 1823, was vigorous:

"Throw yourself on the world without any rational plan of support, beyond what the chance employ of Booksellers would afford you"!!! Throw yourself rather, my dear Sir, from the steep Tarpeian rock, slap-dash headlong upon iron spikes . . . . I bless every star, that Providence, not seeing good to make me independent has seen it next good to settle me upon the stable foundation of Leadenhall . . . . Henceforth I retract all my fond complaints of mercantile employment, look upon them as Lovers' quarrels. I was but half in earnest. Welcome, dead timber of a desk, that makes me live. A little grumbling is a wholesome medicine for the spleen, but in my inner heart do I approve and embrace this our close but unharrassing way of life. I am quite serious.[23]

What a comfortable feeling to know that even if his literary work did not succeed, his monthly budget would not be affected! In his early years the extra money his hack work brought in was all too eagerly consumed, and he was tempted to write what would sell rather than what he wanted to write or what he could best write. As his salary increased, concern for the monetary value of his writing decreased, and he began to write more for pleasure and with consideration of his own peculiar forte. When Southey referred in print to *Elia* as "a book which wants only a sounder religious feeling, to be as delightful as it is original," Lamb feared the comment would affect the sale. But on July 10, 1823, writing to Barton, whom he had persuaded to remain at his bank job, he showed the security he felt: "Let it stop. There is corn in Egypt, while there is cash at Leadenhall. You and I are something besides being Writers. Thank God."[24]

When one notes the large number of letters written by Lamb with the superscription "East India House," it is obvious that, like John Stuart Mill, he found considerable leisure in the intervals between auctions. On October 9, 1822, near the end of his business career, he declared to Barton: "For six hours every day I have no business which I could not contract into two, if they would let me work Taskwork."[25] He made no secret of spending office time on his correspondence; after all, it was common practice. "I have a habit," he told Walter Wilson in a letter of December 16, 1822, "of never writing letters, but at the office—'tis so much time cribbed out of the Company . . . ."[26] He directed his friends to address others as well as himself at the India House because the Company paid the postage on all the letters it received. "Send what letters you please by me," he invited Coleridge on February 5, 1797, "& in any way you choose, single or double. The India Co. is better adapted to answer the cost than the generality of my friend's correspondents."[27]

Not only Coleridge but even Wordsworth and Sir John Stoddart, Chief Justice and Justice of the Vice-Admiralty Court in Malta, defrauded the East India Company by addressing letters and having letters addressed to themselves and their wives through Lamb. At one time such correspondence was distinguished by the simple expedient of adding the letter *e* to Lamb's name,[28] but enclosures were also used. Writing to his sister Sarah, later the wife of Hazlitt, on July 16, 1802, Sir John Stoddart, soon to become the King's Advocate at Malta, advised: "Address your answer to me as above, seal'd, and inclosed in a cover to Mr. Chas. Lamb India-house London—thus we save half-postage, and half a loaf you know is better than no bread—In the cover you may give your remembrances to Miss Lamb."[29] Miss Lamb herself encouraged this practice; writing to Miss Stoddart on July 21 of the same year, she added a postscript: "Remember I pay no postage, and you do, and you can always scribble a few lines to me, when you are disposed to enclose a letter to any other friend, and you know it is not any inconvenience to my brother to receive them."[30]

When in 1816 the generous Company finally felt obliged to abolish this fringe benefit, Lamb complained bitterly, with accusations that anticipate those made against his employees' ambitions by Dickens' Mr. Bounderby:

It is with infinite regret I inform you that the pleasing privilege of receiving letters, by which I have for these twenty years gratified my friends and abused the liberality of the company trading to the Orient, is now at an end. A cruel edict of the Directors has swept it away altogether. The devil sweep away their patronage also. Rascals who think nothing of sponging upon their employers for their Venison and Turtle and Burgundy five days in a week, to the tune of five thousand pounds in a year, now find out that the profits of trade will not allow the innocent communication of thought between their underlings and their friends in distant provinces to proceed untaxed, thus withering up the heart of friendship and making the news of a friend's good health worse than indifferent, as tidings to be deprecated as bringing with it ungracious expense. Adieu, gentle correspondence, kindly conveyance of soul, interchange of love, of opinions, of puns and what not . . . . The upshot is, you must not direct any more letters through me . . . . Write *to* us, but not *by* us, for I have near ten correspondents of this latter description, and one or other comes pouring in every day, till my purse strings and heart strings crack. Bad habits are not broken at once.[31]

Not only letters, but poems, jokes, and probably more than one essay were penned at the office. On January 9, 1802, he wrote to John Rickman of "busy days and riotous nights, doing the Company's business in a morning, straining for Jokes in the afternoon, and retailing them (not being yet published) over punch at night."[32] "The Good Clerk" (1811) contains the statement that it was "sketched, in an interval of business, to divert some of the melancholy hours of a Counting House." "A Dissertation upon Roast Pig," "Grace before Meat," "The Old Benchers of the Inner Temple," "Mackery End in Hertfordshire," "Dream-Children," and "Imperfect Sympathies" were all written on East India House paper, and it is tempting to conclude that they were written on office time. However, he probably "borrowed" some paper for use at home; a company that paid the postage on personal correspondence would hardly have objected. "Remarkable Correspondent" (or "The Twenty Ninth of February"), published in Hone's *Every-Day Book* for May 1, 1825, one month after his retirement, was also written on India House paper.[33]

Lamb himself says very little in his letters about his habits of writing. After the early correspondence with Coleridge and Wordsworth, where there is no dearth of comment and criticism both of his own and of others' writing, the extant letters become more and more barren of information about his own compositions, but we can make some general observations. For one thing, unlike Dr. Johnson, who discounted the necessity of waiting for mood and time to conspire, Lamb insisted on freedom from pressure. Writing theatrical reviews for the *Morning Post*, he found that it was impossible to continue: "It is most probably the last theatrical morceau I shall do," he wrote Rickman on January 14, 1802, "for they want 'em done the same night, and I tried it once, and found myself non compos. I can't *do* a thing against time."[34] Sometime later he wrote to Godwin, November 10, 1803: "I (an author by fits) sometimes cannot put the thoughts of a common letter into sane prose. Any work which I take upon myself as an engagement will act upon me to torment."[35] He had the all-too-human weakness of putting things off: "Charles often plans but never begins," wrote his sister, somewhat exasperated, to Dorothy Wordsworth on October 13, 1804, for they had promised themselves a journey to Grasmere on the first money he earned by writing certain books.[36]

It was this fickleness of spirit that made it needful for sister, friends, and editors to encourage and prod him along the whole path of his essay writing. At first, he was willing enough, but the correspondence convinces one that we owe a large part of Lamb's work to the efforts of his friends in overcoming his inertia. As early as July 21, 1821, after one

year on the staff of the *London Magazine,* he wrote John
Taylor, the editor, "For myself I feel almost exhausted, but
I will try my hand a little longer . . . ."[37] A year later, on
March 20, 1822, he confided to Wordsworth his desire to
withdraw, fearful of going from dull to worse, but a sense
of obligation or loyalty, intensified by the departure of
Hazlitt and De Quincey, prevented him.[38] After still another year, we find him writing to his friend Barton on
March 11, 1823, "They have dragged me again into the
Magazine, but I feel the spirit of the thing in my own mind
quite gone."[39] Two months later, in a letter to the same
person, dated May 3, 1823, we read: "I cannot but think
the London drags heavily . . . I would give a clean sum
of money in sincerity to leave them handsomely. But the
dogs—T. and H. I mean—will not affront me, and what can
I do? must I go on to drivelling? Poor Relations is tolerable—but where shall I get another subject—or who shall
deliver me from the body of this death? I assure you it
teases me more than it used to please me."[40] From the end
of 1823 until September, 1824, Lamb wrote nothing of
which we know. "The London must do without me for a
time, a time, and half a time," he wrote Barton on January
23, 1824, "for I have lost all interest about it, and whether
I shall recover it again I know not."[41] And to the same on
May 15, 1824: "It is in vain to spur me on. I must wait. I
cannot write without a genial impulse, and I have none.
'Tis barren all and dearth."[42] Finally, under much pressure,
another effort is made, "Blakesmoor in H——shire," of which
Lamb has this to say in another letter to Barton, of August
17, 1824: "I wish all the ink in the ocean dried up, and
would listen to the quills shivering up in the candle flame,
like parching martyrs. The same indisposit^n to write it is
has stopt my Elias, but you will see a futile Effort in the
next No., 'wrung from me with slow pain.' "[43] On Decem-

ber 28 of this same year, he answered the request of Alaric Watts for a contribution to his *Annual* thus: "My poor prose, which is near exhausted, is the London's, and my dry spring is not likely to overflow to a second reservoir."[44]

Much of Lamb's "indisposition to write" was the result of the gradual decline of the *London*. After the change in ownership and management, following Scott's death, Hazlitt, Procter, and Wainewright withdrew from the staff, taking with them a noticeable degree of the high quality that had distinguished the periodical. Other writers too began to feel reluctant about the continued association of their names with a failing publication. Lamb was well aware of the decline as early as April 15, 1822, when he analyzed the trouble for J. A. Hessey, one of the owners:

What is gone of the Opium Eater, where is Barry Cornwall, & above all what is become of Janus Weathercock—or by his worse name of Vink——something? He is much wanted. He was the genius of the Lond. Mag. The rest of us are single Essayists.

You must recruit. You will get too serious else. Janus was characteristic. He talkd about it & about it. The Lond. Mag. wants a personal character of its own too much. Blackw^d owes all to that.[45]

Lamb continued, however, as he termed it in a letter to Hunt, "a poor, worn mill-horse, in the eternal round of the damn'd magazine"[46] because he was well paid and was permitted absolute freedom in his contributions. Finally, when the magazine passed into the hands of Henry Southern in September, 1825, he wrote Barton in anticipation on August 10, that he stood "like Xtian with light and merry shoulders."[47]

It is indicative of the perverseness of his muse that, freed from editorial pressure, he began to write for another magazine, the *New Monthly*, as early as January of the following year. He protested as before: "I used up all my best thoughts in that publication, and I do not like to go on writing worse & worse, & feeling that I do so."[48] Having produced his *Popular Fallacies* throughout 1826, he broke away once more from writing: "I have at last broke the bonds of business a second time, never to put 'em on again," he wrote Wordsworth on September 6 of that year. "I pitch Colburn and his magazine to the divil."[49] But the following year he was contributing to Hone's *Table Book,* and in 1831 he was adding prestige to Moxon's *Englishman's Magazine.* When the latter was abandoned after three numbers by Moxon, Lamb wrote him on October 24, 1831: "By the by, to shew the perverseness of human will—while I thought I must furnish one of those accursed things monthly, it seemed a Labour above Hercules's 'Twelve' in a year, which were evidently Monthly Contributions. Now I am emancipated, I feel as if I had a thousand Essays swelling within me. False feelings both."[50]

It should be abundantly clear from the evidence presented that composition was a difficult task for Lamb throughout his life and that most, and the best, of his work was wrung from his brain "with slow pain." Yet ability and an irresistible urge to express himself, together with external considerations, forced him to undergo the mental effort. His high standards kept him from being easily satisfied and thus contributed to the difficulty he felt. Near the end of Lamb's life, Crabb Robinson wrote in his Diary for April 9, 1833: "Lamb says that he can write acrostics and album verses, and such things, at request, with a facility that approaches that of the Italian Improvisatori; but that he has great difficulty in composing a poem or piece of prose which he himself wishes should be excellent. The things that cost nothing are worth nothing. He says he should be happy had he some literary task."

Considering Lamb's temperament and the difficulty he

experienced with literary composition, it seems unlikely that he found the atmosphere of the India House conducive to essay writing although he did some creative work there. His frequent complaints of the interruptions in his letter writing show that it often required a good deal of persistence to get through a friendly epistle. If we may believe his lines in the *Popular Fallacy: "That We Should Lie Down With the Lamb,"* he preferred to write at night: "We love to read, talk, sit silent, eat, drink, sleep, by candle-light . . . . By the midnight taper, the writer digests his meditations . . . . No true poem ever owed its birth to the sun's light . . . . Even ourself, in these our humbler lucubrations, tune our best measured cadences (Prose has her cadences) not unfrequently to the charm of the drowsier watchman, 'blessing the doors'; or the wild sweep of the winds at midnight." Procter tells us that Lamb worked at a table, at the opposite side of which was "his sister, engaged in some domestic work, knitting or sewing, or poring over a modern novel."[51] Mary Lamb confirms this in a description written to Sarah Stoddart of how they wrote the *Tales from Shakespear:* "You would like to see us, as we often sit, writing on one table . . . I taking snuff, and he groaning all the while, and saying he can make nothing of it, which he always says till he has finished, and then he finds out he has made something of it."[52]

As time went on, Lamb acquired more and more friends, and consequently more and more evening visitors. No one was a better host, or liked company better, than Lamb, but with so many callers, there was no time to write. The creative urge was too strong in him to submit to this condition easily, and the bold solution to the problem was announced triumphantly in a letter to Hazlitt on February 19, 1806: "Have taken a room at 3/– a week, to be in between 5 & 8 at night, to avoid my *nocturnal* alias *knock-eternal* visitors.

The first-fruits of my retirement has been a farce which goes to manager tomorrow."[53] The farce, *Mr. H.*, was the first and last fruit. The room was soon given up; it was too lonely, and his conscience was bothered by the knowledge that his sister was alone. Another solution presented itself several years later, when they discovered four untenanted and unclaimed rooms in a garret adjoining theirs in Temple Lane. Mary's sisterly cooperation is evident as she describes the acquisition in a letter to young Barbara Betham on November 2, 1814:

And last winter, my brother being unable to pursue a work he had begun, owing to the kind interruptions of friends who were more at leisure than himself, I persuaded him that he might write at his ease in one of these rooms, as he could not then hear the door knock, or hear himself denied to be at home, which was sure to make him call out and convict the poor maid in a fib. Here, I said, he might be almost really not at home. So I put in an old grate, and made him a fire in the largest of these garrets, and carried in one table, and one chair, and bid him write away, and consider himself as much alone as if he were in a new lodging in the midst of Salisbury Plain, or any other wide unfrequented place where he could expect few visitors to break in upon his solitude. I left him quite delighted with his new acquisition, but in a few hours he came down again with a sadly dismal face. He could do nothing, he said, with those bare whitewashed walls before his eyes. He could not write in that dull unfurnished prison.[54]

So Mary rounded up some old rugs, and they spent a week busily cutting all the prints from the books in his library and pasting them on the walls. Crabb Robinson described the result in his Diary for June 29, 1814: "Called on Lamb in the evening. Found him as delighted as a child with a garrett he had appropriated and adorned with all the copperplate engravings he could collect, having rifled every

book he possesses for the purpose. It was pleasant to observe his innocent delight. Schiller says all great men have
a childlikeness in their nature."

Thus, Lamb came to write in the proverbial attic, but
not for long did it remain his private retreat; the inevitable
happened. They had made it so attractive that it became
known as the print room, "and," added Mary in her letter
to Barbara Betham, "is become our most favorite sitting
room."

Lamb's employment at the India House was not a handi-
cap but a decided advantage, as he himself recognized in
his more serious moments. It gave him a feeling of security
and stability, without which he might have produced less,
or more mediocre, literary work. As it was, he could afford
to set and maintain the highest standard for himself and
refuse to lower it even though there was a ready market
with good pay for every essay he could write. While im-
pelled by an innate desire to create and criticize literature,
he could not meet his exacting standards unless his mood
conspired with time and place. It was torture for him to
write under pressure; yet without it, he would have written
very little. The leisure he enjoyed in business hours was too
irregular and full of interruptions to promote effective writing. He seems never to have been long settled in a place
agreeable to producing literary work. Even when external
difficulties were temporarily removed or modified, his care-
fulness and attention to details of expression slowed his
writing and resulted in constant revision. It is this actual
composition, the conscious creative process itself, that we
must be concerned with next.

FIVE

"Fine Things in Their Ore"

THE CRAFTSMAN

Apart from a few general remarks in books, and one or two isolated articles, no investigation—much less any extended study—has ever been made of Lamb's method of writing. How he wrote his essays and how his polished prose was created are questions that have been answered only by the assumption that his lines flowed easily and naturally to paper from Lamb's facile mind. But it has often been observed that the easier a piece of prose is to read, the harder it was to write. The truth of this dictum is confirmed by a study of the essays of Elia, which are as pleasant and delightful reading as can be found—for their author labored hard in their evolution.

Lamb himself would be the last to sanction a detailed examination of his manuscripts. We know that he liked to think of the literary masterpieces of his predecessors as springing Athena-like from their brains. In a footnote to "Oxford in the Vacation," printed with the essay in the

London Magazine but omitted from the collected edition, he plays with this idiosyncrasy:

> There is something to me repugnant, at any time, in the written hand. The text never seems determinate. Print settles it. I had thought of the Lycidas as of a full-grown beauty—as springing up with all its parts absolute—till, in evil hour, I was shown the original copy of it, in the library of Trinity, kept like some treasure to be proud of. I wish they had thrown them in the Cam, or sent them, after the latter cantos of Spenser, into the Irish Channel. How it staggered me to see the fine things in their ore! interlined, corrected! as if their words were mortal, alterable, displaceable at pleasure! as if they might have been otherwise, and just as good! as if inspirations were made up of parts, and those fluctuating, successive, indifferent! I will never go into the work-shop of any great artist again, nor desire a sight of his picture, till it is fairly off the easel; no, not if Raphael were to be alive again, and painting another Galatea.

It would be interesting to have Lamb's reaction to the fact that a one-and-one-quarter-page manuscript of one of his own letters sold at auction in 1955 for twenty-three hundred dollars; or to the fact that the manuscript of his famous "Dissertation upon Roast Pig" once sold for ten thousand dollars and would probably bring more if it were to be offered today.[1]

It is not unusual to find Lamb's attitude that inspection destroys illusion echoed by critics of his own work. Editors have even hesitated to identify quotations and half-recollections of phrases and lines of poems in his work on the grounds that such annotation detracts from the ultimate pleasure. Macdonald took this attitude in preparing notes to his edition of the *Works*.[2] For those who read for pleasure only, this may be a valid approach; but it is the business of critical scholarship to observe the subtle processes of literary composition, and scholars today are probing deeper and deeper into the minds of authors, even into that "deep well of unconscious cerebration."

As long ago as 1871 Charles Pebody recognized how valuable a study of Lamb's manuscripts would be: "It is surprising how little we can trace the hand of Charles Lamb in his essays and farces . . . . But where are the MSS. of his contributions to the *Reflector* and the *London Magazine?* When, where, and how did he write the Essays of *Elia?* Questions like these we ask and ask in vain; for Lamb, like Handel, kept a lock and key on his desk, shut himself up when he was at work, gave orders to his maid that he was not at home, and, unlike Sheridan, guarded against the inquisitive eye of his biographer by burning all his rough drafts if he had any, all his first attempts, and all his unfinished essays and plays."[3] No longer need we ask Pebody's questions in vain, for—aside from the juvenile notebooks and other early pieces destroyed after the tragedy of 1796—there is no evidence that Lamb burned any drafts. True, he did not leave his papers carefully preserved and labeled for future biographers—it never occurred to him that anyone would ever study him or his literary works; but neither did he take pains to cover his creative tracks, either by "lock and key" or by fire. Then too, most of his correspondents preserved his letters, which, in the course of time, have been collected by men of means and literary taste, who have bequeathed them to various libraries. Although these manuscript letters show innumerable erasures and revisions, it would not serve the same purpose to examine them as it would to examine the essays, for the letters were not intended for publication, and it cannot be assumed that Lamb would have made the same changes or limited himself to those changes if he had been writing for print. Nevertheless, since the general purpose behind revision in the letters, as well as in the essays, was exactness of thought, and, to some extent, improvement of style, a few broad observations may be made.

Many of the cancelled words and lines in the manuscript letters are made illegible by the use of heavy ink and a very effective method of cancellation consisting of a series of closely connected loops—a method that Lamb frequently employed also in the manuscript essays. Whereas erasures in the essay manuscripts are sometimes carefully made with a knife blade, those in the letters rarely show such pains. Some words blotted by the pen were deliberately crossed out still more completely. More often than not, therefore, his letters are anything but neat. Those cancellations that can be deciphered usually prove to be the ordinary composition errors. Repetition errors were frequent. Often he wrote a word or sound recollected from a phrase immediately preceding: "I certainly intend some time in my life to see life . . . ," he wrote in a letter to Manning on September 24, 1802, when he meant to write "Paris," and had to correct it accordingly.[4] Some of the cancellations were the result of the desire to give more accurate information; writing of Coleridge in the same letter, he first said, "He dwells in the very heart of Keswick," but changed it to read, "He dwells upon a small hill by the side of Keswick." A small matter, but it exemplifies significantly Lamb's persistent attention to detail and exactness, which may be observed as well in the essay manuscripts.

As one would expect, Lamb was more interested in accuracy of information and clarity of expression in his letters than he was in stylistic devices and emotional effects. When he pretends concern for the latter in his letters he is facetious, as in his letter to Coleridge of August 14, 1800, where, after crossing out six lines so heavily that it is impossible to detect what he wrote, he continued: "Is it not a pity so much fine writing should be erased—but to tell truth I

began to scent that I was getting into that sort of style
which Longinus and Dionysius Halicarn[assus] aptly
called the affected."[5] There may well be serious revisions
in the letters for improvements in style, but it is the manuscript essays that provide a rich field for this aspect of our
study.

Aside from the uncritical hesitancy to subject the prose
blossoms to scrutiny for fear of shattering their perfection,
the difficulty of locating and seeing the extant essay manuscripts is the chief reason for the absence hitherto of any
revealing examination. Only one such attempt has been
made, an interesting one, but limited to a single essay.[6]
Perhaps, too, the frequent difficulty of deciphering the cancelled words and lines has deterred more extensive study.
But the comparatively recent acquisition of collections of
Eliana by the outstanding research libraries in the United
States and abroad has now made accessible a sufficient
number of manuscripts for a revealing insight into Lamb's
craftsmanship. The following discussion is based on over
twenty manuscript essays, whose publication dates range
from 1821 to 1833.[7] Of this number twelve are of major
status, included in *The Essays of Elia* and *The Last Essays
of Elia*. They were published in five different periodicals,
including the famous *London Magazine*. With such representative material on which to formulate conclusions, it is
hardly likely that additional manuscripts would materially
change our impressions of Lamb's mind at work. As we
observe his methods of correcting and improving, the final
stage in the evolution of Elia now comes to light.

In any examination of this sort it would be helpful to
know that a particular manuscript was the only draft, the
second, third, or *n*th. In most cases it is not possible to
resolve this problem; but the presence of such a large number of revisions as exist in some of the manuscripts indi-

cates that it would have been extraordinary for Lamb to have written an essay of any length for the first and final time in a clear hand with no desire to improve it. Thus, a clean manuscript, such as that of one of his *Popular Fallacies* entitled "That the Poor Copy the Vices of the Rich," is almost certainly a revised draft or a copy made by Lamb for a friend. There are no erasures, cancels, blots, or revisions in this manuscript. The four pages are unfolded and carry no postmark. The laboriousness involved in copying such a long piece, or its availability in print cannot be valid objections to the possibility of its being a copy, because it was customary for Lamb and his contemporaries to transcribe their literary pieces for their friends. We find Mary, for example, making copies of Lamb's play *Mr. H.* for her friends to read.[8]

Two other *Popular Fallacies* exist in clearly written holograph manuscripts: "That Verbal Allusions are Not Wit, Because They Will Not Bear a Translation" and "That the Worst Puns are the Best." There are no corrections in the one and one-half pages of the first nor in the six pages of the second. The manuscript of the extant fragment of "A Quaker's Meeting" shows only two unimportant corrections, but Lamb was copying in part from an earlier draft.[9]

"The Child Angel" is another essay of major importance which shows few revisions in the extant manuscript. The one interesting change is in the title. Lamb first wrote "The Angel's Gossiping: a dream." Then he crossed out "Gossiping," substituting "Child" above it with a caret: "The Angel's Child: a dream." Finally, "Child" is crossed out and inserted with a caret between the first two words to form the present title: "The Child Angel: a dream." In at least one other instance, Lamb revised a title before publication: "Dream-Children" was first entitled "My Children."[10] No one will hesitate to agree that the change was judicious and in keeping with the mood of reverie that pervades what is perhaps Lamb's best-loved essay. In one case the title of a printed essay differs from that of the extant manuscript: "In Re Squirrels" is the heading of Lamb's little essay printed in the *Every-Day Book* for October 17, 1825, and subsequent editors have, properly, continued to use this title. But the extant manuscript, postmarked "October 24, 1825," clearly has "The Squirrel" as the title. Lamb may have made a fair copy from this draft, changing the title in the process.

Lamb's prejudice against envelopes ("I never inclosed one bit of paper in another, nor understand the rationale of it.")[11] enables us to recognize certain manuscripts as printer's copy. "The Squirrel" is only one of many essays that bear an address and postmark. "Grace before Meat," a four-sheet, folio manuscript, was folded so that the address and postmark ("Oct. 1, 1821") appear on page eight. The verso of the second folio leaf of "My First Play" contains the address and postmark. The verso of the fourth sheet of "Imperfect Sympathies" shows the address and postmark.

However, the absence of a postmark and address on an extant manuscript need not prevent us from classifying it as the printer's copy. With the exception of minor changes in punctuation, capitalization, and spelling that were made by the editor, by Lamb himself on the proof sheets, or—sometimes perversely—by the compositor, the extant manuscripts of "Mackery End in Hertfordshire," "Dream-Children," "A Dissertation upon Roast Pig," and "The Defeat of Time" show no differences from the first printed texts. Therefore, we can be sure that we have here final drafts. Manuscripts showing no evidence of being transmitted through the post were probably delivered by messenger, by the author himself, or possibly were actually posted inside a covering letter which bore the address panel.

The extant manuscripts of Lamb's contributions to the *Every-Day Book* and the *Table Book* were, for the most part, the copy sent to the printer. The folding, address, and postmark bear witness to this fact and prove that we have the final drafts. "The Humble Petition of an Unfortunate Day," printed under August 12, the day in question, is postmarked August 22, 1825. Also published in Hone's *Every-Day Book*, under the date May 1, 1825, is the contribution signed "The Twenty Ninth of February," postmarked May 2, 1825, and printed under the title "Remarkable Correspondent." "Munden the Comedian" (printed in some modern editions as "The Death of Munden") was posted February 9, 1832, to C. W. Dilke, the editor of the *Athenaeum*, where it appeared on February 11. The revisions in all three of these manuscripts are few in number and minor in importance. If we stopped here, we might assume that Lamb did his major revising in drafts preceding the one he sent to the printer—and the assumption would be erroneous.

Three other essays exist in manuscripts postmarked to William Hone, the editor of the *Every-Day Book* and the *Table Book*: "Mrs. Gilpin's Riding to Edmonton," "Dog Days," and a Letter to the Editor "Of Maid Marian and Robin Hood." A preposition pencilled in by another hand in the first manuscript and two pencilled indications of notes supplied in the printed text of the last contribution are further proof that these were printer's copy. In contrast to the manuscripts just discussed, these three contain as much alteration as one could wish for a study of Lamb's mind at work. It is obvious from these that, although Lamb may have made fair copies of other work, he did not hesitate to correct his manuscripts almost to the point of making parts of them illegible and to submit copy so blotted and cancelled that a modern editor would return it without a second glance. Paper, of course, was more expensive then—although Lamb's access to the ruled accountant's paper of the East India House must have prevented this from being a concern until he left that establishment. If there were more manuscripts available, we might be able to prove what we can now only suspect—that he was increasingly frugal with his paper after his retirement in March, 1825, and henceforth less reluctant to send a messy copy to an editor. At the same time we must note that Lamb was not unique in sending marked-up copy to the printer.

The first of the three manuscripts just mentioned, "Mrs. Gilpin's Riding to Edmonton," postmarked July 17, 1827, seems to have been written hurriedly, for the word "any" in a phrase near the end of the essay, "it is impossible for any Christian climber," was blotted and had to be inserted clearly; "it" in the same phrase was first omitted and when inserted was so blurred it had to be rewritten; and the signature, "A Sojourner at Enfield," was inadvertently cancelled when Lamb attempted to underline it, so that he had to rewrite it on the other side of the paper, this time underlining it twice for good measure! The essay began with facility, except for the change of "by the poet's friend Romney" to "from the poet's friend Romney." The proximity of the similar beginning of the third sentence, "It is to be supposed that," to the beginning of the second, "It is to be regretted that," causes a reader to expect a revision, but it is the latter part of this extremely long sentence that took the author's attention: "It is to be supposed that in the interval between dinner and tea, finding the time to hang upon her hands, Mrs. Gilpin during her husband's involuntary excursion——." And then, intending to move "Mrs. Gilpin" closer to the beginning of the sentence, he struck out the name and began to insert it after "that." But after writing only "Mrs." he changed his mind and struck that out and continued his sentence: "she rambled——." But there was no antecedent, so "she" was cancelled and "Mrs.

Gilpin" inserted where he had intended: "It is to be supposed that Mrs. Gilpin, in the interval between dinner and
tea, finding the time to hang upon her hands, during her
husband's involuntary excursion, rambled out into the fields
with the children, and at one of those high aukward styles,
so embarrassing to Ladies of——." Involved? Lamb thought
so too, and after cancelling as ambiguous the beginning of
an insertion after "children" that would have identified the
"field," he struck a line through everything after the word
"rambled." He continued: "out with the children into the
fields at the back of the Bell, (as what could be more natural?) and at one of those high aukward styles, for which
Edmonton is so proverbially famed, the embarrassment
represented, so mortifying to a substantial City Madam,
might have happened . . ." and so on to the end of the sentence so rapidly that he left out the preposition "in" before
"a state"—someone else inserted it. A dash for a breather
and Lamb is off again: "Now I talk of Edmonton I must
speak a little about those——." After inserting "styles" after
"Edmonton," he continued: "those of Enfield, in its ne——."
The word was never finished; "in its neighborhood" it
would have been, but "its next neighbor" seemed more personal to Lamb, and we find that phrase substituted: "Enfield, its next neighbour, which are so ingeniously contrived, that every rising bar being more & more pro-
tuber——." But a desire to be more exact—a characteristic
motive for changes in his manuscripts—causes Lamb to
strike out everything after "ingeniously" to make room for
a qualifying phrase: "ingeniously contrived, particularly
on the south side of it, so th——." But, on second thought,
the qualification makes the sentence too unwieldy; he
strikes out the whole line so sweepingly that two words,
"contrived" and "that," are cancelled and have to be rewritten. He continues: "ingeniously contrived that every rising

bar——"; "bar" is changed to "step" immediately: "step to the top becoming . . . ." There is more to say, and this must be a participle, not the main verb of the result clause; so the inserted "that" is struck out to provide for this: "contrived—every rising step to the top becoming more protuberant than the one under it—that is impossible for any Christian climber to get over, without bruising his shins as many times as there are bars." There remain a few touches: "step" becomes "bar" as it was at first—better have repetition than misnomenclature; "it" is inserted after "that"; then, since we are concerned, after all, with a woman, Lamb jots in a parenthetical "(or her)" between "his" and "shins." The rest of the essay gave little trouble. "These inhospitable invitations to a bruis——"; but "bruised" has just been used, so "flay'd" avoids the repetition and adds considerable color. Here is another characteristic alteration in Lamb's manuscripts; seeking to avoid repetition, he hits upon words that enrich the effect. Evidence of hurry is indicated by the echo of a word: "are so troublesomely importunaly." The adverbial termination is tenacious; the whole word is cancelled, and "importunate" is correctly written: "importunate at every little paddock that this . . ."; "here" is inserted at some time after "paddock"—further evidence of Lamb's concern with exactness. "Hecatompolis" is almost identified as the City of the Hundred Gates, but the initial "C" is no sooner on paper than it is crossed out and "Town" substituted—of course, cities don't have stiles; but Enfield abounded in them, on which fact Lamb once punned that it was a very stylish place!

One of the most interesting of Lamb's essays from the standpoint of revision is that entitled "Dog Days," postmarked July 16, 1825, the second of the three manuscripts noted above as bearing postmarks and thus serving as examples of final drafts. In this case the extent of revision tempts us to believe that it was the *only* draft, but of that it is impossible to be certain. The second sentence originally began: "Thousands of us are taken up and executed——," but at this point the author drew a line through the whole clause and began anew: "Warrants are issued out against us and hundreds of us are executed under an obsolete Statute, on bare Suspicion of Lunacy." The grating repetition is removed by substituting "in form" for "against us." The reduction in numbers is drastically continued on better judgment by changing "hundreds" to "whole scores"; from thousands we have come to scores—emotional exaggeration has given way to reason and plausibility. The phrase "taken up" was too good to be let go, and was inserted before "executed." To make the statement more definite, "annually" was inserted after "executed." Finally, "bare Suspicion of Lunacy" is modified to "what is called Suspicion of Lunacy." So the final form was: "Warrants are issued out in form and whole scores of us are taken up & executed annually, under an obsolete Statute, on what is called Suspicion of Lunacy." The next sentence was unchanged although Lamb began to insert the personal phrase "Really, Mr. Edi——" before it; as he wrote, though, he thought ahead and found a better place in the next sentence; so he crossed out what he had put down and jumped into the next. "My pulse for instance, is as temperate as yours, Mr. Editor, and my head as little flighty, but I hardly dare to shew my head"; the repetition is caught, and "head" became "face" immediately. Other than the insertion of "at this present writing" after "for instance," to add vividness, and the change from the less respectful "flighty," descriptive of the Editor's head, to the somewhat safer "rambling," the rest of the sentence remained as written.

Now begins a series of "if" clauses. The first is easy: "If I look up in a stranger's face, he thinks I am going to bite pronounced upon me. I am perfectly swelled with the quantity of ditch water I am forced to swallow in a day to clear me from imputations— ~~With a dose really has the Water ordeal of your old Saxon Ancestors.~~ ...

~~work for fear I should~~ ...

... for fear of being thought raving; if I set up only a little innocent yelp, to clear my throat ~~and~~ ... it is construed into ~~a certain~~ flightiness of conversation. ...

... as much a pleasure to ~~us~~ to ...

... If I bark out-right, I am adjudged to be raving. If I indulge only in a little innocent yelp, it is construed into a sort of ~~flightiness in conversation~~ ... If I snap at a bone I am furious; if I refuse it, I have got the sullens, and that is a bad symptom. I dare not bark out-right for fear of being adjudged to rave. It was but yesterday that I indulged in a little innocent yelp only on occasion of a cart-wheel going over my leg, and the populace was up in arms, as if I had betrayed some marks of flightiness in my conversation. —

Slightly reduced from original.

Dog Days

"Now Sirius rages"

To the Editor of the Every-Day Book

SIR,—I am one of those unfortunate creatures, who, at this season of the year, are exposed to the effects of an illiberal prejudice. Warrants are issued out in form, and whole scores of us are taken up and executed annually, under an obsolete statute, on what is called suspicion of lunacy. It is very hard that a sober sensible dog, cannot go quietly through a village about his business, without having his motions watched, or some impertinent fellow observing that there is an "odd look about his eyes." My pulse, for instance, at this present writing, is as temperate as yours, Mr. Editor, and my head as little rambling, but I hardly dare to show my face out of doors for fear of these scrutinizers. If I look up in a stranger's face, he thinks I am going to bite him. If I go with my eyes fixed upon the ground, they say I have got the mopes, which is but a short stage from the disorder. If I wag my tail, I am too lively; if I do not wag it, I am sulky—either of which appearances passes alike for a prognostic. If I pass a dirty puddle without drinking, sentence is infallibly pronounced upon me. I am perfectly swilled with the quantity of ditch-water I am forced to swallow in a day, to clear me from imputations—a worse cruelty than the water ordeal of your old Saxon ancestors. If I snap at a bone, I am furious; if I refuse it, I have got the sullens, and that is a bad symptom. I dare not bark outright, for fear of being adjudged to rave. It was but yesterday, that I indulged in a little innocent *yelp* only, on occasion of a cart-wheel going over my leg, and the populace was up in arms, as if I had betrayed some marks of flightiness in my conversation.

Really our case is one which calls for the interference of the chancellor. He should see, as in cases of other lunatics, that commissions are only issued out against proper objects; and not a whole race be proscribed, because some dreaming Chaldean, two thousand years ago, fancied a canine resemblance in some star or other, that was supposed to predominate over addle brains, with as little justice as Mercury was held to be influential over rogues and swindlers; no compliment I am sure to either star or planet. Pray attend to my complaint, Mr. Editor, and speak a good word for us this hot weather.

Your faithful, though sad dog,
Pompey.

him. If I look down upon the ground——"; Lamb notes the repetition, and the clause becomes: "If I go with my eyes fixed upon the ground, they say I have got the mopes, which is but a short stage from madness." The last word, though perfectly natural, is too personal; it becomes "the disorder." A nice touch of phrasing comes from the change in the next line: "If I wag my tail, I am thought too lively——"; the "thought" is struck out, and by a pen stroke it becomes reality itself. He continues: "if I do not wag it, I am sulky—either of which appearances passes for a prognostic"; another fine touch is the insertion of "alike" after "passes." After writing two sentences without change, Lamb came to the theme of barking, over which he worked more than any other one revision that I have seen.

"I cannot bark for fear I should——" he begins, only to cancel the whole and try again: "If I bark, it is called raving, if I indulge only a little gentle yelp it is construed into a certain flightiness of conversation." He has retained the chain of "if" clauses, but it doesn't suit, and the insertion of "in" after "indulge" is cancelled together with the rest. But he is ironing it out and tries again: "I dare not bark outright for fear of being thought raving; if I set up only a little innocent yelp, to clear my throat, and kep——"; he's sailing so smoothly he spells phonetically and must stop to change it: "and keep my voice in tune, it is construed into a certain flightiness of conversation." No one would be displeased with this—except Lamb, in whose mind the idea of conversation is developed so that he inserts just before this sentence: "I am obliged to keep——"; too colloquial! "I am obliged to abstain from all discourse." But this is too human, so out it goes. Now, abandoning the location of this insertion, he writes, "I must not talk in my language" after the long sentence just written. This needs explanation: "Dogs have a language of their own, and it is doubtless as much a pleasure to us to bark, as it is to you men to speak." But again the creative artist is not satisfied; the sentence is cancelled and a pun tried: "But we are dumbfounded my mouth is stopt." Reconsidered, this goes by the board too. At this point it seems easier to begin the whole thing over, and the long, hard-earned sentence is cancelled before it has stood five minutes, and for all that work there is nothing to show.

Lamb's mind explores the possibilities of expression: "When I bark outright——" he begins, only to strike it out. "I cannot bark outright for then they would——"; it won't do, and the stylist does not hesitate to reject it. He returns to the "if" construction: "If I bark outright, I am adjudged to be raving; if I indulge only in a little innocent yelp, it is construed into a sort of flightiness in conversation." Note the synthesis of this sentence from the phrases previously evolved. A new phrase, "upon any provocation," is inserted after "If." But the sentence is still not the way Charles Lamb wants it, and it is added to the scrap heap. "I broke out into a loud bark——" is a new beginning, but it gets no further, and the author's dissatisfaction—and perhaps exasperation—is apparent in the heavy lines he draws through it. At this point, he does an interesting and sensible thing: he puts aside temporarily the "barking" theme and continues his "if" clauses on another subject which has just as fitting a place in this context: "If I snap at a bone, I am furious; if I refuse it, I have got the sullens, and that is a bad symptom." Having satisfied his desire for another conditional clause, Lamb now abandons this restriction and expresses the "barking" theme without further trouble: "I dare not bark out-right for fear of being adjudged to rave. It was but yesterday that I indulged in a little innocent *yelp* only, on occasion of a cart-wheel going over my leg, and the populace was up in arms, as if I had betrayed some marks of flightiness in my conversation." The paragraph is ended; the final phrase has been retained from its inception; the sentence is shorter than it had been; the "only" has found its best possible position after trying two others; the vague "provocation" has become a definite "cart-wheel"; and further exactness has been added with the insertion of "yesterday."

The remainder of the essay shows little change: after one or two minor corrections, he continues, "fancied a canine resemblance in some star or other that has about as much effect——"; the relative clause is cancelled immediately: "star or other, that was supposed to predominate over addle brains, with as much justice——," changed to "with as little justice . . . ." As a better frame for the composition, "Mr. Editor" was inserted after "complaint" in the last sentence to recall the same personal address in the first part of the essay. Pompey is, after all, addressing his complaint to the editor, and, while he is ever mindful of it, a reader may have lost sight of the fact since the first use of the name. This last sentence seems to have been an afterthought, because, before it was written, Lamb had the ending "I am Sir, Your faithful dog," but before he wrote the signature he deleted this, rounded out the essay with the final plea, and changed the form of the close to "Your faithful, though sad dog, Pompey." How long it took Lamb to perfect this essay cannot be known; perhaps he put the paper aside at some point. But it is doubtful whether the final result could be improved. It is significant that even a minor prose piece such as this commanded the painstaking care evident throughout the composition of all Lamb's efforts.

The last of the three manuscripts noted earlier as exemplifying final drafts is a Letter to the Editor of the *Table Book*, "Of Maid Marian and Robin Hood," postmarked June 27, 1827, replying to a correspondent's comment on one of the *Garrick Extracts*. Corrections of pen slips include the change of "than" to "that" and of "Davenant's" to "Davenport's" in the first sentence and of "Robins Hood's" to "Robin Hood's" near the end. "But neither her," the beginning of the fourth sentence, seems to have been a mental blending of the corrected "But neither he nor." The substitution of "appears" for the colorless "is" in the second sentence is a stylistic improvement; the insertion of "Play" after "which" in the same sentence avoids ambiguity; the change of "authentic notices" to "authentic testimonies" in the last line is more accurate. An extensive cancellation occurs about the middle of the paper, after "Robin's mistress," where originally Lamb wrote, "I would willingly separate them in idea, for a story may be too romantic. To [*illegible*] Some injudicious poet, I think, first wove the two stories together." After changing "stories" to "incidents," Lamb crossed through this whole section. He continued: "Besides the named authorities, old Fuller (I think) somewhere relates, as a matter of Chronicle History, that Matilda was not only [*one or two illegible words*]"; the illegibility is caused by a cancellation of everything after "History" in favor of the substitution "that old Fitzwalter . . . ." Farther down, the "collection, called Robin Hood's Garland" is qualified as "common collection." The sentence is about to conclude "if I remember, of Mar——" when the beginning of Marian's name is crossed out and "of the nobility of Marian" substituted. "Is she not the daughter of plain Squire Gamiel of old Gamiel——" is changed to "plain Squire Gamwell, of old Gamwell Hall?"

The text of this essay as printed in the *Table Book* is the same as that of the corrected manuscript. With the exception of changing the phrase "old faithful servant, the banished Fitzwalter" to "old faithful servant, Fitzwalter," Percy Fitzgerald printed a faithful text in his edition.[12] But W. C. Hazlitt, who first collected this essay with Lamb's works in 1874,[13] not only exercised his editorial license, as all succeeding editors have done, to correct "confound" in the fourth sentence to "confounds" but changed the text wantonly: "as far as" in the third sentence, was changed to "so far as"; "Fitzwalter" became "Fitzwater" throughout, thus making Lamb's explanatory parenthesis in sentence five completely useless; in the same sentence, "old faithful servant, the banished Fitzwalter" is changed to "old servant, the banished Fitzwater"; and the next to the last sentence, reading "Is she not the daughter of plain Squire Gamwell, of old Gamwell Hall?" became "Is she not the daughter of old Squire Gamwell, of Gamwell Hall?" Lucas, Macdonald, and Hutchinson printed from Hazlitt's defective text; Macdonald and Hutchinson added to the errors by omitting the word "enough" from the second sentence, making it read, "It oddly happens." It would appear that until Lamb's essays are edited by someone of integrity who makes certain of his texts, we cannot be sure that we are reading what Lamb intended us to read.

The text of "An Appearance of the Season" as printed in the *Every-Day Book* for January 28, 1826, differs so much from the one in the two-page holograph manuscript that it is obvious the manuscript is not the final draft. Fitzgerald, who first collected this essay with Lamb's works in 1875, acknowledged his indebtedness to Frederick Locker, who "possesses the MS. of these essays in Lamb's writing . . . ." Locker's manuscript is now in the possession of the Huntington Library; its text is the same as that printed by Fitzgerald except for his omission of the last few lines. However, Lucas and subsequent editors have taken their texts from the *Every-Day Book*, which is assumed to be the text of Lamb's final draft. Since a comparison of the manuscript draft with the final printed version shows significant improvement in the latter, it is worth looking at the two side by side. The text of the manuscript follows:

An Appearance of the Season

Christmas has been among us so lately, that we need not apologise for introducing a character, who at this season of the year comes forth in renovated honours and may aptly be termed one of her *ever blues*: it is the

Beadle of St. ——?'s
[*symbol drawn by Lamb for the Beadle*]

No personal application, reader, we entreat of you. It is not this or that good man—but the *Universal Parish Beadle* not peculiar to either of the Farringdons, or limited to St. Giles' in the Fields, or him of Cripplegate. Such as he is in any one of the wards within the Bills—the same you shall find him in all. [*quotation: same in both versions*] For the verbal description of him we are indebted to an agreeable writer in the London Magazine for Dec. 1822. His corporal lineaments we have borrowed from a Carricature* [sic] (if we may give it so low a name) just published in which this figure is the very gem & jewel in a grouping of characters of all sorts and denominations brought together with infinite skill and fun to illustrate the many shapes of Cant in this canting age: a piece of satire without ill nature, of character rather than of carricatura [sic]; too broad and comprehensive to admit of particular and invidious application: [*Fitzgerald's text stops here*] in which men of every class introduced (for they are class-characters, not persons) may shift the ridicule from their own tribe by retorting upon their neighbour. "Brother, brother, we're both in the wrong."

* "The Progress of Cant": invented and etched by one of the authors of "Odes and Addresses to great persons" Sold by Maclean, Haymarket; and Ralfe Cornhill.[14]

Only a few alterations are evident in this manuscript: "honours" in the first sentence had originally been "attire," and the note had first read: "published by," then "published for," instead of "Sold by." That there are no more revisions is explained by the probability that at this point Lamb re-wrote the entire piece. This next version may have been that from which Hone printed, or there may have been in-mediate versions. At any rate, the text printed in the *Every-Day Book* shows considerable change:

An Appearance of the Season

Apology will scarcely be required for introducing a character, who at this season of the year comes forth in renovated honours, and may aptly be termed one of its *ever-blues*—not a peculiar of either Farringdons, nor him of Cripplegate, or St. Giles in the Fields, or of any ward or precinct within the bills: not this or that "good man"—but the universal parish beadle. [*quotation*] For the pleasant verbal description we are indebted to an agree-able writer in the "London Magazine";* his corporal lineaments are "borrowed" (with permission) from a new caricature,† if it may be given so low a name, wherein this figure stands out, the very gem and jewel, in a grouping of characters of all sorts and denominations assembled with "infinite fancy" and "fun," to illustrate the designer's views of the age. It is a graphic satire of character rather than caricatura; mostly of class-characters, not persons; wherein the ridicule bears heavily, but is broad and comprehensive enough to shift from one neighbour to another.

* For Dec. 1822
† "The Progress of Cant"; designed and etched by one of the authors of 'Odes and Addresses to Great People'; and published by T. Mac-lean, Haymarket, L. Ralfe, Cornhill; and Dickenson, New Bond-Street.

The main result achieved by this version over the earlier, manuscript draft is compression of the material with no loss of effect. This, with some change in the order of certain phrases, has resulted in a more polished piece of prose.

One other relatively brief prose composition by Lamb is available in an early draft, which can profitably be com-

pared with the printed version. It is the introductory letter
to Lamb's essay entitled "Letter to an Old Gentleman
Whose Education Has Been Neglected." De Quincey's
"Letters to a Young Man whose Education has been Neglected" appeared in the *London Magazine* from January
to July of 1823. The date of Lamb's good-natured parody,
"April 1, 1823," and other evidence indicate that Lamb
wrote and submitted his composition while De Quincey's
"Letters" were still appearing, but it was not published until
January, 1825. The first draft of the introductory letter is
referred to by Lamb in an undated letter to J. A. Hessey, of
the *London*, which, we may deduce, was written on April
2, 1823: "I enclose for Lion's head, instead of that which
I wrote last night . . . . I particularly beg you to sign the
Letter to the Old Gentleman, *Elia* instead of S T P T . . . ."[15]
The enclosure was apparently the version ultimately
printed—not in the "Lion's Head" department, but immediately before the essay.

The manuscript of the first draft, which Lamb "wrote
last night," is in the Widener Collection of the Harvard
University Library. It now acquires significance in this particular study of the development of Lamb's expression.
Here is a paper, revised and marked up, only to be discarded in favor of an almost entirely new introduction. The
entire composition is placed in square brackets to avoid
confusion with the body of the work. Above a line drawn
at the top he has written the note "Either to be prefix'd to
the Letter, or put in Lion's Head." Below this line is the
title: "To the Author of the 'Letters to a Young Gentleman,
whose Education had been neglected.'" The introduction
follows:

Dear Sir,

I was in a mixed party the other night, in which the discontinuance of your "Letters to a young Gentleman whose Educa-

tion has been neglected" was the Subject of our general condolence. A sensible old Gentleman present, who owes possibly
more to Nature than cultivation, took up the Subject, & expressed his fears that he was of an age, to be placed beyond the
possibility of your instructions. When I got home, a whimsical
notion strook me, of addressing a Letter to a person, at *his* years,
who had never received *any education whatever*. The following is the result. Our readers, I hope, will consider it as a mere
interlude between your more serious music; as none among them
will be more happy than myself, if this occasional banter should
prove a means of awakening you to a resumption of Letters,
which I am most anxious to see brought to a conclusion.

I am Sir,

With sincerest respect,
Your friend
& hble Serv. STPQ[16]

This first draft has been repeated in its corrected form.
The phrase "the discontinuance" was originally "your discontinuance"—a change made to avoid repetition. The article before "young Gentleman" was inserted later. "Education" began erroneously as "Edut——" but was immediately
corrected to "Educations," from which the final "s" had to
be struck. The phrase "has been neglected" was originally
"was neglected." The verb "be" was at first omitted from
the phrase "will be more happy." These errors, together
with the fact that in three cases a word is repeated and
has to be cancelled, indicate either haste or a late hour.
More positive alterations include the change of "condolence" to "general condolence." The second sentence
began: "A sensible old gentleman present . . ."; Lamb
crossed out "sensible" and inserted "pleasant" above, but
the similarity of sound is unintentional and objectionable:
"A pleasant old gentleman present," so "pleasant" is deleted. But after thinking vainly for a better word, he began
to use it after all: "plea——"; thus far only, and he changed

his mind again and decided on the original "sensible" after all. Another change of mind follows: "who ac——" he began the clause, but cancelled the beginning of the word to continue: "who owes more to Nature . . . ." However, he returned to insert the originally intended "accidentally" only to delete it in favor of a qualification inserted later: "who owes possibly more to Nature . . . ." The next sentence began: "When I got home, a whimsical notion struck me, of writing a Letter to a person, at those years . . . ." Just as "addressing a Letter" was better than merely "writing a Letter," so also was there more artistry, as well as a double compliment, in the change of "a mere interval between serious work" to "a mere interlude between your more serious music." Lamb's decision in his letter to Hessey to sign his essay with his pen name rather than with "S T P Q" must have been reached only after most careful consideration. This manuscript shows that he originally intended a brisk ending by putting "S.T.P.Q." immediately after the word "conclusion," but it must have been too brusque for Lamb; he crossed out the four letters and wrote instead, "I am Sir, With the sincerest respect for our our [sic] Late Opium Eater, Your friend & your hble Serv. Elia." Improvement was made by cancelling "the" before "sincerest" and the repetitive "your" before "hble Serv." Then, recollecting that the letter was addressed to the Opium Eater himself, he crossed out "for our our Late Opium Eater," thus bestowing his respect on De Quincey directly. At the same time, or perhaps later, the question of anonymity recurred, and he replaced "Elia" with "S T P Q."

The printed text of this prefatory letter shows even more extensive changes:

Dear Sir,—I send you a bantering Epistle to an Old Gentleman whose Education is supposed to have been Neglected. Of course, it was *suggested* by some Letters of your admirable Opium-Eater; the discontinuance of which has caused so much regret to myself in common with most of your readers. You will do me injustice by supposing, that in the remotest degree it was my intention to ridicule those Papers. The fact is, the most serious things may give rise to an innocent burlesque; and the more serious they are, the fitter they become for that purpose. It is not to be supposed, that Charles Cotton did not entertain a very high regard for Virgil, notwithstanding he travestied that Poet. Yourself can testify the deep respect I have always held for the profound learning and penetrating genius of our friend. Nothing upon earth would give me greater pleasure than to find that he has not lost sight of his entertaining and instructive purpose.

I am, dear Sir, yours and *his* sincerely,

Elia.

It will be noticed that Lamb thus decided to address the letter to the Editor of the *London Magazine* rather than directly to De Quincey. More attention is given to maintaining his assertion that his paper is in no way to be construed as a ridicule upon De Quincey's "Letters." Also, we see that Lamb changed his mind once more: both this introductory piece and his "Letter to an Old Gentleman" were signed "Elia" in print.

There is no discernible difference in the amount of effort spent by Lamb in perfecting one of his shorter pieces for a minor periodical and that devoted to a longer or better known essay written for a major periodical. However, in order to supplement the analyses already made, as well as to refute any objection that the revisions in the shorter or less profound essays cannot be valid bases for generalizations, it may be desirable to turn our attention to the extant manuscript of the best-known essay, "A Dissertation upon Roast Pig." There are fewer revisions than one would expect in six folio sheets. Of course, there may have been previous drafts; the careful writing flows so smoothly that I should be surprised if there had not been.

The first sentence that shows any change is that beginning, "While he was thinking what he should say to his father, and wringing his hands over the smoking remnants of one of those untimely sufferers . . . ." The words "smoking remnants" are in small writing and appear to have been written over an erasure of a shorter phrase or a single word; "untimely sufferers" was a happy thought in place of the weak and trite "unfortunate little victims." There is no further alteration until we reach the seventh paragraph: "and Ho-ti himself, which was the more remarkable, instead of chastising his son . . . ." This was originally: "and Ho-ti himself, which was the more remarkable, instead of being angry with his son . . . ." Near the end of this same paragraph, Lamb wrote: "and the clearest charge which Judge had ever again . . . ," and on to the end of the paragraph; not until later did he catch this apparent oral error and insert the correct "given." Lamb may have had someone read his manuscript to him in order to facilitate making a fair copy, but it seems more likely that this is just another case where the sound of the word is confused in his mind and translated to the pen. The same error is made in the paragraph after the next: "Without placing too implicit faith in the account above again," he wrote distinctly. Here, too, the error is not detected until after the line was completed; the correct "given" may not have been inserted until the entire manuscript was finished and reread. In this connection, a passage from a letter Lamb wrote to Bernard Barton on May 16, 1826, some four years later, is interesting. He is suffering from a bad head cold and complains that it affects his reading: "I can hardly read a book, for I miss that small soft voice which the idea of articulated words raises (almost imperceptibly to you) in a silent reader.

I seem too deaf to see what I read." It is possible that this "small soft voice" raised by "the idea of articulated words" affected Lamb's writing as well as his reading and was responsible for this confusion of two words that are somewhat similar in sound.

The eighth paragraph of the essay contains a few minor changes. The three words "his Lordship's townhouse" are written over an erasure that is illegible. "People built slighter and slighter every day" at first read "every were," a mistake in spelling for the "where" that was intended. Although modern editors do not preserve a distinction between Lamb's initial capitals and lower case letters and although to his mind they were frequently and perhaps usually interchangeable, yet he is sometimes careful to indicate which he intends, as he does in this same paragraph by changing the originally small letter of the first "manuscript" to a capital. It seems to make no difference here, but one wonders if his use of capitals in other places—letters as well as essays—might not often indicate an emphasis or shade of meaning which modernized texts do not pass on to us.[17]

The manuscript shows no further change until we come to the paragraph beginning: "Pig—let me speak his praise—is no less provocative . . . ." From here to the end of the essay there are more revisions than in the longer, preceding portion. In this sentence, "provocative" was first "tentatory," and we are glad for the sense of it that Lamb made the change. In the same short paragraph, "the weakling refuseth" was first "the weakling rejecteth." The next paragraph gave no trouble; the following one did. It began: "I am one of those, who freely and ungrudgingly impart a share of the few good things, in his kind, which fall to my lot, among my friends. I protest——"; here Lamb crossed out everything after "impart a share" and continued: "of the good things of this life which fall to their lot (few as mine are in this kind) to a friend." Having thus clarified his meaning, he continued: "I protest I take as great an interest in my friend's relishes——"; the last word is immediately cancelled as the idea is expanded to appear second in the series: "in my friend's pleasures, his relishes, and proper satisfactions, as in mine own." One other sentence in this group was revised: "Methinks there is an ingratitude, to speak it without profaneness to the Giver . . ."; the ambiguity is avoided by cancelling "to speak it without profaneness," and the "ingratitude" is properly directed "to the Giver."

The story of his encounter with the beggar on London Bridge, which, as we have seen in Chapter III, was a typically disguised personal experience which he truthfully related in a letter to Coleridge of March 9, 1822, gave some trouble. "In my way to school (it was over——"; the preposition is changed to "up," but whether this was intended to be "upon" or whether he thought of changing the scene (in the letter it is "In my way home through the Borough") we cannot know, for it is crossed out and "over" inserted. He continues: "over London Bridge) a grey-headed old imp——"; the beginning of "impostor" is cancelled—perhaps he wasn't, but he was certainly a beggar, and "beggar" is used: "old beggar saluted me; (I have no doubt at this time of day that he was an impostor)." For some reason "impostor" is cancelled in favor of "counterfeit." "I had no pence to console him with, and in the vanity of self-denial, and the coxcombry of charity . . . ." Intensified meaning is created by inserting "the very" before "coxcombry": "of charity, school-boy like, I made him a present of—the whole cake! I walked on a little, buoyed up, as one is on such occasions, with a sweet feeling of self-approbation, but before I had got fairly upon the Bridge my better f——";

here, in danger of repeating "feeling," Lamb deleted everything back to and including "on such occasions," with which words he had begun page five of his manuscript, turned the sheet over, and continued: "on such occasions, with a sweet soothing of self-satisfaction, but before I had got to the end of the Bridge, my better feelings returned . . . ." Again, by avoiding repetition Lamb has discovered a far better word, "a sweet soothing of self-satisfaction"; but for the necessity of shunning a repetition of "feeling," the euphonious phrase would never have been. Note too how a definite time is assigned for the development of his "better feelings" by the change of the scene in relation to the Bridge. The last part of the paragraph ran: "and how disappointed she would feel that I had parted——"; but he had used "to part with" earlier in the long sentence, so "parted" is deleted, and the thought changed: "that I had never had a bit of it in my mouth at last—&——"; the ampersand is expanded to "and"—a strange alteration for Lamb, who made no distinction and whose editors automatically expanded the symbol. Continuing: "and I blamed my impertinent alms——"; "alms" is cancelled and incorporated as "spirit of alms-giving." The sentence ends with "old grey impostor"; "grey" was cancelled only to be immediately rewritten, and "impostor" was cancelled only to be inserted after, apparently, a better word was not forthcoming.

At this point the manuscript originally began a conclusion: "With this story I shall conclude, leaving thee, reader, if thou be'st any thing of a Casuist, to determine imposture impostor——"; the entire is cancelled and the conclusion held in abeyance while a new paragraph is started. "What should his sau——"; but the question of sauces was to be considered in the last paragraph. After cancelling this first intention, Lamb began again: "Our ancestors were nice in their methods of sacrificing these tender victims." Perhaps this was the time that Lamb stopped long enough to return to the first part of his essay and change "victims" to "sufferers." "We read of pigs whipt to death with something of a shock, as we hear of any other obsolete practice." Later, probably when he used "practice" near the end of this paragraph, he came back and inserted "custom" for this use of "practice." Lamb did not always change the second occurrence of a word when the repetition jarred; just as frequently he made a substitution for the first use. "The age of discipline is gone by, or it would be curious to enquire (in a physiological light m——"; the term fits the subject, but it is changed to "philosophical light merely) what effect this process might have towards intenerating and dulcifying a substance, naturally so mild and dulcet as the flesh of young pigs."

The first sentence of the next paragraph shows the only other important revision: "I remember a thesis argued upon when I was at St. Omers, and maintained with much learning and pleasantry by——"; the preposition is changed immediately: "on both sides . . . ." The phrase "by the young students" was first inserted after "St. Omers," then cancelled and inserted after "argued upon." Lamb couldn't decide whether to write "thesis" or "hypothesis." First, "thesis" was cancelled and "hypothesis" written above it with the proper change made in the article from "a" to "an." Then this insertion was struck out and "thesis" written after it with the introduction of the article "a" after the revised "an" had been cancelled. Finally, Lamb deleted both these and wrote, after crossing out "I remember"— since there was no more room for insertions: "I remember an hypothesis" at the beginning of the line. To an ordinary reader it would make little difference which word was used, but to an extraordinary writer the difference was important enough to warrant considerable thought.

One of the manuscripts extant is that of Lamb's prose paraphrase of Thomas Hood's long poem "The Plea of the Midsummer Fairies," published in 1827 with other poems and dedicated to Lamb. "I heard she [Mrs. Hood] and you were made uncomfortable by some unworthy to be cared for attacks, and have tried to set up a feeble counteraction thro' the Table Book of last Saturday," Lamb wrote in announcing his effort.[18] He called his paraphrase "The Defeat of Time; or a Tale of the Fairies"; it was published on September 15, 1827. The manuscript is replete with alterations that show the great amount of time and trouble he expended voluntarily in an effort to offset the harsh criticism of his friend's poem. As a paraphrase, it is of special interest in revealing his method.

As might be expected, the beginning is more nearly complete in its synthesis of the poem than is the latter part. The plea of the second fairy is shortened by omitting the last part; the speech of the third fairy is confined to the first of Hood's three stanzas; the second of the three stanzas of Time's answer is omitted; the five-stanza speech of the little forester is compressed into a short paragraph; stanzas fifty-four to seventy-eight of Hood's poem, containing further pleading of the fairies with a narration of their duties and deeds, are skipped; and the last thirty-three stanzas are summed up in a brief compass. In spite of these abbreviations, the manuscript runs to seven folio pages; so it is hardly correct for Lamb to say, as he does at the end, that "the above is nothing but a meagre and a harsh, prose-abstract." It is certainly a good deal more than meagre.

And it is far from being a harsh abstract. Lamb followed the thought closely and utilized many of Hood's words and phrases, sometimes—as particularly in stanzas seventy-nine to eighty-one and eighty-three to eighty-six—whole lines. In both versions the figure of Time is "a melancholy shape";

the huddled fairies are compared to sheep; the first fairy is "clad all in white like a chorister"; and the speech of the little forester includes the phrases: "clad in green," "We be small foresters," "Training the young boughs," "show blue snatches of the sky," "close intricacies," "as our tiny hatchets ply, Men say the tapping woodpecker is nigh," "we scoop the squirrel's hollow cell," "carve quaint letters on trees' rind"—all phrases common to both versions. In some cases the manuscript reveals that Lamb came back to Hood's word choice after first trying another. In one place he first wrote: "Then TIME made answer, striking the ground with his hurtful scythe . . . ." The phrase "in his wrath" was inserted before "striking" after a short-lived intention to write "wrathful," and "ground" is made "harmless ground," thus repeating Hood's exact phrase, as does also "hurtful scythe." Hood had written of Time's "enormous tooth"; Lamb naturally enough wrote "enormous teeth" but, apparently feeling that he should be as close to the details of the original as possible, he changed it immediately to "tooth." In the forester's speech, Lamb omitted "we frame all shady roofs and arches rude," but returned to insert it. There is no doubt that he had the poem before him and referred to it constantly. Another similar change occurs in Puck's answer: "The morsel from the Gossip's fork," as Hood's line reads, was first written with "mouth" in place of "fork," but Lamb changed it to conform. Near the end of the paraphrase, there occurs the phrase "stray deer, stealthy and bold," just as in the poem; but Lamb's manuscript shows that he had first written "spritely" for "bold."

In many cases Lamb was just as concerned to depart from Hood's phraseology. The description of the forester's cap as "an acorn's cup," as Hood has it, was first included in Lamb's paraphrase of this section, but he later crossed it out. Similarly, Hood's poem had described Time standing "like a leaden statue" while lovers were apart; this was Lamb's first choice, but he changed it to "motionless statue." The Queen's "dark misgivings" in Hood's poem became "melancholy forebodings" in Lamb's version. Hood's description of Time as "that ancientest of Kings" was first converted by Lamb to "old Wisard," then "ancientest of Rulers," and finally "ancientest of Monarchs." His "barren poll," as Hood puts it, is simply "bald top" in Lamb's words. Hood's "veil'd nuns, meek violets" become "violets, like nuns," and his "lonely harebells, quaking" tempted Lamb to write so far as "lo——," but he omitted the word and wrote "quaking hare-bell." Hood's phrase "come fair or storm" became Lamb's "in storm or in sun," but he revised it to read "foul weather or fair," perhaps preferring Macbeth. The "loud unusual note" of Hood's grasshoppers became Lamb's "small concert"; but then he started to insert "loud unus——" between the two words, crossed it out and inserted "but loud" instead. Hood describes Time beginning "to clutch his mortal engine," but Lamb first wrote "clutched again his mighty Scythe," which he altered to "grasped fast his mighty Scythe." One of Puck's duties, in the poem, is to "stop the sneezing Chanter in the middle of a verse"; Lamb first wrote the same phrase then revised it to read: "stop the sneezing Chanter in mid Psalm." Such changes suggest Lamb's desire to be specific, to avoid a too slavish imitation of the original wording, and to confine his terms to simple and restrained prose.

Sometimes Lamb departed not only from the phrasing but from the plain sense of his original, and too, he sometimes added to his material. Thus, the Queen in Hood's poem hid from Time in an acorn cup, but in Lamb's account "the most courageous among them crept into acorn cups." Hood had expressed his ignorance whether King Oberon and Titania had had a quarrel or whether his absence was occasioned by his leading a war against the Gnome; Titania does not lament his absence nor wish his presence. Lamb wrote: "Titania's first impulse was to lament the absence of her Lord, King Oberon, who was far away, following a strange Beauty, a Fay of Indian Land; that with his good lance and sword he might defend her against TIME." On further consideration, he converted "lament the absence" to "wish the presence" and inserted "false" before Lord and "like a faithful knight & husband" after "sword." Again, when Titania enfolds the knee of TIME in Hood's poem she does so as a gesture of despair, but Lamb changes her reason to "being overcome with fear," which he later changed to "waxing speechless with fear." Again, the idea of Hood's fairies sitting at even in sweet bow'rs above Lovers, shaking rich odours on the air and keeping off the owl and bat from their privacy is slightly changed by Lamb. He has them sitting at evening shaking rich odours from sweet bowers upon discoursing lovers, and adds the idea that the odours "seem to be their sighs," which is altered for clarity to "that seem to each other to be their own sighs"; in addition to the bat and the owl, Lamb includes "the ill-boding whistler." The portion of the poem that relates how the abandoned infant Sir Thomas Gresham was found by means of the chirping of grasshoppers is told by a female fairy, but Lamb changed the sex without any obvious reason or deliberation. Furthermore, Lamb identified the infant by name, whereas the poem does not. Similarly, he identifies the Apparition that routs Time as Shakespeare, whereas Hood had left it to the reader to guess. Also, Hood had made Puck and Robin Goodfellow partners, but Lamb conjoined them.

In concluding his paraphrase, Lamb described the work as "a most agreeable Poem, lately put forth by my friend

Thomas Hood . . . ." The manuscript reveals that he had first written: "the most——"; but he had cancelled the superlative at once for the more conservative phrase. Perhaps the tedium of his labor had dulled his enthusiasm. Perhaps, too, it was at this very moment that Thomas Westwood, his next-door neighbor, acquired his copy of Hood's poem. We recall his account of how Lamb's distaste of modern books led him to dispose of copies which were presented to him: he would skim a Leigh Hunt through the apple trees, roll a Bernard Barton downstairs after him, leave a Barry Cornwall on his damp windowsill, "and," wrote Westwood, "the *Plea of the Midsummer Fairies* I picked out of the strawberry-bed."

The analyses and comparisons made thus far reveal several facts about Lamb's creative habits. For one thing, he seldom, if ever, wrote an essay without subjecting it to careful and thoroughgoing revision. Even when he may have been copying from an earlier draft, he took the opportunity of making changes in the title and the text as he transcribed. Lamb always strove for further improvement—no matter how many times he had transcribed from an earlier version. He did not always concern himself with preparing a fair copy for the printer. In the process of writing, a word or phrase would often be cancelled before it was finished and the revised reading continued; on the other hand, re-reading after the sentence or essay was completed is indicated by the use of carets to insert words and phrases above the line of writing. Frequently Lamb changed his mind about a revision, sometimes choosing yet another and sometimes returning to the first choice. Frequently words and phrases that were tried and rejected separately find a synthesis in the ultimate reading. Lamb's concern with the exact, the specific, the definite is evident in his revisions that furnish location, number, time, or person. In addition to mechanical improvement, his revisions are productive of stylistic gain and frequent compression of single sentences and of the whole. Of particular interest is the fact that Lamb was peculiarly sensitive to the sound of words; many changes are made to avoid unpleasant repetition of sound, and many pen slips are committed because of retention or anticipation of the sounds of nearby words. Finally, the usually thorough methods of cancellation by horizontal lines, joined up-and-down strokes, and closely connected loops suggest Lamb's unhesitating rejection and a dissatisfaction so determined that frequently adjoining words are inadvertently struck out and have to be rewritten.

In analyzing the types of manuscript alterations made by Lamb, it is convenient to adopt, with considerable modification and amplification, the two major categories formulated by Professor French: negative and positive. Those made "simply for avoidance of errors" he labels "negative alteration."[19] We may employ this term to cover (1) the correction of pen slips including miswriting and the inadvertent omission of words—articles, prepositions, adverbs, auxiliary verbs, pronouns, and nouns; (2) the correction of sound confusion; (3) the correction of retention and anticipation errors; (4) the correction of undesirable repetition if no other gain is achieved; (5) the correction or improvement of grammatical constructions, including capitalization, spelling, paragraphing, location of a phrase or clause, and change from a main clause to a sentence or to a subordinate clause; and (6) the cancellation of what may be termed first intentions.

Examples of the first kind of pen slips, miswriting, are the immediate correction of "times" to "time" in the phrase "will take you some times" and the subsequent correction of "invidually" to the correct word in the phrase "and invidiously suppress the exceptive clause" ("Remarkable

Correspondent"). Lamb began to write "neigt" for "neither" in the phrase "were implied in it neither" ("Barrenness of the Imaginative Faculty in the Productions of Modern Art"). In the same essay the word "Eliphaz" was slightly blotted and for that reason was cancelled and rewritten; similar blotting necessitated the rewriting of "Amphibium" ("The Child Angel"). The immediate correction of this type of error is a characteristic of Lamb's essay manuscripts.

The omission of words may be exemplified by reference to several manuscripts. There are the insertions of definite articles in the clauses "I wonder my shameless Rival can have ⟨the⟩ face" and "but where are ⟨the⟩ evidences of this first birth?" ("The Humble Petition of an Unfortunate Day"), as well as in the clause "which I have already mentioned as ⟨the⟩ indispensable concomitant of his visits" ("Poor Relations");[20] and there is the insertion of the indefinite article in the phrase "maketh matters worse by ⟨an⟩ excess of participation" ("Mackery End in Hertfordshire"). The omission of prepositions is illustrated by the clauses "she lived in it ⟨in⟩ a manner" ("Dream-Children") and "when men should cease ⟨to⟩ believe in them" ("The Defeat of Time"). Adverbs omitted include "not" in "And did ⟨not⟩ know till lately" ("Poor Relations") and "forth" in "shot ⟨forth⟩ intolerable rays" ("The Defeat of Time"). Verbal changes are made by the insertion of "had" in "under which it ⟨had⟩ been her seeming" ("Poor Relations"), of "have" in "They seem to ⟨have⟩ been superseded" ("In Re Squirrels"), of "could" in "as brimful of rogueries & inventions as you ⟨could⟩ desire" ("The Old Benchers of the Inner Temple"), and of "having been long" in "nature ⟨having been long⟩ confined" (first written "nature being confined") in the same essay. The pronouns "they" and "her" respectively were later inserted in "so ⟨they⟩ would have remained, stupor-fixed" ("Barrenness") and in "what should I say to ⟨her⟩ the next time" ("A Dissertation upon Roast Pig"); the noun "life" had to be added to the clause: "he would speak of his former ⟨life⟩" ("The Old Benchers"), the word "childhood" was omitted from the first phrasing "I have wished that sad ⟨childhood⟩ might have a mother" in the same essay, the explanatory phrase "of the Task" is an insertion after "Author" in the line "The Author ⟨of the Task⟩ somewhere speaks" ("In Re Squirrels") and "hostess" has to be supplied in "mine ⟨hostess,⟩ not very indistinctly" ("Imperfect Sympathies"). It is revealing to observe here that, without exception, not one of these omissions was supplied until the original sentence had been continued and, possibly, concluded; it was not until Lamb reread the line that he detected the lacuna.

The mental confusion of the sound of one word with that of another, which we saw operating in "A Dissertation upon Roast Pig," caused Lamb to write "Who are what sort of persons" for "Who or what sort of persons" ("Mackery End"), "hark to the midnight charm" for "hark to the midnight chime" ("The Defeat of Time"), "Not a word is spoken of its been seen" for "Not a word is spoken of its being seen" ("Barrenness"), "prettinesses heightened by fair" for "prettinesses heightened by fear [*later changed to* "consternation"]" in the same essay, and "Do take any slice" for "Do take another slice" ("Poor Relations"). In most cases of this sort, the insertion of the correct reading above the line indicates that the error was not detected until the sentence had been continued; however, in the last two examples given, the error was corrected at once.

Just as Lamb's mind sometimes confused sound, so it frequently retained letters and words already written and caused the pen to repeat them. Thus, he wrote "inoffef——" before immediately cancelling it for "inoffensive" ("The Defeat of Time"). Did Lamb's tendency to stutter carry over into his writing? He wrote of "our less-known relations in in that fine corn country" and, of Bridget (his sister), "She is excellent to be be at a Play with" ("Mackery End"). He speaks of "this thi——" (cancelled immediately) "chimerical notion of *affinity constituting a claim to acquaintance,* may subject the spirit spirit of a gentleman" ("Poor Relations"). And he first wrote how the fairies were empowered "to live in live in the minds of mind men, while verse shall have power to to charm" ("The Defeat of Time"). The correct "men" written after the cancelled "mind" shows that this error was detected immediately, but there is no way of knowing whether the other superfluous words were cancelled immediately or afterwards. The extra preposition in the phrase "to charm" was never cancelled—the printer must have recognized it as an error, or Lamb corrected it in the proof. The same is true of the extra preposition in the phrase "fond of of affirming" ("Imperfect Sympathies").

Just as frequent an error as the retention of words is the anticipation of letter and word sound combinations. There is the immediate cancellation of "comp——" for "contemptible" ("Remarkable Correspondent") and the later correction of "prepossing" to "prepossessing" ("The Old Benchers"). He writes of "an old woman, who persists in calling her 'her son Dick'" ("Poor Relations"). This was not corrected to "him" until later. "While for you have time, it will be well for you" shows Lamb thinking ahead ("Remarkable Correspondent"). "But let us seen" ("Barrenness") is obviously a synthesis of "But let us see in the text . . . ." And a verb seems to have been influenced by the sibilant termination of the demonstrative adjective in "before he sents this [*later changed to* "these"] incondite manuscript" ("The Old Benchers").

Occasionally the repetition of a word is avoided without any other stylistic gain; such changes are almost never made immediately. He makes the comparison of "names and circumstances still crowding back upon her, as words written in lemon come back upon exposure to a friendly warmth" ("Mackery End"). The second usage is altered to "out." Speaking of a horse, he wrote how their uncle would "make him carry him" ("Dream-Children"); the first "him" is changed to "it." Writing "An air of discomfort sate upon the Queen, and upon her tiny Courtiers. Their merry friskings . . . ," he changed "merry" to "tiny" and avoided repetition by deleting the first use of the word ("The Defeat of Time"). The repetition of "time" in "C. gave away 30,000 £ at one time in his life-time" ("The Old Benchers") is avoided by changing "at one time" to "at once." The word "pinions" had been used seven lines before Lamb wrote how the infant "was shorn of its aspiring pinions, and fell fluttering" ("The Child Angel"); so the second use was cancelled, leaving the somewhat odd "was shorn of its aspiring, and fell fluttering . . . ." Lamb wrote originally of "a perfect moon-struck character" ("Munden the Comedian"), but he deleted "perfect" when he found a better use for it in the appositives: "a perfect abstraction from this earth . . . ." Noting the repetition of "act" when he quoted from Heywood at the end of a footnote ("Imperfect Sympathies"), Lamb converted his use of the word two lines before to "deed": "could give no other reason for the deed . . . ."

The manuscripts reveal numerous alterations made, in general, to correct or improve grammar and style. Some were made immediately; some, later. The spelling of "gambles" is changed to "gambols" ("The Defeat of Time"), of "inviting" to "uninviting" ("The Old Benchers"), and of "apolouge" to "apologue" ("Remarkable Correspondent"). "All-Georges-Day" ("The Humble Petition") was first written with a lower-case letter for "all," and "men" was capitalized after the initial lower-case letter was written in the phrase "ambitious Children of Men" ("The Defeat of

Time"). "S. was his opposite" ("The Old Benchers") began a new paragraph after the first two words were written at the end of the former one.

Other alterations made to improve style include such changes as "What I have done" to "What have I done" ("Remarkable Correspondent"); of "long ago, in those pretty pastoral walks about Mackery End" to "in those pretty pastoral walks long ago about Mackery End" ("Mackery End"); of "Here John slyly deposited a bunch of grapes which, not unobserved by Alice, he had meditated dividing with her, back upon the plate . . ." to "Here John slyly deposited back upon the plate a bunch of grapes . . ." ("Dream-Children"); and of the beginning of a main clause "and I aw——" to "and immediately awaking, I found . . ." ("Dream-Children"). The conversion of a clause, "and the murmers [sic] of mine hostess . . ." to a sentence is achieved by adding a period, deleting the conjunction, and overwriting the initial letter of the definite article with a capital: "The coach drove off. The murmers of mine hostess . . ." ("Imperfect Sympathies").

Last in the category of negative alterations are cancellations of first intentions, of words and phrases that would have modified or amplified the thought, of ideas later considered not pertinent, and of words that were subsequently recalled to service after being deleted. The line beginning "Here Alice put out . . ." first began "At mention of . . ." ("Dream-Children"), but this was abandoned, perhaps as superfluous. Similarly, the beginning of the word "between" was deleted as unnecessary in the sentence reading "Many and hot were the skirmishes bet——" ("Poor Relations"). The line beginning "When the spirit appeared before Eliphaz . . ." ("Barrenness") was an afterthought, for Lamb began to write, "But let . . . ," which is the start of the following sentence. The fate of the fairies ("Defeat of Time") is said to be "dependent upon the"—capricious & ever mutable faith of men, it would have been, but Lamb cancelled the definite article in order to include a commentary: "dependent upon so fickle a lease, as the capricious & ever mutable faith of man." In the same essay Lamb began to insert the word "quickly" after the description of Time's "great throat [*originally* "swallow"] that seemed capable of devouring [*originally* "swallowing"] up the earth quick——," but he cancelled it and crystallized the idea in the terminating phrase: "earth and all its inhabitants, at one meal." Such changes were all made immediately.

Words and phrases that would have modified the thought are occasionally cancelled. We read of the Inner Temple, "What a cheerful liberal look hath that portion of it, which, from three sides, overlooks the greater garden . . ." ("Old Benchers"). After writing the sentence, Lamb inserted the phrase "in particular" after "it," but either then, or later, the insertion was deleted. Later on in the same essay, Wharry is described as having a "singular gait, on the Parade which was performed by three steps and a jump regularly succeeding." The phrase "on the Parade" was cancelled, possibly because it is used in the last sentence of the essay although that is hardly close enough for anyone to have noticed.

Occasionally, Lamb's mind began to go off on a tangent as he amplified an idea, and these undeveloped thoughts were sometimes cancelled in the interests of unity and economy. After describing how the fairies sheltered themselves from the "intolerable" rays of the full moon ("The Defeat of Time"), Lamb added the explanation "For the moon is their sun." Apparently he thought it was sufficiently clear without the line and so cancelled it. Later in the same essay he wrote of "cowslips which shep——," intending to introduce some association with shepherds, undoubtedly, for he cancelled this much immediately to convey the idea as "pastoral cowslips." When Bridget's memory, stimulated by meeting some newly discovered cousins to whom she had introduced herself, "warmed into a thousand half-obliterated recollections of things and persons, to my utter astonishment, and her own . . ." ("Mackery End"), Lamb inserted after "persons" the defensive "sufficient at least to prove we were no impostors." But this expression of a lack of self-confidence was cancelled, perhaps after reflecting that it would be ungenerous to attribute suspicion where none was felt by the hospitable Gladmans of Hertfordshire. Writing of the chaplain "proceeding with the grace" ("Barrenness"), Lamb originally continued: "which if we're at all adequate to the profusion of the . . . ," a departure from the thought and therefore judiciously deleted. Again, Lamb related how a tense situation arose when his aunt invited Mr. Billet, the poor relation, to have more pudding, " 'for you do not get pudding every day.' The old gentleman said nothing at the time— . . ." ("Poor Relations"). Here Lamb originally continued with "I for my part thought I should have dropped——"; but the personal reference was heavily cancelled.

Careful reconsideration is indicated by the frequent decision to use a word after it had been written and cancelled. In only one instance in the extant manuscripts does this occur with an inserted word: writing of the receding figures of the children "which without speech ⟨strangely⟩ impressed upon me the effects of speech" ("Dream-Children"), Lamb inserted the adverb "strangely" after "speech," cancelled it, then rewrote it. The other examples of this sort involve the cancelling of words originally written in the line and the rewriting of the same word. This rewriting is occasionally in the space above: "Rome" in the phrase "that had been Emperors of Rome" ("Dream-Children"), "money" in "pulled out their money ⟨silver⟩, and formally" ("Imperfect Sympathies"), and "whim-whams" in "and a thousand whim-whams," which, after the first deletion, is partly inserted and cancelled, then completely inserted and cancelled, before a fourth writing, which is retained ("Imperfect Sympathies"). Usually it is rewritten after the cancellation—evidence of a change made immediately. Such is "in spite" in the phrase "of my father, who in spite of an habitual general respect" ("Poor Relations"); "moulted" in the phrase "bracelets, moulted upon the occasion," "fright" in the phrase "But is this vulgar fright, this mere animal," and "adequate" in "alarm of fire has been given—an adequate exponent" ("Barrenness"); and "Nymphs" in "And she knew how that the race of the Nymphs" ("The Defeat of Time"). Sometimes the cancellation is made before the word is completely written, an indication of too hasty judgment which had to be revised.

Of more interest than the negative alterations, and almost twice as numerous, are the positive or artistic alterations, designed (1) to increase the precision of the expression, either by using a more specific word or by qualifying the first phrasing; (2) to add vividness and intensity; (3) to enrich the connotation; (4) to perfect the rhythm, variety, or concision of the structure; and (5) to avoid repetition with concomitant improvement. Additional examples of each of these types of positive alterations will be found in the Appendix.

Changes made to increase the precision of the expression are approximately twice as numerous as any of the other types of positive alterations. Many of them illustrate Lamb's concern with being specific in matters of time and place; of this type some were made immediately:

Guy Faux preposterously blazing in——	*Guy Faux* preposterously blazing twice over in the *Dog-days.*
	["Humble Petition"]

I could never learn since whether he were alive or dead——

He was among the first who perished before the walls of St. Sebastian

[*"Poor Relations"*]

However, most changes resulting in a more specific time or place were made after the phrase or sentence had been completed:

to read how that the Angel

to read how that once the Angel

[*"Child Angel"*]

with myself closing up the rear, who thought I could not do better than follow the example of such grave and warrantable personages. The steps went up.

with myself closing up the rear, who thought I could not do better than follow the example of such grave and warrantable personages. We got in. The steps went up.

[*"Imperfect Sympathies"*]

who did indeed know something more of us when she almost knew nothing

who did indeed know something more of us, at a time when she almost knew nothing

[*"Mackery End"*]

Exactness also involved the frequent change from a pronoun to a noun; some were changed at once:

He wots not ——

The good man wots not

[*"Old Benchers"*]

of one of them——

of one of these little gentry

[*"In Re Squirrels"*]

Some pronouns were not converted until later:

Twopenny would often railly him upon it . . . .

Twopenny would often railly him upon his leanness . . . .

[*"Old Benchers"*]

I reconciled it to my ideas	I reconciled the phenomenon to my ideas
	["Old Benchers"]
whatsoever victims he should clutch	whatsoever victims TIME should clutch
	["Defeat of Time"]

Alterations in other parts of speech show Lamb's constant striving for the word that would convey the precise meaning intended; some were immediate:

Cherry-coloured ribbands and what not——	Cherry-coloured ribbands and favors.
	["Remarkable Correspondent"]
I awoke childless in my bachelor armchair——	immediately awaking, I found myself quietly seated in my bachelor armchair
	["Dream-Children"]

Much more frequently, such alterations were not made until after the line had been completed:

He once struck a sword out of the wrist of a man	He once wrested a sword out of the hand of a man
	["Old Benchers"]
in these accursed times	in these serious times
	["Munden the Comedian"]

Approximately half as frequent as these changes for exactness are those made for the purpose of adding vividness and intensity to a statement. Here too, many of these were made during the composition of the phrase:

nor did he look wo——	nor did he look, or walk, worth a moidre less
	["Old Benchers"]
powerless to do him honour——	powerless to add any worthy trophy to his renown
	["Defeat of Time"]

More such changes for added vividness and intensity were made after the line had been completed, probably at various times:

a creature that might have sat to a painter for the Image of Welcome	a creature that might have sat to a sculptor for the Image of Welcome ["Mackery End"]
a dish of plain mutton	a dish of plain mutton with turnips[21] ["Grace before Meat"]

Changes made to improve the connotation by using different words are almost as frequently found in the manuscripts as those changes just considered. Again, those made at once are less numerous than later alterations:

the smile——	the soul of the first Alice looked out at her eyes ["Dream-Children"]
the blighted——	the chilling touch of man's incredulity ["Defeat of Time"]

Changes of this type that were made at some later stage include:

sometimes almost to the revival	sometimes almost to the recommencement ["Poor Relations"]
that in the days of infancy I was her tender charge—as I have been her troublesome care since	that in the days of weakling infancy I was her tender charge—as I have been her care in foolish manhood since ["Mackery End"]

Fewer by half than the changes made thus for connotative value are those that effect either condensation of an expression or a rhythmical or varied structure. Some are made at once:

Let us turn to the words in Daniel. He has The King——

From the words of Daniel it appears that Belshazzar
["Barrenness"]

We have seen——

Just this sort of consternation we have seen
["Barrenness"]

More often, changes of this type are made at a later time:

the turbot being a small one

the turbot being small
["Poor Relations"]

The children of Alice W——n call Bartrum father

The children of Alice call Bartrum father
["Dream-Children"]

Not infrequently, when seeking to avoid objectionable repetition, Lamb hit upon a word or expression which proved to be a definite embellishment. Occasionally such alterations were made at once:

The guests were select and admirable——

The guests were select and admiring. The Banquet profuse and admirable.
["Barrenness"]

that I stood in doubt which of them was present——

that I became in doubt which of them stood there before me, or whose that bright hair was,—and both the children gradually grew fainter" *changed to:*

"that I became in doubt which of them stood there before me, or whose that bright hair was, —and while I stood gazing, both the children gradually grew fainter
["Dream-Children"]

As in other alterations, most changes to avoid objectionable repetition were made later:

It had been a lucrative promotion. But L. chose to forego
the promotion because

It had been a lucrative promotion. But L. chose to forego
the advantage because
["Old Benchers"]

Her dress is

Her garb is [The verb
"dresses" occurs some four
lines earlier.]
["Poor Relations"]

The [?good lady] was very
clamorous

Mine hostess was very clamorous ["good lady" occurs in
the following sentence]
["Imperfect Sympathies"]

One final example of manuscript revision, showing both negative and positive alterations, is a passage forming part of the conclusion of "Imperfect Sympathies." Finishing page 6 (verso of third sheet), Lamb reached for the first of the two folio double sheets (since separated into single sheets by a collector) on which the essay was written and continued on what he apparently mistook for page 7 (recto of fourth sheet). But this double sheet, on which he had already written pages 1 and 2 (recto and verso of first sheet, respectively), had become folded so that page 8 (verso of fourth sheet) was on top and upside down. Lamb wrote several lines before he realized that the address panel had to appear on that page, and he would overrun that space if he continued. So he cancelled the entire passage and turned the sheet back to page 7 right-side up, where he took the opportunity of making further improvements as he re-wrote. The cancelled passage can be almost entirely deciphered:

my conscience, which the whimsical scene had for a time suspended, beginning to give me twitches, I waited in hopes that

some justification would be offered by these grave persons for the seeming injustice of their conduct. Not a [illegible] passed on the subject during the rest of the journey. "Hast thee heard how Indigos go at the India House"? asked the youngest of them just before we got to W [illegible] and the question operated upon my conscience as a soporific as far as Exeter.—

The number of improvements desired by Lamb apparently made it expedient to rewrite the entire passage rather than correct what he had written; even with the revision two further improvements were inserted later:

my conscience, which the whimsical scene had for a while suspended, beginning to give some twitches, I waited in the hope that some justification would be offered by these serious persons for the seeming injustice of their conduct. To my great surprise not a syllable passed [*later altered to* "was dropped"] on the subject. They sate as silent as in [*later altered to* "mute as at"] a Meeting. At length the eldest of them broke silence by enquiring of his next neighbour "Hast thee heard how Indigos go at the India House"?—and the question operated as a soporific on my moral feeling as far as Exeter. Elia [inserted after originally being written beneath the first footnote, which follows the passage just quoted].

The change of "grave persons" to "serious persons" avoids the partial repetition of "grave personages," some five lines before. His own reaction is amplified, and a simile vivifies the situation. The question is now asked by the eldest, the same who had led the procession from the coach-stop after the altercation over the bill; variety has given way to consistency. The question is not thrown out at random but put naturally to an individual. Lamb's "conscience" had already twitched, so the effect is applied to his "moral feeling." The echo of "silent" in the "silence" of the adjoining sentence is avoided by the felicitous "mute as at."

Lamb's revisions did not cease with the dispatch of the

manuscript to the publisher. His correspondence contains many letters to the editors of the *London* and the *New Monthly* magazines, requesting not only minor changes but major ones as well. His mind continued to work on problems of phrasing even after he had been obliged by deadlines or common sense to relinquish the copy. An example of this careful consideration of an essay after it had been once approved and transmitted is seen in a letter postmarked March 16, 1826, to Charles Ollier of the *New Monthly:* "If not too late, pray omit the last paragraph in 'Actor's Religion,' which is clumsy. It will then end with the word Mugletonian. I shall not often trouble you in this manner, but I am suspicious of this article as lame."[22] His concern with the appearance of his literary work exactly as he wished it is evident in his indignation in two instances: when the editor of the *Philanthropist* distorted "Confessions of a Drunkard" to serve his own ends at the expense of Lamb's intentions; and when Gifford of the *Quarterly Review* cut and altered the review of Wordsworth's "Excursion." On the latter occasion, Lamb wrote to Wordsworth: "I assure you my complaints are founded. I know how sore a word altered makes one, but indeed of this Review the whole complexion is gone. I regret only that I did not keep a copy."[23]

Still another opportunity was available for making alterations—printers' proofs, which Lamb frequently writes of returning. Several essays which have no postmarks are not so closely in agreement in their corrected form with the first printed text that we can say categorically that they represent final drafts, nor are they so dissimilar as to persuade us that another draft would have been needed. I refer to the extant manuscripts of "Barrenness of the Imaginative Faculty in the Productions of Modern Art" (Part 2), "A Quaker's Meeting," "The Child Angel," "Poor Relations," and "The Old Benchers of the Inner Temple." Two good examples, from the first of these essays, of the sort of error that may well have been corrected by an editor are the deletion near the end of the sixth paragraph of the repetitious "report" in the manuscript's phrase "at the report only of a report of a gun having gone off" and the correction of "indivuality of posture" at the end of the eleventh paragraph of the manuscript to "individuality of posture" in the printed essay in the *Athenaeum*. With only these two discrepancies between the manuscript and the printed text, I think we may safely assume that there was no intervening draft.

The existence of discrepancies between the text in the *London Magazine* and the extant manuscript of "Imperfect Sympathies," which, by virtue of an address panel and postmark, we know was the copy sent to the editor by Lamb, strengthens the assumption that these other manuscripts were printers' copy. In the absence of proof sheets or other evidence, we cannot assign categorically the credit for these variations to either editor or author. In the case of this essay, the editor probably silently corrected Lamb's spelling of "Lionardo da Vinci," "Smollet," "Sallads," and "murmer." He may also have altered "demi-consciousnesses" to the more common but less Elian "semi-consciousnesses," thereby obliterating a shade of connotation. It is unlikely, however, that he would print "Jael" for Lamb's "*Sisera*," even though that was the proper name for Lamb's reference; here is probably an authorial correction in the proofs.

A change probably made by Lamb in reading his proof occurs in "A Quaker's Meeting," where the manuscript begins: "Reader, would'st thou know what true peace and quiet mean; would'st thou find a refuge from the noises and clamours of the multitude; would'st possess the depth of thy own spirit in stillness, without being shut out from the consolatory faces of thy species . . . ." The insertion of a clause for the *London* seems to confirm the suggestion, expressed earlier, that Lamb was condensing this version from an earlier draft: "Reader, would'st thou know what true peace and quiet mean; would'st thou find a refuge from the noises and clamours of the multitude; would'st thou enjoy at once solitude and society; would'st thou possess the depth of thy own spirit in stillness . . . ." Here again, there is no reason to suppose a later draft. In the same category belongs, I believe, the extant manuscript of "The Child Angel." Only two changes prevent the text of the corrected manuscript and that printed in the *London* from being identical: in the first paragraph the manuscript reads, "I chanced upon the prettiest, oddest, fantasticalist thing of a dream the other night, that you shall hear of." The printed version in the *London* reads "fantastical." In the fifth paragraph, "Lord, what an inextinguishable titter," in the manuscript, is printed without "Lord."

Somewhat more important alterations are evident in the *London* text of "Poor Relations" when compared with that of the extant manuscript; yet neither their number nor their complexity is such as to presuppose the necessity of an intervening draft. In the fourth paragraph of the periodical version we read: "He thought himself ridiculous in a garb, under which Latimer must have walked erect . . . ." The manuscript reads: "He thought himself ridiculous in a garb with which Chillingworth must have walked erect . . . ." This is certainly not an editorial change. Nor, I think, is the subtly fortuitous one in the first paragraph, from a series of descriptive phrases punctuated as sentences to the use of the same series separated with commas and indicative dashes. The avoidance of repetition and the increased emotional effect of substituting "The old gentleman" for the

pronoun in the sentence "He said nothing at the time . . . ,"
in the fifth paragraph, is another change that Lamb probably made in the proofs. The insertion of the indefinite article in the next to the last sentence, "never been obliged to
any man for *a* sixpence" and of the missing adverb in the
fourth paragraph, "It was the principle of self-respect carried as far *as* it could go . . ." may have been made at the
same time by Lamb or automatically by the editor.
Strangely enough, the phrase ending the first paragraph as
printed in the *London*, "–the bore par excellence," is unmistakably cancelled in the manuscript. It is omitted in the
1833 text of *The Last Essays of Elia*. The cancellation must
have been made after the periodical publication; perhaps
Lamb began to use the manuscript to indicate changes desired in the collected edition, but if so, the intention was
short-lived because other changes between the periodical
and book versions are not so indicated: "that your other
guests take," of paragraph 2, became "that your guests
take"; "and a Lady with a great estate," of paragraph 4,
became "and a lady of great estate"; "A supposed interest
with some of the Heads of Colleges," of paragraph 4, became "A supposed interest with some of the heads of the
colleges"; and, in the same paragraph, "the poor student
slunk from observation" became "the poor student shrunk
from observation."

This further opportunity given to Lamb to revise his
essays when they were collected in book form as *Elia* (1823)
and *The Last Essays of Elia* (1833) was utilized to the utmost and shows the author's continuing affectionate and
paternal interest in the children of his fancy. Alterations at
this last stage of the evolution of Elia included omissions,
rearrangement of material, changes in titles, changes of
names of places and people, and even some artistic alteration of words. Were the material that Lamb omitted when

preparing his essays for book publication combined, it would amount in bulk to several essays; on the other hand, his additions are very few. A comparison of the essays in the collected editions with their first appearance in the periodicals shows that the largest type of omission was the footnote, which often gave references to quotations or additional information to the magazine readers. Some of these notes were quite long; some had lost their timeliness; others were omitted as nonessential. Most of those that were retained were incorporated into the text.

In addition to this type of omission, both long and short passages were deleted from the text itself. In the *London*, for example, there were two paragraphs before, and three after, what appeared in *The Last Essays of Elia* as "Preface By a Friend of the Late Elia." "On Some of the Old Actors" originally included a long passage after the fifth paragraph. In "The Superannuated Man," after the query "It is Lucretian pleasure to behold the poor drudges, whom I have left behind in the world, carking and caring; like horses in a mill drudging on in the same eternal round—and what is it all for?" there came originally a long passage quoting from Cowper, transcribing his own sonnet on "Work," and referring the reader to a sonnet in the *London* for April, 1821, "by a daintier pen than I can pretend to. I subscribe to that Sonnet *toto corde*." Of course he would subscribe to it—it was his own sonnet "Leisure"! A long passage came originally just before the last paragraph of "Oxford in the Vacation." The first paragraph of "Modern Gallantry" in the *London* read: "In comparing modern with ancient manners, we are pleased to compliment ourselves upon the point of gallantry as upon a thing altogether unknown to the old classic ages. This has been defined to consist in a certain obsequiousness, or deferential respect, paid to females, as females." In the collected *Elia* the passage reads: "In comparing modern with ancient manners, we are pleased to compliment ourselves upon the point of gallantry; a certain obsequiousness, or deferential respect, which we are supposed to pay to females, as females." The thought has been modified and the expression condensed. Before the last sentence of "The Old and the New Schoolmaster" the following personal reflection appeared in the periodical: "These kind of complaints are not often drawn from me. I am aware that I am a fortunate, I mean a prosperous man. My feelings prevent me from transcribing any further."

Some passages were deleted because of a change of attitude or of situation. A quotation from the letters of Lady Mary Wortley Montague is dropped from "The Old Benchers" after Lamb apparently realized that the association of his Samuel Salt with the "S" [S^{te}] in the letter would not be creditable to Salt.[24] Again, in "Detached Thoughts on Books and Reading," published in the *London* in 1822, he wrote: "As in these little Diurnals I generally skip the Foreign News, the Debates—and the Politics—I find the Morning Herald by far the most entertaining of them. It is an agreeable miscellany, rather than a newspaper." But about the time Lamb wrote this, the paper suddenly gave less attention to social gossip and much more to politics. Therefore, his remarks were no longer apposite and were removed for the text of 1833. In like manner, "Recollections of Christ's Hospital" contained, in its first appearance in 1813, a long opening passage which attempted to answer the criticism that favoritism was being shown in granting admission to the school. Since this was no longer an issue in 1818, the passage was deleted when the essay was revised for inclusion in Lamb's *Works*, published in that year. Also, in "Guy Faux," a passage referring to members of Parliament was omitted as being no longer appropriate. Timeliness, or

rather the lack of it, was also the reason for the deletion of
a reference to Gifford's 1816 edition of Jonson when Lamb
expressed his preference for folios and his lack of sympathy
with octavo editions, in the *London* version of "Detached
Thoughts on Books and Reading." Perhaps more mature
consideration led to the cancellation in "Imperfect Sympathies" of the passage concluding his observations on
Burns: "I have a great mind to give up Burns. There is certainly a bragging spirit of generosity, a swaggering assertion of independence, and *all that* in his writings."

An apparent moderation of once stronger feelings dic-
tated the deletion of the long paragraph before the present
last in "Detached Thoughts on Books and Reading," which
told of Lamb's persistence in reading while in a theater
crowd and of his determination not to yield before their
protests as his farce had been forced to do a few nights
earlier. Affectation, even when labelled, as here "affected,"
was uncongenial to Lamb. A similar fear that a literal
reader would react uncharitably toward his character probably led him to delete the following passage from the *Popular Fallacy* "That Home Is Home Though It Is Never So
Homely": "O the comfort of sitting down heartily to an
old folio, and thinking surely that the next hour or two will
be your own—and the misery of being defeated by the useless call of somebody, who is come to tell you, that he is
just come from hearing Mr. Irving! What is that to you?
Let him go home, and digest what the good man said to
him. You are at your chapel, in your oratory."

Some omissions seem to have been prompted by a sense
of delicacy. Thus, "To the Shade of Elliston," printed in the
Englishman's Magazine for August, 1831, included the subordinate clause, omitted from the 1833 book edition: "while
with uplifted toe retributive you inflict vengeance incor-
poreal upon the shadowy rear of obnoxious author, just

arrived . . . ." The book version also omitted the close: "Thy friend upon Earth, though thou did'st connive at his d——n, Mr. H," in reference to Elliston's playing the lead in Lamb's ill-fated farce *Mr. H.* A similar reason apparently prompted the change in the *Popular Fallacy* "That Such a One Shows His Breeding" from "Are there no other topics— as, to tell him his father was hanged—his sister made a ———" to "Are there no other topics—as, to tell him his father was hanged—his sister, &c. ——— . . . ."

Some omissions seem to make little or no difference. "He stood in a posture of idiot wonder" originally appeared after the word "crackling" near the end of the first paragraph of "A Dissertation upon Roast Pig." Possibly the printer of *Elia* lost it. Similar is the loss of the initial word "Two" in the *Last Essays* version of the *Popular Fallacy* "That Home is Home Though It Is Never So Homely"; in the periodical it read: "Two homes there are, we are sure, that are no homes: the home of the very poor man, and another which we shall speak to presently." That the printer, rather than the author, was responsible for the omission is indicated by a manuscript of this essay, said to be the slightly revised text used by the printer of *Last Essays*. It is described as showing the word "Two" "immediately following the title on the first line (the only word of the text on this line)."[25] Defending black as the proper color of his clothes in "The Wedding," Lamb wrote "to have appeared in some lighter colour—a pea-green coat, for instance, like the bridegroom's —would have raised more mirth at my expense, than the anomaly had created censure." The example is omitted from *The Last Essays of Elia.* The deletion of "His coat is coeval with Adam's" from the 1823 text of "A Complaint of the Decay of Beggars in the Metropolis" possibly was the result of the reflection that the exaggeration, even when applied to beggars, was too extreme to be effective.

The preparation of the essays for book publication included collection of parts, rearrangement of material, division of a longer essay, and change of title. Where an essay had been divided between two numbers of a periodical, as had "The Superannuated Man" in the *London*, the parts were naturally combined and the quotation introducing the second part, if one had been used, subjoined to the first quotation. The three articles on "The Old Actors" underwent considerable reorganization to form "On Some of the Old Actors," "On the Artificial Comedy of the Last Century," and "On the Acting of Munden." The position of "Edax on Appetite" before "Hospita on the Immoderate Indulgence of the Pleasures of the Palate" in the *Reflector* was reversed in the *Works*. "To the Shade of Elliston" and "Ellistoniana" had originally appeared in the *Englishman's Magazine* under the title "Reminiscences of Elliston." Numerous changes in titles were made: "Newspapers Thirty-Five Years Ago" was first printed as "On the Total Defect of the Faculty of Imagination Observable in the Works of Modern British Artists"; "Stage Illusion" was originally "Imperfect Dramatic Illusion"; "Imperfect Sympathies" was first called "Jews, Quakers, Scotchmen, and Other Imperfect Sympathies"; and the two *Popular Fallacies* "The Genteel Style in Writing" and "The Sanity of True Genius" had appeared first under the respective titles "That My Lord Shaftesbury and Sir William Temple are Models of the Genteel Style in Writing" and "That Great Wit is Allied to Madness." We observe a salutary trend toward brevity in these titular modifications.

More interesting are the changes of names of places and persons for book publication. Some seem to have been made in the interests of greater accuracy and others to avoid specific reference to people originally designated, but in many cases there is no ascertainable reason for the revision.

"My First Play" originally began: "At the north end of Russel Court there yet stands a portal, of some architectural pretensions, though reduced to humble use, serving at present for an entrance to a wine vault." In the collected edition, the location is "Cross Court," and the use is "a printing-office." In "The Old Margate Hoy" the phrase "Aldermanbury, or Watling-street" became "Thames, or Tooley Street" in *The Last Essays of Elia*. "I am no longer J——s D——n," wrote Lamb in "The Superannuated Man," which he signed: "J. D., Beaufort-terrace, Regent-street; late of Ironmonger-court, Fenchurch-street." But in *The Last Essays* the signature is omitted and the first statement changed to "I am no longer ******." The "Earl of Flanders" in the *London* version of "A Complaint of the Decay of Beggars" became the "Earl of Cornwall" in *Elia*, although, strangely enough, it is the "Earl of Leicester" in the ballad referred to. The "Mr. ———" in "All Fools' Day" springs into life as "Raymund Lully" in *Elia*. The "noble patient in Horace," as the *New Monthly* prints the phrase in the *Fallacy* "That a Sulky Temper is a Misfortune," becomes "noble patient in Argos" in the revised version. The "favourite critic of our day" in "Defence of the Sonnets of Sir Philip Sidney" is identified as "W. H." in "Some Sonnets of Sir Philip Sydney," as the essay is retitled; and "Mr. Hazlitt" becomes, in the same transition, "The Critic." In the same essay, "the loves of Catullus" became "the loves of Tibullus." The phrases "paintings . . . of M——," in the *Athenaeum* essay "On the Total Defect of the Quality of Imagination, observable in the Works of Modern British Artists," is changed to "paintings . . . of a modern artist" in "Barrenness of the Imaginative Faculty in the Productions of Modern Art," as the new title runs.[26] "Emery" in "On the Acting of Munden," published in the *Examiner* of 1819, became "Farley" when it was reprinted in the *Lon-*

don. "Mirzah," occurring twice in the *London* version of "The Child Angel," became "Adah" in the *Last Essays*. The personal "Joey Munden" in the *London* version of "Distant Correspondents" became the unqualified "Munden" in *Elia*.

Finally, Lamb did not hesitate to take the opportunity of making substitutions of words and phrases when he collected his essays into book form. If some of his word choices have seemed consciously learned, here is ample evidence that, far from striving for pedantry, Lamb aimed at simplicity. Thus, representative examples of changes found in a dozen essays collected in *Elia* and *The Last Essays of Elia* include the substitution of "statue" for "stony gaberdine," of "joke" for "jest," of "gone over" for "traversed," of "unseasoned" for "unfledged," of "to want reverence" for "to be unreverend," and of "mistake" for "fallacy." An effort at greater exactness of meaning motivated other changes: "the claimant's" for "a person's," "inculcate" for "explicate," "to be adduced" for "to be more than hinted at," "so deadly a disunion" for "such a mighty antipathy," "inquisitive to explore" for "that wished to explore," "visage" for "visnomy," and "apathies" for "dispathies." Lamb's continuing concern to attain the exact term is exemplified in the "Post script" to "The Old Benchers of the Inner Temple": the manuscript shows that he had first written "The good man wots not, peradventure, of the license which magazines have arrived at in these personal days . . . ." He altered this, first to ". . . which we magazine writers alas! have arrived at in this Age of Ebony . . . ," and then to ". . . which Magazines have arrived at in this Age of Ebony." In the *London* for September, 1821, the sentence read: "The good man wots not, peradventure, of the license which Magazines have arrived at in this personal age . . . ." Apparently he had revised it again in the proof. Finally, when the essay was collected in *Elia* the line read: "The good man wots not, peradventure, of the license which Magazines have arrived at in this plain-speaking age . . . ."

"I am as slow as a Fleming Painter when I compose anything," Lamb wrote early in his writing career to his friend Robert Southey, who was to become Poet Laureate.[27] The ease and facility of composition which he attributed to Milton—and which a cursory reader of the essays of Elia might erroneously attribute to him—were never to be among his attainments. Throughout his manuscripts there are, it is true, whole sections of beautiful prose that show little or no evidence of alteration; for example, this long and complex sentence from the beginning of "Dream-Children":

Then I went on to say, how religious and how good their great-grandmother Field was, how beloved and respected by every body, though she was not indeed the mistress of this great house, but had only the charge of it (and yet in some respects she might be said to be the mistress of it too) committed to her by the owner, who preferred living in a newer and more fashionable mansion which he had purchased somewhere in the adjoining county; but still she lived in it in a manner as if it had been her own, and kept up the dignity of the great house in a sort while she lived, which afterwards came to decay, and was nearly pulled down, and all its old ornaments stripped and carried away to the owner's other house, where they were set up, and looked as awkward as if some one were to carry away the old tombs they had seen lately at the Abbey, and stick them up in Lady C.'s tawdry gilt drawing-room.

It is possible that such sentences were immediately achieved; it is equally possible that they went through an earlier draft—or several.

Certainly, we may deduce from our examination of the manuscript essays that Lamb customarily wrote with difficulty and that many of his most delightful lines were the product of long thought and tedious trial and error. At times his thoughts did seem to outrun the ability of his pen to transcribe them, and in his attempt to keep pace he committed errors of the sort common to all but the most inspired writers. But such spurts were short lived. The frequency of unintentional repetition attests to his usual slowness, for, had he written swiftly at all times, potential repetition would have been caught and avoided before being committed. As it was, he often failed to note it until he reread his work. Far from being a loss, however, such faults were actually steps toward a higher achievement; only by the attempt to avoid such repetition were many memorable phrases given existence.

The preponderance of positive alterations over the negative type reveals Lamb's greater concern with the search for evocative, memorable words to increase the suggestiveness and vividness of his thought. His abnormal sensitivity to the sound of words, particularly the retention or anticipation of the sound, led to errors that had to be corrected, but it also produced euphonious prose. Concern with conveying the precise meaning with the desired overtones is suggested by Lamb's careful attention to capitalization—a key to his meaning, which, along with italics, has largely been lost through the carelessness of successive editors.

Sometimes his teeming brain beguiled him into inserting ideas that more mature consideration realized would cause diffusion and lack of unity. On the other hand, a simple idea was often interrupted in its conception to admit a happy afterthought which enriched without diluting.

Lamb's continual and meticulous attention to the details of composition made revision an unending task—while his essays were still in his workshop and after they had left it. The difficulty he experienced in expression was caused, in large part, by his own high standards; he was his own most exacting critic—his reach constantly exceeding his grasp. But by persistent reaching he attained an immortal niche in the annals of literature.

SIX

"A Self-pleasing Quaintness"

THE STYLIST

In Leigh Hunt's *London Journal* of October 17, 1835, there is a collection of colloquies, one of which runs as follows:

"What a fine style X. has!" said a poetaster. "Excellent," echoed another person; "don't you think so, Mr. Lamb?"—"I'm no judge of styles," was the answer; "I only know what pleases myself."

In the same way, Lamb's critics have been pleased with his style but have resorted to vague phrases and generalizations in attempting to define its ingredients. We read of the *quaintness* and agree that this word denotes one of the charms of Lamb's prose. Hazlitt, in "Elia, and Geoffrey Crayon," admitting the originality of Lamb's feelings and observations, charged him with a "certain mannerism." "His sentences," he wrote, "are cast in the mould of old authors; his expressions are borrowed from them." This "certain quaintness and singularity of style," he went on, "is an agreeable relief to the smooth and insipid monotony of modern composition." In his essay "On Familiar Style" the same critic called Lamb an "imitator of old English style," but adds that "he is so thoroughly imbued with the spirit of his authors that the idea of imitation is almost done away with."

It is usually implied or alleged by those who write on Lamb's style that his quaintness resulted from his saturation in the old authors. Finding a few verbal parallels between Lamb's essays and the books he read, they have attempted, with questionable success, to trace certain of Lamb's stylistic devices to these various authors. In the present chapter we shall review this question of Lamb's indebtedness and seek to measure its extent more exactly than has hitherto been done. Furthermore, other factors in Lamb's life, which have been previously overlooked in connection with his style, will be seen to have had considerable influence. As a means of showing that many of his stylistic characteristics were natural to him, rather than consciously imitated by him, we shall note their presence in his correspondence, where artificiality and mannerism were less likely to exist. Finally, Lamb's use of quotations must be carefully considered, for they are of considerable importance in producing the quality of quaintness. Beyond this, an analysis of these quotations serves to throw new light on his favorite reading and also on the nature of his memory.

Had Lamb been intended for the East India Service when he was enrolled in Christ's Hospital, he would not have been placed in the Grammar School, as he was, but in the Writing School. The five schools of the institution were kept quite distinct at that time: "so that," as Leigh Hunt tells us in his *Autobiography*, "a boy might arrive at the age of fifteen in the grammar-school, and not know his multiplication-table; which was the case with myself. Nor do I know it to this day!" Hunt goes on to say that the Writing School "was for those who were intended for trade and commerce . . . and the grammar-school for such as were designed for the Church, and to go to the University." The course of studies Lamb pursued in the latter certainly influenced his literary career more than that of the Writing School would have done, even though he did not rise above the rank of Deputy-Grecian (next to the highest) to go on to the university. Indeed, if Lamb had been subjected to the curriculum of the Commercial School at that formative and impressionable time of his childhood, he might never have come to write his famous essays.

The emphasis on the Bible at Christ's contributed to the development of his prose style as well as to his character. "On Sundays," wrote Hunt in his *Autobiography*, "the school time of the other days was occupied in church, both morning and evening; and as the Bible was read to us every day before every meal, and on going to bed, besides prayers and graces, we rivalled the monks in the religious part of our duties." In addition to providing Lamb with illustrative material, the Bible was the source of many words and expressions that helped produce the effect of quaintness.

Christ's Hospital was also, unquestionably, the place where he first came upon many of the Latin expressions and classical allusions found throughout his essays and letters. Hunt's *Autobiography* informs us that the "Deputy-Grecians were in Homer, Cicero, and Demosthenes," and Talfourd states that Lamb read "Virgil, Sallust, Terence, selections from Lucian's Dialogues and Xenephon; and had evinced considerable skill in the niceties of Latin Composition both in prose and verse." It is noteworthy that the weekly scheme of lessons given by the Reverend William Trollope in 1834 included Homer, Virgil, and Horace "by heart."[1] A modern writer on the institution says that in 1837 the Deputy-Grecians "read Pinnock's *Catechism of Hebrew Grammar,* the Greek Testament, Homer, Demosthenes, Cicero, Horace, the *Georgics,* and Terence. They made 'Latin and English verses and themes.' "[2] It is not possible to trace all of Lamb's classical references to his school work, but many more than have been realized came from the intense drilling and memory work of that period. E. E. Burris, in his helpful study of Lamb's classical culture, writes of the presence of "many reminiscences in Lamb's essays and letters of his study of Virgil . . . . Scattered throughout Lamb's writings we find echoes of his reading of Terence . . . . References to Pliny the Younger are not uncommon . . . . A few references to Horace occur . . . . There are at least two references to Epicurus in the writings of Lamb . . . . References to mythological characters are frequent . . . ."[3]

Lamb did not excel in the Greek language, nor did he ever become proficient in anything but English and Latin. "I do not retain enough of my Greek (to my shame I say it) to venture at an opinion of the correctness of your version," he wrote Charles Lloyd, Sr. on June 13, 1809, in connection with the latter's translation of the *Odyssey.*[4] To the same correspondent, on September 8, 1812, he wrote: "I am no great Latinist . . . I have neglected my Latin (and quite lost my Greek) since I left construing it at School."[5] The several extant letters that Lamb composed in Latin, however, show that he was unusually proficient in that language, but there is no reason to doubt his statements about forgetting Greek. As for German, "You know I am homo unius linguae," he wrote Coleridge.[6] Writing on September 24, 1802, to Manning of his desire to visit Paris, he said: "It was a trivial objection to my aspiring mind, that I did not understand a word of the language, since I certainly intend some time in my life to see Paris, and equally certainly never intend to learn the language."[7] Nor did he, for the occasional French phrases found in his letters are spelled phonetically rather than by any system of French orthography and are frequently accompanied by a "how do ye spell it?" or a "do you understand me?"[8] Charles Lamb was too honest to learn a language for mere ostentatious effect: "I hate the pedantry of expressing that in another language which we have sufficient terms for in our own," he wrote Joseph Hume, a civil servant.[9]

It is probable that this predilection for simplicity was nourished, if not originated, by the zeal of the Reverend James Boyer, Master in Christ's Hospital. In Coleridge's words, he "showed no mercy to phrase, metaphor, or image, unsupported by a sound sense, or where the same sense might have been conveyed with equal force and dignity in plainer words."[10] Boyer's precepts returned to Coleridge in Lamb's letter of November 8, 1796: "Cultivate simplicity, or rather, I should say, banish elaborateness; for simplicity springs spontaneous from the heart, and carries into daylight its own modest buds and genuine, sweet, and clear flowers of expression. I allow no hot-beds in the gardens of Parnassus."[11]

In addition to reading Shakespeare and Milton, Boyer's pupils were required to produce one theme a week. His particular concern for the exact appropriateness of phrase was manifested in his method: According to Coleridge, he allowed several papers of a student to accumulate—"Then placing the whole number *abreast* on his desk, he would ask the writer, why this or that sentence might not have found as appropriate a place under this or that other thesis: and if no satisfying answer could be returned, and two faults of the same kind were found in one exercise, the irrevocable verdict followed, the exercise was torn up, and another on the same subject to be produced, in addition to the tasks of the day." These drastic but effective methods undoubtedly made such a lasting impression that Lamb was mindful of his old schoolmaster's standards when writing his Elian essays thirty-odd years later. His many revisions and the finished perfection of most of the essays indicate that Boyer's trouble had not been taken in vain in his case at least.

Another type of writing exercise required of Lamb and his colleagues is described by Leigh Hunt in his *Autobiography:*

They were upon a given subject, generally a moral one, such as Ambition or the Love of Money: and the regular process in the manufacture was this:—You wrote out the subject very fairly at top, *Quid non mortalia* &c., or, *Crescit amor nummi.* Then the ingenious thing was to repeat this apophthegm in as many words and roundabout phrases as possible, which took up a good bit of paper. Then you attempted to give a reason or two, why *amor nummi* was bad; or on what accounts heroes ought to eschew ambition; after which naturally came a few examples, got out of Plutarch or the Selectae e Profanis; and the happy moralist concluded with signing his name.

The repetition of the thought for emphasis and to show the ingenuity of the author, rather than to advance the argument, was a device frequently utilized by Lamb. This use of a series of short phrases for emphasis may be illustrated by the opening of "Poor Relations":

Poor Relations.

A Poor Relation is — the most irrelevant thing
in nature. A piece of impertinent correspondency.
An odious approximation. A haunting
conscience. A preposterous shadow, lengthening
in the noon-tide of your prosperity. An
unwelcome remembrancer. A perpetually
recurring mortification. A drain on your
purse. A more intolerable dun upon your
pride. A drawback upon success. A
rebuke to your rising. A stain in your
blood. A blot on your 'scutcheon. A rent
in your garment. A death's head at your
banquet. Agathocles' pot. A Mordecai
in your gate. A Lazarus at your door.
A lion in your path. A frog in your
chamber. A fly in your ointment. A
mote in your eye. A triumph to your
enemy. An apology to your friends. The
one thing not needful. The hail in harvest.
The ounce of sour in a pound of sweet. —

Slightly reduced from original.

Poor Relations

A Poor Relation is—the most irrelevant thing in nature,—a piece of impertinent correspondency,—an odious approximation,—a haunting conscience,—a preposterous shadow, lengthening in the noon-tide of your prosperity,—an unwelcome remembrancer,—a perpetually recurring mortification,—a drain on your purse,—a more intolerable dun upon your pride,—a drawback upon success,—a rebuke to your rising,—a stain in your blood,—a blot on your scutcheon,—a rent in your garment, —a death's head at your banquet,—Agathocles' pot,—a Mordecai in your gate,—a Lazarus at your door,—a lion in your path,—a frog in your chamber,—a fly in your ointment,—a mote in your eye,—a triumph to your enemy, an apology to your friends,—the one thing not needful,—the hail in harvest,—the ounce of sour in a pound of sweet,—the bore *par excellence*. [Text of the *London Magazine*, May, 1823]

Two writers on the essay have pointed out that repetition or iteration without progression occurs in the prose of Fuller and Browne in the seventeenth century. "This disjointed fashion of analysis is most characteristic of Fuller," writes Bernard Lake with the suggestion that it was from him that Lamb derived the device.[12] J. S. Iseman, terming it "the style that more than any other is characteristic of Lamb," states: "it is certainly from Browne that Lamb has derived this trick of imaginative iteration . . . . One idea is merely iterated over and over, imaged, exemplified, but not advanced."[13] The combination of a series of short phrases, sometimes intermingled with single words, may be found in both Fuller and Browne, but it is no more fundamental to the style of either than it is to that of Lamb. Nor is it peculiar to them among seventeenth-century writers; it can be found in Burton.[14] Lamb did read these authors, but the required school exercises alone were sufficient to have introduced to him this method of analysis. Long before he read Fuller and Browne, the writing of these academic papers had impressed this device of imaginative iteration on his consciousness. His discovery of the same sort of amplification in his reading must have reminded him of it and even confirmed the validity of its use in literature, but the mere reading cannot equal the exercises as a directing tendency.

If Lamb had been consciously copying this method of writing from examples in his reading, it would not have been natural to him. That it had become natural to him is clear from the fact of its appearance in his correspondence. An excellent example occurs in a letter of January 9, 1824, to Bernard Barton:

> Do you know what it is to succumb under an insurmountable day mare—a whoreson lethargy, Falstaff calls it—an indisposition to do any thing, or to be any thing—a total deadness and distaste—a suspension of vitality—an indifference to locality—a numb soporifical goodfornothingness—an ossification all over—an oysterlike insensibility to the passing events—a mind-stupor—a brawny defiance to the needles of a thrusting-in conscience—did you ever have a very bad cold with a total irresolution to submit to water gruel processes?[15]

A more difficult, but better, school exercise written by Lamb consisted of the abridgment of some paper in the *Spectator*. According to Hunt's *Autobiography,* the necessity of culling the best points gave that periodical an unnatural gravity in the eyes of the pupils. The close study may have had some effect on Lamb's diction; De Quincey thought that his essays "resemble Addison's papers . . . in the diction; which is natural and idiomatic, even to carelessness."[16] Perhaps also the gravity of the *Spectator* stimulated Lamb to attempt something less grave, by way of reaction. Certainly, the practice of abridgment helped to develop the characteristic concision of thought which marks the essays of Elia. In his sketch for the *Annual Biography* of 1835 Barron Field wrote: "Lamb's effusions are short and fragmentary. All his works, both verse and prose, could easily have been dilated into five times their quantity; he was therefore a poor gainer, as a periodical writer, by the sheet. We never knew a man so sensible of the magnanimity of suppression in writing. By a happy word he suggested a whole triad of balanced periods, or rather, he disdained to debase his style into such a calculating machine."

Critics have suggested other influences on Lamb's characteristic concision. De Quincey made an analogy between Lamb's tendency to avoid pomp of cadence or sonorous ascent of clause and his lack of musical sense and rhythm. Further, he offers the remarkable suggestion that his avoidance of the continuous, the elaborate, and the sustained was the result of his habit of reading at bookstalls, where he snatched a few moments to tear the heart out of an author, and of his reading at home in constant fear of interruption by the "endless visitants." In both cases he would be compelled to skim the cream, and the habit carried over into his writing, where he never prolongs his expressions, or repeats—except occasionally where he does so for a humorous effect or for emphasis, as in the passages of iteration. A modern writer strains further to attribute his simplicity of expression to constitutional infirmity: "It was . . . physically impossible for him to pour out a stream of smooth-flowing and uninterrupted sentences. The characteristic style of Elia is the translation of that stammer into literature."[17]

Besides the abridgment of *Spectator* papers, which was the first and probably the most important influence on this habit of compression, there were two other activities which may have aided the tendency. Speaking of his early days as a writer for Fenwick's *Albion*, in "Newspapers Thirty-Five

Years Ago," Lamb wrote that his cue was "to insinuate, rather than recommend, possible abdications." To "insinuate" would require the use of words with wide connotations, and the result would be compression in contrast to the elaboration that would have been required for "recommendation." Aside from this, the composition of jests for Stuart's *Morning Post* nourished the habit, for *by requirement* the jokes had to be of seven lines or less. The other activity that influenced concision in Lamb's essays was his extensive correspondence. Only rarely did he use more than one folio sheet for a letter, and this rather arbitrary limit encouraged him to condense his thoughts to a suitable compass. He frequently expressed a doubt that what he had said was worth even the postage his correspondent must pay. In view of all these conditioning influences, it would seem that the terseness and compression in Lamb's style was less the result of conscious effort than of habitual writing practice.

At this point it may be asked why other essayists of the period did not exhibit similar stylistic characteristics traceable to similar academic work. However he benefited from his intensive study and extensive reading, Hazlitt's irregular and less formalized education could not have had the influence on his subsequent writing that the curriculum of Christ's had on Lamb. But one might expect Hunt, also of the Grammar School, to have formed writing tendencies of a like nature. And it is noteworthy that his essays are described as deriving in manner and method from the *Spectator*—which, as we have just seen, was the basis for a disciplinary study. At the same time, Hunt, like Hazlitt, was a professional writer, guided by considerations somewhat different from those that concerned Lamb. Furthermore, given different temperaments and subjected to additional and diverse modifying forces, Hunt and other essayists of similar academic background can hardly be expected to manifest more than a partial stylistic similarity. For school exercises, while a major influence on style in Lamb's case, were not the only determinants.

To proceed to another of these influences, what part, aside from that just noted, did his prolific letter writing play in the development of Lamb's distinctive style? Undoubtedly, the discipline in writing that it afforded him, in which he could experiment with his humor, his Latin tags, his quotations, and his vocabulary, was of inestimable value. That he was conscious of style even in his letters is evident from several statements in them: "My very style seems to myself to become more impressive than usual, with the change of theme," he wrote in a letter to Barton on December 1, 1824;[18] and to the same correspondent on another occasion, he interrupted his theme to say, "Do I write quakerly and simply, tis my most Master Mathew's like intention to do it."[19] Writing again to Barton on March 20, 1826, he amused himself with the idea of a comparison of his letters, with their superior "delicate irony, judicious reflexions, etc.," to the epistles of Pliny.[20] A postscript to a letter to Ayrton of November 25, 1817, comments on its exceptionally neat wording;[21] and the phrase "we propose postponing," in a letter of July 17, 1821, also to Ayrton, was followed immediately by a parenthetical reflection: "I wonder if these words ever met so close before—mark the Elegancy."[22]

A comparison of Lamb's early letters with the later ones shows a definite advance from the direct, earnest approach to the perfected subtleties of expression associated with the essays. While some of the letters have as much thought content, as much structural development, and as much fancy as some of the essays, yet, as is to be expected, they generally lack the elaborate allusions and the exquisite polish, wrought, as we have seen, with infinite labor. They are naturally more familiar or personal, while the essays are finished, deliberate, carefully written, and steadily progressive. But the conversational qualities of the letters—second thoughts, parenthetical remarks, and the intimacy—are found also in the essays to a high degree, and a comparative reading indicates that the apparent mannerisms of the essays are actually fundamental in Lamb's expression.

Proof of this assertion is to be found in parallel passages, such as those quoted in connection with the development of the essays. An excellent example is a portion of a letter of March 9, 1822, to Coleridge, which is closely similar to part of "A Dissertation upon Roast Pig":

To confess an honest truth, a pig is one of those things I could never think of sending away. Teals, wigeons, snipes, barn-door fowl, ducks, geese—your tame villatic things—Welsh mutton, collars of brawn, sturgeon, fresh or pickled, your potted char, Swiss cheeses, French pies, early grapes, muscadines, I impart as freely unto my friends as to myself. They are but self-extended; but pardon me if I stop somewhere—where the fine feeling of benevolence giveth a higher smack than the sensual rarity—there my friends (or any good man) may command me; but pigs are pigs, and I myself therein am nearest to myself. Nay, I should think it an affront, an undervaluing done to Nature who bestowed such a boon upon me, if in a churlish mood I parted with the precious gift. One of the bitterest pangs of remorse I ever felt was when a child—when my kind old aunt had strained her pocket-strings to bestow a sixpenny whole plum-cake upon me. In my way home through the Borough, I met a venerable old man, not a mendicant, but thereabouts—a look-beggar, not a verbal petitionist; and in the coxcombry of taught-charity I gave away the cake to him. I walked on a little in all the pride of an Evangelical peacock, when of a sudden my old aunt's kindness crossed me—the sum it was to her—the pleasure she had a right to expect that I—not the old impostor—should take in eating her cake—the cursed ingratitude by which, under the colour of a Christian virtue, I had frustrated her cherished purpose. I sobbed, wept, and took it to heart so grievously, that

I think I never suffered the like—and I was right. It was a piece of unfeeling hypocrisy, and proved a lesson to me ever after. The cake has long been masticated, consigned to the dunghill with the ashes of that unseasonable pauper.[23]

This passage admirably illustrates the presence in a letter of many of the qualities for which the essays are most valued. Here is the self-revelation and the familiarity—which we should, of course, expect to find in a friendly letter. But there is also the accumulation of words and phrases to iterate an idea, a parenthetical second-thought, and the marked appropriateness of word choice—for which we also admire the essays. Such phrases as "tame villatic things," "giveth a higher smack," "a look-beggar, not a verbal petitionist," "the coxcombry of taught-charity," "Evangelical peacock," and many others are exactly the sort we associate with the essays. Indeed, many of these found a place in "A Dissertation upon Roast Pig." The conclusion must be that what have been called mannerisms were certainly not affectations.

There is no doubt that Lamb's extensive reading exerted an influence on his prose style, for his impressionable mind retained the flavor as well as the substance of what he read. In "Mackery End" he told how Mary was "tumbled early, by accident or design, into a spacious closet of good old English reading, without selection or prohibition, and browsed at will upon that fair and wholesome pasturage." Lamb's own unmethodical reading in this library of Samuel Salt, a Bencher of the Inner Temple who employed Lamb's father, made him acquainted with the many good authors there represented. It was probably in this "spacious closet" that he came to know the Elizabethan dramatists and what he later spoke of as his childhood favorites, *Pilgrim's Progress* and *The Compleat Angler*. His studies at Christ's Hospital would not have prevented him from reading such popular boys' books as *The Fortunate Blue-Coat Boy* and

The Life and Adventures of Peter Wilkins, as well as works of a more literary nature. Hunt wrote in his *Autobiography* that the curriculum "did not hinder my growing mind from making what excursions it pleased into the wide and healthy regions of general literature. I might buy as much Collins and Gray as I pleased, and get novels to my heart's content from the circulating libraries."

Lamb also read Collins and Gray, but, judging from references in his earliest extant letters, he did not become acquainted with many of his favorites of the sixteenth and seventeenth centuries until he was out of his teens; up to this time he read largely in the early eighteenth-century literature. He continued to like Pope throughout his life; "I can read him over and over for ever," he is reported to have said.[24] Lamb was attracted to the literature of the past just as he was to old scenes; in later years he refused, on the grounds that they were new, to read presentation copies of books written by friends. Even some by Barton and Hunt were tossed over into the yard of his appreciative young neighbor, Thomas Westwood. In his *Popular Fallacy* "That We Must Not Look a Gift-Horse in the Mouth," he declared that "a presentation copy is a copy of a book which does not sell, sent you by the author, with his foolish autograph at the beginning of it; for which, if a stranger, he only demands your friendship; if a brother author, he expects from you a book of yours which does not sell, in return."

Lamb's favorite novelists belonged almost entirely to the eighteenth century: Defoe, Fielding, Smollett, and Goldsmith. While he was acquainted with contemporary fiction and allowed that the vicarious pleasure provided by the circulating libraries was a legitimate one, he disapproved of the tendency to moralize or instruct. Further, the purposeless events of the novels published by the Minerva Press—"those scanty intellectual viands of the whole female reading public, till a happier genius arose, and expelled for-

ever the innutritious phantoms"—were condemned along
with the characters, who "are neither of this world nor of
any other conceivable one . . . ."[25] Although he referred
more than once to the Waverley novels and had met and
corresponded with Scott, there is little enthusiasm.[26]
"Narrative teazes me," he wrote in "Mackery End, in
Hertfordshire." "I have little concern in the progress of
events . . . . Out-of-the-way humours and opinions—heads
with some diverting twist in them—the oddities of author-
ship please me most." Lamb appreciated the insight into
character produced by the epistolary form of *Clarissa;* he
perceived how the autobiographical point of view in *Robinson Crusoe* created verisimilitude; and he objected to being
told by Sterne how he was to feel. As a critic, Lamb understood well the methods and effects of fiction.[27]

It was because of this critical ability that Lamb was imposed upon by amateur novelists as well as by would-be
poets. Writing to Moxon on February 18, 1828, Lamb fore-
stalled any possible gifts of fiction: "Mary does not immediately want Books, having a damn'd consignment of Novels in MS. from Malta: which I wish the Mediterranean
had in its guts."[28] Lady Stoddart, wife of Sir John Stoddart,
Chief Justice and Justice of the Vice-Admiralty Court in
Malta, had written for the *London Magazine* under the
pseudonym "Martha Blackford." As the sister-in-law of
Hazlitt's wife, she had traded on her acquaintance with the
Lambs to the extent of securing their aid in negotiating
with booksellers for more ambitious works. Lamb's vehe-
mence is explained by an examination of the manuscripts of
this persistent writer, now in two large folio volumes with
corrections and alterations made throughout in red ink by
Lamb. It seems that he allowed the office of friendship to
be distorted into the function of unpaid critic; as unrelieved
fiction, the work was particularly uncongenial.

In this connection we may note Lamb's reaction to another task imposed by acquaintance: the correction of Charles Cowden Clarke's prose *Tales from Chaucer,* the idea for which had been planted a quarter century earlier by the Lambs' *Tales from Shakespear*. Lamb's comments were expressed in a letter to the author, here printed for the first time:

Dear C.

The Prioresses Tale is well done & the Cock & fox. But surely, if you have time, you must rub out as much as you can of the technicalities of Alchemy in the pages doubled down. They are scarce interesting to Antiquarians, quite alien from young modern reading. Ben Jonson's Alchymist must have been obsolete in his time. Gamelin I never heard of. Tis some Robin hood garland thing. Not at all Chaucerish.

I write in much confusion. I have made verbal corrections. M.S.S. *submitted to me* kill me, bother me, confound me, nevertheless God prosper yours & your'n—

I don't much think the alchemist will do; tho' tis well done, omitting the slang of art.

Luck to Novelles & Novellos. & mirth to all my good Masters & Mistresses[29]

It would seem that Lamb felt a sense of despair when friendship obligated him to offer his criticism as an imposed task.

Beyond fiction, Lamb read widely although he did not, so far as is known, include travel books in his repertoire. On what he did read and thoroughly understand he came to hold definite opinions, marked by antipathies as well as by affections. These were often based on his reaction to the author rather than to his work, for Lamb was a lover of the biographical part of literature. Thus, he was contemptuous of Shelley and Byron more because of their reputed characters than because of their poetry.[30] He was not interested in the works of Newton or Locke, because one is not curious beyond what he can learn from their writings, while, on the

other hand, the books of Sir Thomas Browne and Fulke
Greville were "riddles, and they themselves the most mys-
terious of personages."[31] His love for the works of the
Duchess of Newcastle, Burns, Cowper, Milton, Spenser,
Chapman, Bourne, and the Elizabethan dramatists is well
known and approved by the verdict of time. His contempt
for Goethe's *Faust,* which he called "a disagreeable canting
tale of Seduction, which has nothing to do with the Spirit
of Faustus—Curiosity,"[32] is not to his credit. But he was
judging the work from a translation. Hazlitt summed up
Lamb's reading in "Elia, and Geoffrey Crayon":

Mr. Lamb's taste in books is also fine, and it is peculiar. It is
not the worse for a little *idiosyncrasy.* He does not go deep into
the Scotch Novels; but he is at home in Smollett or Fielding.
He is little read in Junius or Gibbon, but no man can give a
better account of Burton's *Anatomy of Melancholy,* or Sir
Thomas Brown's *Urn-Burial,* or Fuller's *Worthies,* or John Bunyan's *Holy War.* No one is more unimpressible to a specious
declamation; no one relishes a recondite beauty more. His admiration of Shakespear and Milton does not make him despise
Pope; and he can read Parnell with patience, and Gay with
delight. His taste in French and German literature is somewhat
defective; nor has he made much progress in the science of
Political Economy or other abstruse studies, though he has read
vast folios of controversial divinity, merely for the sake of the
intricacy of style, and to save himself the pain of thinking.

The suggestion that Lamb was conscious of style to the extent that he sometimes read for that alone has nourished the
belief that the old authors, especially those of the seventeenth century, exerted a strong influence on his own modes
of expression. It is unusual and heartening to find a critic
saying, "The influence these authors of the past had on his
work was but slight."[33] We have earlier discounted the alleged influence of Fuller and Browne on his habit of itera-

tion. It remains to consider the question of influence by his other favorite writers.

Lamb's indebtedness to Milton and Spenser has been the subject of several articles and paragraphs, but it was more operative on Lamb's poetry than on his prose. As we have seen, Milton was studied at Christ's Hospital, but beyond pointing out the many quotations from Milton in the essays, a natural result of such an intensive study, it is difficult to assert any concrete evidence of indebtedness. J. Milton French states the case admirably when he says, "Milton's works were continually fresh in Lamb's mind and his constant joy from his earliest to his latest years."[34] In the same way, Lamb's frequent quotation from Spenser and his scattered comments indicate an appreciation summed up in his well-known epithet "the Poet's Poet," but it is going too far to say with Professor French, "for over thirty years Spenser was so close to Lamb's mind that he constantly affected his thought and expression."[35] Frederick Hard objects: "I do not agree with the emphasis which he appears to place upon the significance of Lamb's association with Spenser. . . . This, I think, stretches the point much too far."[36]

There is more of a case for the influence on Lamb of William Cowper's frequent egotism and wit-melancholy. Lamb may have read his prose, as well as his poetry, before the turn of the century; as early as December 5, 1796, he was praising Cowper's "divine chit-chat" to Coleridge. The very definite sympathy between the two men is indicated in a letter written in 1782 by Cowper to the Reverend William Unwin, comparing the innocent humor of his John Gilpin to *la bagatelle* of Swift:

La bagatelle has no enemy in me, though it has neither so warm a friend nor so able a one as it had in him. If I trifle, and merely trifle, it is because I am reduced to it by necessity,—a melancholy, that nothing else so effectually disperses, engages me sometimes in the arduous task of being merry by force. And,

strange as it may seem, the most ludicrous lines I ever wrote
have been written in the saddest mood, and, but for that saddest
mood, perhaps had never been written at all. To say truth, it
would be but a shocking vagary, should the mariners on board
a ship buffeted by a terrible storm employ themselves in did-
dling and dancing; yet sometimes much such a part act I.[37]

Lamb, too, found wit in melancholy and may have
learned from Cowper's "trifling" the use of humor in re-
lieving sadness. Some critics have attributed Lamb's wit to
his reading of Fuller. Leigh Hunt comes closer to the truth
in his *Autobiography* when he writes of "the scholarly turn
of joking which is common to a classical education." Re-
gardless of influences or sources, in the final analysis it is
the individual's own necessitated ability to keep things in
proper perspective that results in expressions and mannerisms that to less sensitive souls are incongruous and sometimes indecorous. Lamb's punning at a funeral "to the consternation of the rest of the mourners,"[38] drawing upon himself "the awful eye of the parson" when he began to make
a joke at the wedding of Sarah Burney,[39] and his attempt to
discountenance an outsider who persisted in intruding on
Wordsworth's solemn intonations at Haydon's Immortal
Dinner[40]—such outbursts of honest spirit are typical of
Lamb; "I cannot divest me of an unseasonable disposition
to levity upon the most awful occasions."[41] Something of the
same sort of mental tendency was, I think, in the mind of
Gamaliel Bradford when, writing of the inner life of Lincoln and his wife, he says:

That she had a trace of the larger humorous attitude seems
unlikely, and it is still more unlikely that she ever grasped or
enjoyed that attitude in the subtle, pervading, dissolving form
in which it was constantly manifest in her husband. The element of Touchstone, of Charles Lamb, the instinct of remote-
ness, of detachment, even in the midst of vast tragic passions,
perhaps most precisely in the midst of such, of illuminating

them with the strange glory of laughter, which was so haunting
and so fascinating in Lincoln, evidently annoyed and perplexed
her, as it has many other excellent people.[42]

It has been alleged that the seventeenth-century author
Jeremy Taylor influenced Lamb's style, but no one has ever
proved any relationship. One verbal parallel unnoted heretofore occurs in "Amicus Redivivus," where Lamb writes of
Dyer's hysteria: "He discoursed of marvellous escapes—by
carelessness of nurses—by pails of gelid, and kettles of the
boiling element, in infancy . . . ." In the first part of Chapter
I of *The Rule and Exercises of Holy Dying* we read: "But
if the bubble stands the shock of a bigger drop, and outlives
the chances of a child, of a careless nurse, of drowning in a
pail of water . . . ." But such a half-recollection does not
prove any stylistic influence.

There is more cause to say that Robert Burton helped to
mould Lamb's style. "Burton is a scarce gentleman, not
much known," Lamb wrote to Thomas Manning on April
5, 1800.[43] Yet general interest in *The Anatomy of Melancholy* was increasing at this very time, judging partly from
the fact that a new edition was published in the same year
and another was issued in 1806. Lamb's copy of the first
edition, 1621, was one of his favorite books, probably because of the interest its author as a person had for him. As
with Cowper, there was a strong affinity of temperament
between the two men: both exhibited traits of melancholy
and of irrepressible humor, passing easily from one state to
the other. Reserved toward strangers, they reveled in their
friendships, only to bewail the consequent lack of solitude.

Burton's influence first showed itself by a direct imitation
—Lamb's "Curious Fragments," printed with his play *John
Woodvil* in 1802 as material "Extracted from a common-
place book, which belonged to Robert Burton, the famous
Author of the Anatomy of Melancholy." Here Lamb has

adopted the distinctive stylistic devices of Burton. "On the
Melancholy of Tailors," published in 1814, is an excellent
imitation of form and spirit, although not of language. Burton's method of anatomising is followed, and authorities
are quoted in the manner of Burton, but they are Lamb's
own favorites. Lake offers the plausible suggestion that
Lamb was influenced to write his "Witches, and Other
Night-Fears" by reading Burton's digression on the "Nature
of Spirits, bad Angels and Devils and how they cause melancholy" and "Of Witches and Magicians, how they cause
melancholy." It might be added that the analytical method
used in "The Convalescent" and the subject treated in the
Popular Fallacy "That a Sulky Temper is a Misfortune" are
both reminiscent of Burton.

"Fantastic" is the adjective applied to the spirit of Burton's prose by Lake, who alleges that Burton's influence is
operating whenever the subject is grotesque enough to admit the fantastic. This is stretching influence beyond the
limits of proof. Lamb often adopted the anatomical style
with its disjointed progression of short phrases, and it is
probable that the *Anatomy* brought this device to Lamb's
attention, but, as we have seen, it was not unique with
Burton. Certainly the conscious imitations of Burton's style
in these counterfeits of form and substance would have resulted in a deeper impression of stylistic devices than could
be gained by mere reading. But Lamb does not follow him
in his superabundance of quotations nor in his Euphuistic
antithesis. Both writers have the habit of digression, an
occasional tendency toward the pedantic word, and a loose-
ness of style contributing to the feeling of familiarity. The
presence of all these traits in Lamb's correspondence as well
suggests that they were natural to his writing habits rather
than the result of conscious imitation. Are not similar temperaments alone sufficient cause for similar expression?

The seventeenth-century author in whom Lamb particu-

larly delighted was Sir Thomas Browne. It is not difficult
to comprehend his affection for Browne's work when we
stop to realize the many points of similarity existing in the
characters of the two writers. Both were amateurs rather
than professionals; both had an intellectual curiosity which
delved into the past; both lived in politically upset times
yet remained out of the turmoil; both were introspective;
and both were concerned with perfecting their prose styles.
In Lamb's essays there are more than twice as many quotations from Browne as from Burton, and these indicate a
specific familiarity with *Religio Medici, Hydriotaphia,
Pseudodoxia Epidemica,* and *Christian Morals.* As with
Burton, some of Browne's influence on Lamb took the form
of direct imitation: "On Burial Societies" follows the manner of *Hydriotaphia,* and *Popular Fallacies* that of *Vulgar
Errors.* Several verbal parallels in the prose of the two authors have been pointed out.[44]

It is difficult to agree with Iseman that "On almost every
page of Lamb we find faint half-echoes of Browne, never
conspicuous, but always endowing his pages with the 'atmosphere' of the older author."[45] This is the sort of broad
assertion made by writers straining to establish an influence
by their favorite writer. Back on more solid ground, Iseman
discovered that "There is a chronological parallel between
Lamb's increasing knowledge of Browne, as shown by his
reference to or quotations from the old author, and the
development of personality in his own writing."[46] Of this
personalized approach, Pater wrote: "The type of this literature, obviously, is not Locke or Gibbon, but, above all
others, Sir Thomas Browne . . . ."[47] The presence of subjectivity, a characteristic excellence of Lamb's essays, in the
Religio Medici, a work with which Lamb was thoroughly
familiar, may have aided him in discovering the appeal of
this approach, but he was conscious of it in the works of
Montaigne and others.

The grandeur and rhythm of the style of *Religio Medici* and of the closing portion of *Hydriotaphia,* so distinctive a mark of Browne's prose, cannot be found in Lamb's essays. His sentences, however, are often as lengthy and as involved. Common to both writers is a copious use of parentheses, of punctuation, and of conjunctions to inaugurate sentences. For these, too, critics are disposed to suggest an indebtedness on Lamb's part. It may be that he was encouraged to write in this way by the authority of the older writer; but Lamb, like Browne, was writing as he thought— or, more accurately, to make the result appear as if this were the case—and since his thinking habits were essentially without logical order, we must be wary of asserting an influence. Lamb's manuscript letters show dashes used for breaks of thought and for relationships not immediately clear; quotation marks often come in the middle of a sentence, where they logically, if not always grammatically, belong. A similarity of temperament, especially of mental processes, and of objective resulted in a similarity of expression.

To say that Lamb derived his special use of an "of" phrase from Browne is difficult of proof. Lamb's "elder Palmer (of stage-treading celebrity)," from the essay "On Some of the Old Actors" is similar to Browne's "Don Quixote of Melodious Memory"; but such a use thus exemplified is hardly distinctive. Highly doubtful also is the suggestion that Lamb learned his alliteration from Browne rather than from Lyly and his followers, because Lyly joined it with balance of clause whereas Lamb used it only when his thought and language are in the same mood with Browne's. The use of such a widely practised rhetorical device as alliteration, so frequent with seventeenth-century writers, can hardly be assigned to familiarity with any one author. A more distinctive device used by both authors is that of reduplicated phrases for imaginative quality and clarity. Lamb may cer-

tainly be in Browne's debt for such a structure as that in
"A certain obsequiousness or deferential respect" from
"Modern Gallantry" or "his periegesis or triumphant pas-
sage throughout this island" from "The Two Races of
Men."[48]

One of the chief features of Lamb's style is his use of
pedantic and archaic words. As early as 1874 W. C. Hazlitt
wrote: "Lamb's style, even for his own age, had an antique
cast and tone about it, not wholly unaffected or unintentional. It would surprise many readers to see a list drawn
up of such words as are scattered through the two series of
Elia, and as will be barely intelligible, in the sense in which
the writer employed them, to the generation now springing
up. I see the remote possibility of a glossary to the *Essays,*
of a Lamb *cum notis variorum!*"[49] A modern student of
obsolete and archaic words in the essays answers this comment: "It is surprising that one can read these without an
unpleasant consciousness of ignorance as to their meaning.
They are used with skill, and in many cases frankly explained in the context, for Lamb is too 'chatty and con-
versible' a friend to intend to leave us in doubt as to his
meaning or send us drudging to the dictionary."[50] While the
words in a list such as W. C. Hazlitt envisaged would be
generally meaningless or obscure, they are clearly appre-
hended in context, where such devices as reduplicated
phrases guarded them against loss through the passage of
time.

Burton, Milton, and other seventeenth-century writers
experimented in the aesthetic value of words, but Browne
is most notorious for his extreme exercise of verbal pedantry. "Browne was greatly interested in the beauty of
words, in their sound, their form, the image that they
raised," wrote Sir Edmund Gosse.[51] His coinages, his archa-
isms, and his frequent Latinisms are outstanding when

compared with, say, Jeremy Taylor's more representative
diction. The conclusion from these facts has been that
Lamb gained "a sense of the importance of the *word*" from
Browne.[52] The discerning French critic Derocquigny terms
Lamb's style a style of words, the opposite of the moving,
easy style like that of Addison.[53] In the analysis of the manuscripts we saw how Lamb sought for the precise word, not
content with any that did not carry the exact connotation—
sometimes embracing several ideas. He was concerned
with the sound and the form of the word. His love of paro-
nomasia or punning was closely allied to this awareness of
the significance of words. "I am sometimes happy in it," he
wrote to Manning on January 2, 1810.[54] Lamb's acquaintance with the works of Browne may have given him a
definite realization of the importance of the word; yet there
seems to have been a natural interest in unfamiliar words
and a curiosity about their form and sound that argues a
more innate concern than can be explained by the reading
of one author. There are many odd and coined words
throughout his correspondence. His parenthetical remark
"I always spell plumb-pudding with a *b*, p-l-u-m-*b*—I
think it reads fatter and more suetty," in a letter to Joseph
Hume of December 29, 1807, is but one example of his per-
vasive playing with words.[55] "I have Ray's *Collection of
English Words Not Generally Used*, 1691," he wrote on
May 19, 1823, to his editor friend William Hone, and there
is no doubt that he used it.[56] The Cowden Clarkes recalled
that this propensity was evident in Lamb's conversation:

He was at this time expecting a visit from the Hoods, and
talked over with us the grand preparations he and his sister
meant to make in the way of due entertainment: one of the
dishes he proposed being no other than "bubble and squeak."
He had a liking for queer, out-of-the-way names and odd,
startling, quaint nomenclatures; bringing them in at unexpected

moments, and dwelling upon them again and again when his interlocutors thought he had done with them. So on this occasion "bubble and squeak" made its perpetual reappearance at the most irrelevant points of the day's conversation and evening fire-side talk till its sheer repetition became a piece of humour in itself.[57]

Browne's verbal pedantry joined with his rhythm, balance, and antithesis to create the effect of grandeur; with Lamb's more natural structure, the effect is that of quaintness.

The most obvious influence of Lamb's general reading on his prose was manifested by his use of quotations. Underlying the feeling that the capacity to appreciate the essays of Elia is indicative of a high degree of literary taste is Lamb's extensive use of quotation, allusion, and recollection. These borrowed threads woven into the texture of the essays must be recognized—although not pulled out for close scrutiny or even necessarily identified—before the associative emotion intended by their use can be elicited and fully savoured. Since Lamb's recollection of his reading played so important a part in determining his style, it is appropriate to examine his reasons for quoting, his methods, and his sources. In so doing we may throw some light on his reading and the nature of his memory. To trace all the echoes would be an enormous undertaking of doubtful value; for the present purpose only definite uses of the phrases of other writers of sufficient extent to merit the term "quotation" will be considered.[58]

It is surprising to find Lamb, who used so many quotations, writing to Barton on September 17, 1823, "Besides, there is a quotation in it, always bad in verse; seldom advisable in prose."[59] Perhaps it was this belief that resulted in his omitting quotation marks more often than he employed them. "It was the primitive clock, the horloge of the first world," he wrote of the sundial in "The Old Benchers"; the

words are from Marvell, from whom Lamb later in the
essay quotes with the source, but here there is no distinction from the context. Several of Lamb's commonplace
books are extant; these were not collections of notes for his
essays but extract books in which he wrote lines, letters,
verses, and whole poems that he had come across in his
reading. He pasted in clippings of his own essays and
copied short pieces written by his friends. A careful examination reveals that very few of the quotations in his essays
are in these extract books. The conclusion must be that he
depended entirely upon his memory, and the almost universal inaccuracy of his quotations substantiates the fact that
he did not supplement it by reference to the originals. Even
when Lamb quoted himself, as he often did, he is frequently
inaccurate. Dishonesty was not his intention, as is clear
from a passage in a letter of February 17, 1823, to Barton:

I have quoted G. F. in my Quaker's meeting as having said he
was "lifted up in spirit . . . and the Judge and Jury were as dead
men under his feet." I find no such words in his Journal, and I
did not get them from Sewell, and the latter sentence I am sure
I did not mean to invent. I must have put some other Quaker's
words into his mouth. Is it a fatality in me, that every thing I
touch turns into a Lye? I once quoted two Lines from a translation of Dante, which Hazlitt very greatly admired, and quoted
in a Book as proof of the stupendous power of that poet but no
such lines are to be found in the translation, which has
been searched for the purpose. I must have dreamed them,
for I am quite certain I did not forge them knowingly.
What a misfortune to have a Lying memory.[60]

All too often Lamb's perverse memory thus led him into
falsehoods, but this very inaccuracy indicates that he assim-
ilated his reading rather than merely catalogued it. When
he wished to memorize, he was capable of doing so, as is

indicated by the following interesting, though probably exaggerated, anecdote, which seems never to have been reprinted since its first appearance in 1849:

Lamb was once invited by an old friend to meet an author who had just published a volume of poems; when he got there (being somewhat early) he was asked by his host to look over the volume of the expected visitor. A few minutes convinced Elia that it possessed very little merit, being a feeble echo of different authors. This opinion of the poetaster was fully confirmed by the appearance of the gentleman himself, whose self-conceit and confidence in his own book were so manifest as to awaken in Lamb that spirit of mischievous waggery so characteristic of the Humorist. Lamb's rapid and tenacious memory enabled him during the dinner to quote fluently, several passages from the pretender's volume. These he gave with this introduction—"This reminds me of some verses I wrote when I was very young"—he then, to the astonishment of the gentleman in question, quoted something from the volume. Lamb tried this a second time; the gentleman looked still more surprised, and seemed evidently bursting with suppressed indignation. At last, as a climax to the fun, Lamb coolly quoted the well-known opening lines of "Paradise Lost," as written by himself. This was too much for the versemonger—he immediately rose to his legs, and with an impressive solemnity of manner thus addressed the claimant to so many poetical honors—"Sir, I have tamely submitted all this evening to hear you claim the merit that may belong to any little poems of my own; this I have borne in silence, but, Sir, I never will sit quietly by and see the Immortal Milton robbed of "Paradise Lost."[61]

In some few instances, quotations were kept fresh in Lamb's memory by his use of them in letters or in other essays.[62] Only seldom, however, were quotations used more than once. It is possible that Lamb often quoted without being conscious of borrowing. "I am Retired Leisure. I am to be met with in trim gardens," he wrote near the close of "The Superannuated Man," recalling lines 49–50 of *Il Penseroso:*

> And add to these retired Leisure
> That in trim gardens takes his pleasure.

Speaking of the "fair sepulchre in the grateful stomach of the judicious epicure," in "A Dissertation upon Roast Pig," he wrote that the pig "for such a tomb might be content to die," recalling Milton's epitaph on Shakespeare: "That Kings for such a tomb would wish to die." "Bridget's was more a waking bliss than mine," he wrote in "Mackery End": "waking bliss" is a phrase in Milton's *Comus.*[63] Examples of this unconscious or half-conscious recollection could be multiplied many times over, but these, picked at random, are enough to suggest that Lamb's reading was so thoroughly absorbed that it was often manifested in a natural use of the original words.

By and large, however, Lamb was conscious of his frequent quotation from and allusion to his reading, although he probably could not always have pointed to the exact source on demand. His purpose was often to brighten thoughts that he desired to emphasize, as in "Imperfect Sympathies," where we read: "For myself—earth-bound and fettered to the scene of my activities," followed by a line from *Paradise Lost:* "Standing on earth, not rapt above the sky." Usually, the quotation is introduced naturally into the context: "These were bright visitations in a scholar's and a clerk's life—'far off their coming shone' " he wrote in "Oxford in the Vacation," quoting again from *Paradise Lost.* Often the quotation is, in part or in whole, a repetition of the same thought, with a resulting grace and beauty. Speaking of the sundial in "The Old Benchers," Lamb wrote: "How would the dark line steal imperceptibly on,

watched by the eye of childhood, eager to detect its movement, never catched, nice as an evanescent cloud, or the
first arrests of sleep!" Then, slipping in easily and naturally
two lines from Shakespeare's 104th Sonnet, he substantiates
and embellishes the idea:

> Ah! yet doth beauty like a dial-hand
> Steal from his figure, and no pace perceived!

Herein lies one difference between Lamb's use of quotations and Hazlitt's manner of borrowing. Hazlitt searches
for quotations; they are seldom integrated with his own
words. Lamb's quotations give a very echo to his own expressions; Hazlitt's substitute for his. De Quincey maintained that Hazlitt's practice "is at war with sincerity, the
foundation of all good writing, to express one's own
thoughts by another man's words."[64] Lamb's use of quotations almost constantly in addition to his own words, rather
than in place of them, gave him more freedom in adapting
the original to suit his context, which he did unhesitatingly.
"For myself, I must spoil a little passage of Beaumont and
Fletcher to adapt it to my feelings," he wrote to Coleridge;[65]
and this was his policy in his essays as well. One example
suffices to show how he compressed the original into a
smaller space and rearranged the order of words. Lines
83–84 of *Il Penseroso* run:

> Or the bell-man's drowsy charm
> To bless the door from nightly harm.

Near the end of Lamb's *Fallacy* "That We Should Rise with
the Lark," we read: "Even ourself, in these our humbler
lucubrations, tune our best measured cadences (Prose has
her cadences) not unfrequently to the charm of the drowsier watchman, 'blessing the doors.'"

Another liberty Lamb took in quoting was frequently to
employ lines in entirely different contexts from those originally used. Thus, two lines of Coleridge's "Epitaph on an
Infant,"

> Ere sin could blight, or sorrow fade,
> Death came with timely care—

are applied to the pig in his "Dissertation." At such times
a new meaning and a new emotion are given to the original;
where this occurs, Lamb is so far from being a copier that
he himself becomes the creator.

Lamb was not limited in his quoting to the literature of
any one country or any one period.[66] However, his comparatively small amount of reading in foreign literature
accounts for the scarcity of quotation therefrom: one from
Tasso in Fairfax's translation; one from Erasmus in Latin;
and one each from Dante, Cervantes, and Zimmerman in
translation. In classical literature, Virgil is the most quoted,
with sixteen uses of the *Aeneid,* two of the *Eclogues,* and
one of the *Georgics.* Book I of the *Aeneid* is the most drawn
upon, but quotations, adaptations, and allusions are derived
from Books II, III, V, VI, and X as well. Some appear in
Latin; some in translation. Four quotations from the *Aeneid*
are found also in the letters. Most quoted after Virgil of
the classical authors is Horace: phrases and lines, almost
all in the Latin, from *Ars poetica, Epistles, Lament for
Quinctilius, Satires,* and the *Odes.* Of the five quotations
from Terence, the phrase "Taedet cotidianarum harum
formarum" had a particular attraction:[67] in "Many Friends"
and the essay "On the Genius and Character of Hogarth"
it is only slightly changed; but in a letter of June 16, 1796,
to Coleridge, he wrote: "In the words of Terence, a little
altered, 'Taedet me hujus quotidiani mundi.' I am heartily
sick of the every-day scenes of life"; and to Wordsworth

on March 20, 1822, he complained, "Taedet me harum quotidinarum formarum, these pestilential clerk faces always in one's dish . . . ."[68] Other quotations from the classics are taken from the *Iliad,* Ovid's *Metamorphoses* and *Tristia,* Juvenal's *Satires,* and the works of Catullus, Cicero, Quintilian, and Seneca. In some cases, these are found also in the letters.[69] It will be remembered that Lamb's Christ's Hospital studies included most of these authors. The fact that Virgil and Horace were used for memory work explains why these two authors were quoted more in the essays than other classical authors. With minor exceptions, the classical quotations and allusions are traceable to Lamb's school days rather than to his general reading.

In the same way, the sixty-odd quotations from, and allusions to, the Bible are largely the result of association with it in Christ's Hospital. Lamb's heavy dependence on the Bible in this way had as much, if not more, to do with giving his style a quaintness than did his borrowings from Spenser and Milton. It is of interest to note that there are almost twice as many uses of the Old Testament as of the New and that the Psalms and Proverbs are the most quoted.[70] Other books of the Old Testament used are I and II Kings, Judges, Joshua, Genesis, Exodus, Job, Jeremiah, Ecclesiastes, Deuteronomy, Song of Solomon, I Samuel, Esther, and Daniel. From the New Testament there are four or five quotations each from Luke, I and II Corinthians, Matthew, Revelation, and Acts, while there is one each from Romans and James. There are also two references to the Apocrypha.

In English literature exclusive of the drama, Milton was the author most quoted in the essays. Here again, the explanation lies basically in Lamb's intensive study of Milton as an academic lesson. The quotations from *Paradise Lost,* the most quoted poem, are, to a large extent, taken from rather definite sections—just those places of sufficient excellence to merit being given special attention by a schoolmaster. Thus, out of ten quotations from Book I, six are taken from lines 502 to 569.[71] The five quotations from Book II are more scattered,[72] but six of the nine in Book III come from lines 445 to 493.[73] Two of the five quotations from Book IV are close together in the poem.[74] Book X supplied four, Book VI two, and Book XI one phrase used twice.[75] Books VII, VIII, IX, and XII supplied one each.[76] Lamb made only seven quotations from *Paradise Regained* —five from Book II and two from Book IV.[77] Six quotations come from *Comus*, four from *Il Penseroso*, three from *Lycidas*, and one from *Samson Agonistes*.[78] It would seem that, like most readers, Lamb was better acquainted with the first books of *Paradise Lost* than with the later ones, and more with this masterpiece than with other of Milton's poems.

A much smaller number of quotations can be traced to Spenser. Most of these come from the *Faerie Queene:* three quotations and a reference to Book I, one quotation and three references to Book II, one reference to Book VI, and a quotation from Book VII. Stanzas 19 and 21 of the *Hymne in Honour of Beautie* and a phrase from the dedication of the *Shepheards' Calendar* to Sidney are incorrectly quoted. One verse from stanza 8 of the *Prothalamion* is twice quoted,[79] and there is one from the *Epithalamion*.

It is surprising to find about the same number of quotations from Pope as from Spenser. They are scattered: three from *Moral Essays III* and one each from *The Rape of the Lock*, the *Essay on Man*, the *Epistle to Dr. Arbuthnot*, the *Ode on St. Cecilia's Day*, and *Moral Essays I*; and a reference to *The Narrative of Dr. Robert Norris*. Other eighteenth-century poets quoted are Thomson, Gray, Prior, Gay, Collins, Cowper, and Vincent Bourne, who each contributed three or four, and Young, David Mallet, Burns, and John Armstrong, who each contributed one.[80]

In view of the tendency to associate Lamb with writers of the seventeenth century, it is startling to discover that there are more quotations in his essays from poets of the eighteenth century than there are from those of the fifteenth, sixteenth, and seventeenth centuries put together, still excluding the drama. Aside from lines quoted from several songs and ballads that may derive from the fifteenth century, there is only one, and that a doubtful, reference to anything in the fifteenth century.[81] The sixteenth century is a little better represented: he quoted from six of Shakespeare's sonnets and once from "The Rape of Lucrece"; then besides several sonnets from *Astrophel and Stella* in the essay on Sidney, there is only one quotation each from Leland's *Itinerary,* a lyric by Richard Barnfield, and Chapman's *Eugenia,* and two from Matthew Roydon. Of the seventeenth-century poets, Cowley, Marvell, and Drayton lead in the number of quotations they supplied, although there are only three from each. One or two phrases—half-recollections—come from Jonson. Other seventeenth-century poets quoted are represented by only one each: Fletcher's "The Faithful Shepherdess," Waller's "On the Foregoing Divine Poems," Beaumont's "On the Tombs in Westminster Abbey," Wither's "Shepherds' Hunting," Daniel's "Hymen's Triumph," Donne's "Eclogues," John Cleveland's "Poem on the death of Edward King," Fulke Greville Lord Brooke's "Silence augmenteth grief . . . ,"[82] Richard Flecknoe's "Poems of All Sorts," Charles Cotton's "The New Year," and Thomas Randolph's "Ode to Master Anthony Stafford."

Wordsworth was the most quoted of the contemporary poets. Besides several passages of the *Excursion* in his review, Lamb quoted one other in another place. In addition to several phrases that may be recollections of lines from other poems, there are two quotations from the *Ode on Intimations of Immortality* and one each from *The Fountain, Peter Bell,* the sonnet to Thomas Clarkson, *Tintern Abbey,* lines *Written in March,* and *Yarrow Visited.* Lamb's use of a stanza from the last poem provides an example of an uncharacteristic concern with accuracy in quotation. The manuscript of "Mackery End in Hertfordshire" shows that he first wrote:

> And thou, that didst appear so fair
> to bland Imagination,
> Dost rival in the light of day
> Her delicate creation!

In a letter to Wordsworth of April 28, 1815, he had mentioned *Yarrow Visited* "with that stanza, 'But thou that didst appear so fair—' than which I think no lovelier stanza can be found in the wide world of poetry . . . ."[83] The manuscript of the essay shows that he corrected "And" to "But" and "bland" to "fond." Then when the printer's proof showed him that "day" had been changed to "air," to rime with "fair," Lamb wrote the editor, John Taylor, on June 8, 1821, "DAY is the right reading, and I *implore you to restore it.*"[84]

Quotations from Coleridge's poems were almost as numerous as those from Wordsworth's. Lamb took one quotation each from *The Ancient Mariner, Kubla Khan,* the *Epitaph on an Infant,* the *Ode to Tranquillity,* and *Religious Musings.* The *Ode on the Departing Year* supplied two quotations, one of which was used twice. Other contemporary poets quoted include Landor (whose *Gebir* was quoted from once and referred to once), Hunt (whose *Foliage* was quoted from once), Thomas Moore (whose *Loves of the Angels* was referred to as an "extraordinary

legend"), Procter (to whose *Dream* Lamb referred once),
and Watts (from whose *Songs for Children* Lamb quoted
in a note). It should be added that Lamb quoted twice from
his own *Poetry for Children* and once each from his sonnets
"Wish" and "Work."

Of the dramatic writers quoted in the essays, Shake-
speare is, by far, the author most drawn upon. *Hamlet,
Lear, Macbeth,* and *I Henry IV* each provided about a
dozen quotations. Slightly less used were *As You Like It,
Richard II, Twelfth Night,* and *The Tempest.*[85] Three or
four quotations each were taken from *Othello, Henry V,
III Henry VI, II Henry IV, A Midsummer Night's Dream,
Love's Labour's Lost, The Merry Wives of Windsor,* and
Timon of Athens. Two quotations each come from *Antony
and Cleopatra, Cymbeline, The Merchant of Venice,
Richard III, Romeo and Juliet, The Taming of the Shrew,
The Winter's Tale,* and *Troilus and Cressida.* The total of
twenty-four plays is a wide range, and the inaccuracy of
many of the quotations shows that Lamb quoted from
memory. Once again, his study and required memory work
at Christ's Hospital helps to explain the large number of
quotations from Shakespeare. The plays used are well divided among the tragedies, comedies and histories, with
only a slight preference for the first two, which is natural
in view of the exclusion of the histories from his and Mary's
Tales from Shakespear.

Lamb's well-known familiarity with the Elizabethan
drama would lead us to expect more quotations from that
than from Restoration drama, but the fact is that, exclusive
of Shakespeare, there are as many from the Restoration
drama as there are from the Elizabethan and Stuart periods
together. Heywood's *Four 'Prentices of London,* Kyd's
Spanish Tragedy, Marlowe's *Edward II,* and Marston's
Antonio's Revenge are each drawn upon for only one quota-

tion. There are two from Tourneur's *Revenger's Tragedy*, one from Middleton's *Mayor of Quinborough*, a possible one from Webster's *Duchess of Malfi*,[86] and one each from Jonson's *Alchemist* and *The Poetaster*. From the Restoration plays we find one quotation from Congreve's *Love for Love* and an adaptation from his *Mourning Bride*, one from Dryden's *All for Love* and a reference to his *Conquest of Granada*, a quotation from Sir Robert Howard's *Vestal Virgin*, one from Thomas Killigrew's *The Parson's Wedding*, and one from Vanbrugh's *Relapse* which is used twice. There are also mere references by the use of character names to Wycherley's *Love in a Wood*, Farquhar's *Inconstant*, Etherege's *Man of Mode*, and Buckingham's *Rehearsal*. Drama more nearly contemporary with Lamb was referred to in this same way, except for Home's *Douglas*, from which a short phrase is taken. Other eighteenth-century plays, which are merely referred to, are Thomas Arne's *Artaxerxes*, Foote's *Liar*, Sheridan's *School for Scandal* and *The Rivals*, Garrick's *High Life below Stairs* and *Miss in Her Teens*, Morton's *Children in the Wood*, Coffey's *The Devil to Pay*, and Ireland's *Vortigern*.

In the category of prose, the quotations come preponderantly from the seventeenth century. The sixteenth century is represented only by several passages from some of More's *Dialogues* in his "Sir Thomas More" and by the mere mention of some of the characters in Sidney's *Arcadia*. In the eighteenth century, there is a quotation from Mackenzie's *Julia de Roubigné*, one from Defoe's *Complete English Tradesman*, two from Dr. Johnson, and one from Edmund Burke's "Letter to a Noble Lord." There are also references to Thomas Amory's *Life of John Buncle*, Fielding's *Joseph Andrews*, Mandeville's *Fable of the Bees*, Smollett's *Roderick Random*, Swift's *Ars Punica, sive Flos Linguarum*,[87] Richardson's *Clarissa*, and Sterne's *Tristram*

Shandy. Quotations from the prose of the seventeenth century are more than twice as numerous as those from that of the eighteenth. As we should expect, there are several from Sir Thomas Browne: three from the *Religio Medici,* three from *Hydriotaphia,* and one from *Christian Morals.* In his "Specimens from the Writings of Fuller," Lamb naturally used excerpts, which are, however, often inaccurately transcribed. One other, from Fuller's *Holy State,* is in "Imperfect Sympathies." Burton's *Anatomy of Melancholy* furnished three quotations. Taylor's *Gunpowder Treason* sermon furnished one, and his *Discourse of the Nature, Offices, and Measures of Friendship* another. There is one from Bunyan's *Pilgrim's Progress,* several from Sir William Temple's *Essays,* and two or three probable recollections of Walton's *Complete Angler.* A line from Collier's *Biographical Dictionary* was quoted, and a passage in his essay *On Musick* from *Essays upon Several Moral Subjects* was used in *Dryden and Collier* and *The Ass.* The phrase *lumen siccum* (dry knowledge) from Bacon's *Novum Organum* was used in two places, and there is one reference to his *New Atlantis.* Finally, there is one quotation each from Jonson's *Timber;* Burnet's *History of His Own Time;* John Ogilby's *Accurate Description of Africa;* Howell's *Epistolae Ho-Elianae;* Elias Ashmole's *Institutions, Laws and Ceremonies of the Order of the Garter;* Tom Brown's *Observations on Virgil, Ovid and Homer;* Simon Patrick's *Parable of the Pilgrim;* and from Mrs. Hannah Woolley's *The Queene-like Closet.*

The enumeration of the sources from which Lamb took his quotations is of value in many ways. The list of books known to have been in his library and his epistolary references to his reading help us to know very accurately what he read, but the vast extent and variety of his reading are emphasized by observing the sources of his quotations. We may be certain that the books from which he quoted were, for the most part, his favorites or the ones that had made the strongest impression and had often influenced his thinking. Furthermore, this analysis is a commentary on the exceptional retentiveness of his memory, for he quoted in all from more than one hundred thirty authors and from a much larger number of individual works. While he sometimes used a quotation in a letter that he had previously used, or later used, in an essay, within the essays themselves he rarely used the same quotation twice and never more than twice. It is doubtful that he made any conscious effort to memorize passages after his schooldays, nor did he use his commonplace books for the purpose of preserving them for future use. Accuracy was unimportant for his purposes and even in a review he did not bother to consult the original. Undoubtedly he was aware of the transmutation the lines had undergone in his mind, but rather than arresting the change, he furthered it by condensing, transposing, and substituting until the original fit his context with a natural smoothness. This was more important to Lamb than the mechanical preservation of the original; he had no blind reverence for the words of his predecessors. In this respect, at least, Lamb's essays are superior to those of his professional colleague, William Hazlitt, who employed a multitude of quotations—albeit apt—to express, rather than embellish, his own thoughts. Lamb's subtle use of quotation, allusion, and half-recollection throughout his essays infused them with a literary quality that helps to distinguish them. The preponderant use of the Bible, the classics, Milton, and Shakespeare—resulting chiefly from academic emphasis on these literatures at Christ's Hospital—in particular contributed to a result termed, among other appellations, quaint. One final observation based on the foregoing analysis of Lamb's quotations is that most of the authors quoted have come to be regarded as the most outstanding of their times. While much of Lamb's reading was off the beaten path and some of his quotations derive from works hardly remembered and little read today, it is a tribute to his critical appreciation that his emphasis was on the literature whose worth has been confirmed by time.

As for Lamb's prose style as a whole, evidence suggests that it was more completely and essentially his own than we have been led to believe by critics who have passed on traditional opinions. There is no question that Lamb absorbed into the texture of his expression many words and some devices of phrase construction found in his reading. But it is incorrect to assume that he was a conscious imitator of the older writers merely because of these similarities. His mental affinity to several favorite writers goes far to explain similarities of expression. His interest in words, in their sound, their spelling, and their connotation, has been clearly demonstrated. While the "antique modes and phrases," as Lamb himself expresses it in the Preface to *Last Essays,* may seem affected to us, we err in concluding that they were affected by Lamb. "Better is it that a writer should be natural in a self-pleasing quaintness, than to affect a naturalness (so called) that should be strange to him," he wrote in this Preface. The presence in the correspondence of many of his apparent affectations supports this statement; for him they were not such but natural expressions which he was accustomed to use in writing to friends. In the same way, his occasional compression of thought and the analytical method of imaginative description may be found in the letters; the academic exercises and early journalistic work had formed this tendency—it was not affected from seventeenth-century prose. So, too, the frequently occurring Latinistic words, while encouraged by the authority of Browne's prose, derived from the resourceful brain of Charles Lamb, another accomplished Latinist.

Above all, the familiar and conversational tone of the essays was natural, not imitative. Consciously aware of his purpose, he practiced this quality in his letters. "The order of our thoughts should be the order of our writing," he maintained in a letter to P. G. Patmore.[88] Edward Moxon commented: "He always spoke as he wrote, and did both as felt; and his letters—they were unpremeditated—are in the style of his other writings . . . ."[89] Lamb's use of dashes and irregular punctuation resulted naturally from his feeling expressed to William Hone that "prose feeds on grosser punctualities" than verse.[90]

Attempts to define and label the style of Lamb's essays have been numerous; the encomiums have been multitudinous. But William Wordsworth contented himself with a single sentence, eloquent in its simplicity: "Charles Lamb, my friend, writes prose exquisitely."[91]

The perfection of Lamb's work, which so many critics have sought in vain to explain only to fall back on the magic word "genius," is owing to his painstaking attention to the details of literary expression and to his refusal to publish an essay until he had perfected it by arduous labor and careful revision to conform to his own high standards. Our survey of the directing influences at work on Lamb and on his essays explains why he came finally to express himself in the essay form and how he attained eminence in that medium. The selective use of Lamb's correspondence and other reliable sources of information reveals how he worked and what precisely his contribution to literature was. The examination of representative original manuscripts of the essays unveils the actual process of his literary creation. All this makes the uniqueness of the essays more comprehensible; Lamb is seen as an essayist shaped by logical causes, and his essays as the result of definable forces.

To understand the background of a piece of literature

need not detract from the appreciation of it. To discover the tendencies that informed and molded the mind of Charles Lamb and the steps by which his essays grew from partial idea to polished idiom does not lessen our affection for the essayist nor the appeal of his essays. On the contrary, to see the difficulties under which he worked and over which he triumphed, and to see the toil and thought that went into the creation of his prose lyrics is to see the greatness that was Elia. His steady growth in excellence—his progressive evolution—makes appropriate to him the words of his lifelong friend, Samuel Taylor Coleridge: "You will find this a good gage or criterion of genius—whether it progresses and evolves, or only spins upon itself."[92]

Additional Examples of Positive Alterations in the Essay MSS

I. TO INCREASE PRECISION OF MEANING

A. Changes made immediately

whose affairs had be——	whose affairs were beginning to flourish
	["Poor Relations"]
about to embark for C[*illegible*]	about to embark for Portugal
	["Poor Relations"]
fallen upon a recollection——	fallen upon a recital so eminently painful
	["Poor Relations"]
The houses of the ancient city are——	The houses of the ancient city of Lincoln are
	["Poor Relations"]
she beckoned to her chief attendants . . . to pl——	she beckoned to her chief attendants . . . to come forth from their hiding places, and to plead
	["Defeat of Time"]

In page——	In column 310 ["Remarkable Cor- respondent"]
so you quot——	so you transcribe ["Remarkable Cor- respondent"]
He looked——	He walked blustering—— *changed again to:* He walked burly ["Old Benchers"]
the letter——	the aspirate ["Old Benchers"]
ascending——	walking upon the earth ["Old Benchers"]
hardly common attentions. He was a perfect gentleman, it must be acknowledged, in his shyest moods, a pattern of genteel behaviour. In his youth I have heard that he was reckoned handsome, but his eye lacked lustre, and he wanted——	hardly common attentions. He had a fine face and person, but wanted methought the spirit that should have shewn them off ["Old Benchers"]
a pantomime hoax got up between——	a pantomime hoax got up by the ingenious Mr. Farley ["Barrenness"]
visible to all Babylon—as the countenance of Belshazzar was troubled——	visible to all Babylon—as the knees of Belshazzar were shaken, and his countenance troubled ["Barrenness"]*

---

* Had Lamb added the phrase about the knees, instead of inserting it, the order would have followed the description in *Daniel,* from which he had just quoted.

B. *Changes made later*

We made an excursion together a summer or two ago

We made an excursion together a few summers since
["Mackery End"]

that had married a Bruton

who, by marriage with a Bruton, had become Mistress of the old Mansion
["Mackery End"]

But this *adopted Bruton* was better

But this adopted Bruton in my mind was better
["Mackery End"]

But the name of kindred, and of cousinage

But the name of kindred, and of cousinship
["Mackery End"]

With what corresponding kindnesses we were received —how

With what corresponding kindnesses we were received by them also—how
["Mackery End"]

Children love to listen to stories about their elders, when *they* were young

Children love to listen to stories about their elders when they were children
["Dream-Children"]

a great sulky pike hanging down the water

a great sulky pike hanging midway down the water
["Dream-Children"]

kept up the dignity of the great house while she

kept up the dignity of the great house in a sort while she
["Dream-Children"]

with all the sweet garden smells

with all the fine garden smells
["Dream-Children"]

but of their grandmother Field

but of their greatgrandmother Field
["Dream-Children"]

were seen in the heavenly distance

were seen in the uttermost distance
["Dream-Children"]

The Rev****, the admired

the Revd****, the then admired
["Barrenness"]

objections to our theory

objections to the theory of our Motto
["Barrenness"]

On that side the imagination halts

On that side the imagination of the artist halts
["Barrenness"]

a mob of Courtiers

a mob of Brigton [sic] courtiers
["Barrenness"]

confined to the phantasy of Belshazzar

confined to the fancy of Belshazzar
["Barrenness"]

founded upon an old Prophecy

founded upon an ancient Prophecy
["Defeat of Time"]

demurring whether it shall settle upon this sweet flower or that, set forth

demurring whether it shall settle upon this sweet flower or that, before it settles—set forth
["Defeat of Time"]

Titania, with her moonlight Elves

Titania and her moonlight Elves
["Defeat of Time"]

and the least courageous

and the most courageous
["Defeat of Time"]

she besought the All-Destroyer

she besought the Spectre
["Defeat of Time"]

an ancient Prophecy that the date

an ancient Prophecy, laid up in the records of Fairyland, that the date
["Defeat of Time"]

seems to decline entertainment

seems to despair of entertainment
["Poor Relations"]

he would never be taken

he would be in no danger of being taken
["Poor Relations"]

welcome comparisons

favorable comparisons
["Poor Relations"]

the boys who lived above (however agreeing in a common school)

the boys who lived above (however brought together in a common school)
["Poor Relations"]

where he had long held a comfortable independence

where he had long held, what he accounted, a comfortable independence
["Poor Relations"]

and with two pounds, fourteen shillings

and with five pounds, fourteen shillings
["Poor Relations"]

making the Sovereign

making your Sovereign
["Humble Petition"]

Divide me by twenty four

Divide me into twenty four
["Remarkable Correspondent"]

was a known toast of the Ladies

was a known toast with the Ladies
["Old Benchers"]

in all this

in this, as in all
["Old Benchers"]

He resigned his title almost of respect

He resigned his title almost to respect
        ["Old Benchers"]

as Izaac Walton would have liked to go a fishing with

as Izaac Walton would have chosen to go a fishing with
        ["Old Benchers"]

but generally with one hand or both folded behind

but generally with both hands folded behind
        ["Old Benchers"]

cheeks were colourless even to pallor

cheeks were colourless even to whiteness
        ["Old Benchers"]

resembling that of our great Philanthropist

resembling (but without his sourness) that of our great Philanthropist
        ["Old Benchers"]

from the effects of which he never probably recovered

from the effects of which probably he never thoroughly recovered
        ["Old Benchers"]

became after a [? few furlongs] inaudible

became after a time inaudible
        ["Imperfect Sympathies"]

to this self-watchfulness

to this imposed self-watchfulness
        ["Imperfect Sympathies"]

can be no antipathy

can be no direct antipathy
        ["Imperfect Sympathies"]

I have been hitherto speaking upon the subject of what I would [*illegible word(s)*] *imperfect sympathies.*

I would be understood as confining myself to the subject of *imperfect sympathies.*
        ["Imperfect Sympathies"]

II. TO ADD VIVIDNESS AND INTENSITY

A. *Changes made immediately*

keeps me out of my day——

keeps me out of my dues and privileges
["Humble Petition"]

I am the youngest of the——

I am the youngest of three hundred and sixty-six brethren
["Remarkable Correspondent"]

instead of its——

instead of the Title it now vaunts
["Remarkable Correspondent"]

as their——

as he their poor uncle must have been
["Dream-Children"]

which was no——

which was in no case to be violated
["Poor Relations"]

that he would overlook . . . as no——

that he would overlook . . . as too diminutive
["Defeat of Time"]

who had no existence beyond a dream; and lived but in the fancy of men——

who had no existence beyond a dream; frail objects of a creed; that lived but in the faith of the believer.
["Defeat of Time"]

| And they came forth—— | And one of them came forth ——*changed again to:* And one of those delicate creatures came forth——*changed again to:* And one of those little delicate creatures came forth—— *changed again to:* And one of those small delicate creatures came forth—— ["Defeat of Time"] |

B. Changes made later

acknowledgment of my existence	acknowledgment of my occasional visitation ["Remarkable Correspondent"]
"to poison the sparrows"	"to poison the sparrows by my orders" ["Old Benchers"]
which I have made to rise and fall to the astonishment	which I have made to rise and fall how many times! to the astonishment ["Old Benchers"]
that I find	that I for one find ["Mackery End"]
the whole story was carved out in the wood	the whole story of the Children and their cruel Uncle was to be seen fairly carved out in wood ["Dream-Children"]
for seven years	for seven long years ["Dream-Children"]
I courted the fair Alice—and	I courted the fair Alice W——n; and ["Dream-Children"]

It was in the lane leading	It was in the fine lane leading ["Poor Relations"]
the eye of fashion	the critical eye of fashion ["Barrenness"]
following a strange Beauty	in the pursuit of a strange Beauty ["Defeat of Time"]
the mighty Oberon albeit the stoutest Champion	the mighty Oberon himself, albeit the stoutest Champion ["Defeat of Time"]
This was that Sir Thomas Gresham	This was that famous Sir Thomas Gresham ["Defeat of Time"]
partial illuminations, embryo conceptions	partial illuminations, "dim instincts," embryo conceptions ["Imperfect Sympathies"]
in your presence before he quite knows	in your presence to share it with you before he quite knows ["Imperfect Sympathies"]
a shoulder of mutton but such	a leg of mutton & turnips but such ["Munden the Comedian"]

III. TO ENRICH THE CONNOTATION

A. *Changes made immediately*

A stately Being—let out——	A Captive—a stately Being, let out ["Poor Relations"]
The eye was perfectly di——	The eye was perfectly dazzled ["Barrenness"]
his less Epicurean Brothers——	his less Epicurean brethren ["Old Benchers"]

the child Elia gazed on your predecessors——

the child Elia gazed on the Old Worthies, your predecessors that lived before ye—— *changed to:* the child Elia gazed on the Old Worthies, that solemnized the Parade before ye!

["Old Benchers"]

quaking hare-bell is in our protection——

quaking hare-bell is in our wardship

["Defeat of Time"]

B. *Changes made later*

had now invited him

had now induced him

["Poor Relations"]

slender ties, that are slight

slender ties, that prove slight

["Mackery End"]

a huge transparency was visible in which

a huge transparency was discovered, in which

["Barrenness"]

his new livery

his smart new livery

["Old Benchers"]

in those days but generally

in those days "as now our stout Triumvirs sweep the streets"—but generally

["Old Benchers"]

the same superstitious respect with which

the same superstitious veneration with which

["Old Benchers"]

so deadly a Giant

so huge a Giant

["Defeat of Time"]

the Lark, when he is mounted out of sight; or if ever you have listened with a pleasant ear to the Night Bird

the Lark, as he mounts to Heaven's gate, beyond the ken of mortals; or if ever you have listened with a charmed ear to the Night Bird

["Defeat of Time"]

some age-worn temple, which	some age-worn Edifice, which ["Defeat of Time"]
haunting the forests, till their	haunting the woods, till their ["Defeat of Time"]
as that little skipping animal makes	as that pretty little chirping creature makes ["Defeat of Time"]

IV. TO CONDENSE, VARY, OR CREATE RHYTHM

A. Changes made immediately

the Queen herself, to whom the writing appears to have been related to Belshazzar. It is——	the Queen herself, who merely undertakes for the interpretation of the phenomenon, as related to her doubtless by her Husband ["Barrenness"]

B. Changes made later

all this huddle and vulgar consternation	all this huddle of vulgar consternation ["Barrenness"]
the transparency in the real scene at Brighton. The huddle, the flutter, the bustle, the escape, the vulgar fear [*changed to:* fright], and the mock alarm; the prettinesses heightened by fair [*changed to:* fear]	the transparency in the anecdote. The huddle, the flutter, the bustle, the escape, the alarm, and the mock alarm; the prettinesses heightened by consternation ["Barrenness"]
with much formality and apology	with much formality of apology ["Old Benchers"]
Jackson as he was called	Jackson he was called ["Old Benchers"]

V. TO AVOID REPETITION, WITH
CONCOMITANT IMPROVEMENT

A. Changes made immediately

had been the Guardians of the sacred woods, and of the silver woods——

had been the Guardians of the sacred woods, and of the silver fountains, of the consecrated w—— *changed to:* had been the Guardians of the sacred floods, and of the silver fountains, and of the consecrated hills and woods

["Defeat of Time"]

B. Changes made later

Maiden aunts keep these animals as they do

Maiden aunts keep these creatures, as they do *changed to:* Maiden aunts keep these "small deer" as they do

["In Re Squirrels"]

courtiers, sympathising with the well-acted surprise of their sovereign; all this, and no more, is exhibited by the well-dressed Courtiers in the hall

courtiers, sympathising with the well-acted surprise of their sovereign; all this, and no more, is exhibited by the well-dressed Lords and Ladies in the Hall

["Barrenness"]

Not only the dresses and jewelry, in Mr. M's picture exposed to the eye of fashion, as minutely as the Dresses in a Lady's magazine

Not only the female attire and the jewelry exposed to the critical eye of fashion, as minutely as the Dresses in a Lady's magazine, in Mr. M's picture

["Barrenness"]

NOTES

BIBLIOGRAPHY

INDEX

LIST OF PERIODICAL ABBREVIATIONS

ELH	Journal of English Literary History
HLQ	Huntington Library Quarterly
MLQ	Modern Language Quarterly
N&Q	Notes and Queries
PMLA	Publications of the Modern Language Association of America
SP	Studies in Philology
TLS	London Times Literary Supplement

NOTES

Introduction

1. David Daiches, "Reflections on the Essay," *A Century of the Essay* (New York, 1951), pp. 2, 4.

2. B. I. Evans, "Charles Lamb," *Nineteenth Century,* CXVI (Dec., 1934), 681.

3. C. T. Winchester, "Leigh Hunt," *A Group of English Essayists of the Early Nineteenth Century* (New York, 1910), p. 247.

4. Robert St. John, *From the Land of Silent People* (New York, 1942), p. 248.

5. Odell Shepard, "Emerson's Collected Letters," *The New York Times Book Review,* May 28, 1939.

6. *The Letters of Charles Lamb: To Which Are Added Those of His Sister Mary Lamb* (hereafter referred to as *Letters*), ed. E. V. Lucas, 3 vols. (London, 1935). Whenever possible, the quotations from the letters have been collated with the originals in order to avoid the frequent inaccuracies of this edition; see George L. Barnett, "A Critical Analysis of the Lucas Edition of Lamb's Letters," *MLQ,* IX (Sept., 1948), 303–14 and "Corrections in the Text of Lamb's Letters," *HLQ,* XVIII (Feb., 1955), 147–58.

Chapter I

1. Walter Pater, "Charles Lamb," *Appreciations* (New York, 1911), p. 117.

2. *Letters,* III, 286; II, 64.

3. Ibid., III, 258.

4. Ibid., I, 303 note.

5. Ibid., p. 176.

6. Jan. 27, 1835. Quoted in *The Letters of Charles Lamb,* ed. H. H. Harper (Boston, 1905), I, 66.

7. Algernon Black, "Charles Lamb," *Macmillan's Magazine,* XXXIX (Mar., 1879), 431.

8. This is the last part of a sonnet by Edward Hovell-Thurlow, second Baron Thurlow (1781–1829), entitled "To a Bird, that Haunted the Waters of Lacken, in Winter." Lamb copied it in his "Holcroft" album as well as in the one he compiled for Emma Isola, his adopted daughter. De Quincey described in his *Recollections* how Lamb used to read it aloud. In a letter of December 5, 1828, to Bernard Barton, Lamb asked, "know you Lord Thurlow's sonnet to a Bird of that sort on Lacken water? If not, 'tis indispensable I send it you . . . ." And a footnote to "Some Sonnets of Sir Philip Sidney" (1823), omitted from the collected edition, read: "A profusion of verbal dainties, with a disproportionate lack of matter and circumstance, is I think one reason of the coldness with which the public has received the poetry of a nobleman now living; which, upon the score of exquisite diction alone, is entitled to something better than neglect. I will venture to copy one of his Sonnets in this place, which for quiet sweetness, and unaffected morality, has scarcely its parallel in our language." See also his letter of April 7, 1815, to Wordsworth.

9. George Gilfillan, *Sketches of Modern Literature and Eminent Literary Men (Being a Gallery of Literary Portraits)* (New York, 1846), I, 383.

10. Printed in *The Works of Charles and Mary Lamb,* ed. E. V. Lucas (London & New York, 1903–5), II, 354 (hereafter cited as *Works*), where Lucas states that the manuscript is in the Dyce and Forster Collection at South Kensington; however, Arthur Wheen, former Keeper of the Library of the Victoria and Albert Museum at South Kensington, London, informed me by letter that "we have no record that the MS. of Lamb's essay 'Witches, and Other Night-Fears' was ever in this Library" (Oct. 3, 1955).

11. *Letters,* I, 40.

12. See ibid., pp. 21, 61, 72.

13. See ibid., pp. 54 f., 66, 106, 132; III, 152.

14. See ibid., I, 55.

15. Ibid., p. 58.

16. Ibid., III, 62.

17. Ibid., I, 405.

18. Ibid., II, 77.

19. Ibid., p. 148.

20. Ibid., p. 332.

21. Ibid., p. 436.

22. *The Indicator*, Jan. 31, 1821.

23. *Letters*, II, 449 note.

24. Ibid., III, 339.

25. This item is reproduced by permission of the Henry W. and Albert A. Berg Collection of the New York Public Library. Classified there as a letter, it should follow No. 925 in the Lucas edition. For a letter and references to Harriet Isola, see *Letters*, III, 172, 181, 286, 388.

26. *Letters*, I, 266.

27. Ibid., p. 271.

28. Ibid., p. [432].

29. Ibid., p. 268. Lamb's comment is made in reference to his suggestions for Godwin's play "Faulkener."

30. Ibid., p. 120.

31. "Charles Lamb and Some of His Contemporaries," *Quarterly Review*, Jan., 1867, and *Miscellaneous Prose Works* (London, 1868), I, 119.

32. *Letters*, II, 74; I have followed the punctuation of the original letter here, which Lucas modernizes.

33. Ibid., III, 105.

34. Ibid., p. 110; see also his letter to Barton of Aug. 10, 1827 (ibid., p. 117).

35. This item is reproduced by permission of the British Museum. Its existence was pointed out by Newman I. White (*TLS*, Sept. 10, 1938, p. 584), who erred in stating that it has been in the Museum since 1866, that it follows page 264 of Vol. X, and that it was written to "a friend of the actor John Kemble . . . ." It was acquired by the Museum in 1861; it follows page 262 of Vol. X; and it was written to a friend of Charles Kemble, not his brother John, who had died in 1823.

36. *Letters*, III, 121, where he refers to Jameson as "a particular friend of mine and Coleridge."

37. Ibid., p. 124, where Lucas omits the second sentence; it was printed in the seventeenth catalogue of the Bodley Book Shop (New York, 1937), Item 233 (see N&Q, CLXXIV [Jan. 8, 1938], 28).

38. Ibid., p. 131. In "Barbara S——" (Apr., 1825) Lamb had written: "I have chatted with ever good-humoured Mrs. Charles Kemble. I have conversed as friend to friend with her accomplished husband."

39. Hood's *Whims and Oddities* was published in two series in 1826–27, and the Lambs were lodging with Mrs. Leishman in August, 1827, before taking a house. Although the day of the month appears to be "20" (it is so read by White), it is ambiguous and could be "27," which also fell on Monday in 1827; evidence for the latter reading is Lamb's letter of August 28, to Barton (III, 122), which includes the sentence: "Yesterday I sent off my tragi comedy to Mr. Kemble."

40. *Letters*, I, 362–63.

41. *The Letters of Thomas Manning to Charles Lamb*, ed. G. A. Anderson (New York, 1926), p. 74.

42. *Letters*, I, 85.

43. W. F. Bryan and R. S. Crane, *The English Familiar Essay* (New York, 1916), Introduction, pp. xxxvii–xxxviii.

44. See M. R. Watson, "The *Spectator* Tradition and the Development of the Familiar Essay," *ELH*, XIII (1946), 189–215, for a more thorough analysis of Boswell as an essayist. The same author's *Magazine Serials and the Essay Tradition, 1746–1820* (Baton Rouge, 1956) may also be profitably consulted.

45. "Notes of an Interview with the Late Charles Lamb," signed "T. W.," *Eliza Cook's Journal*, III (May 18, 1850), 36.

46. *The Monthly Review*, XXII (Jan., 1760), 38.

47. *Letters*, II, 432.

48. October 18, 1819; quoted from a typed copy at Harvard University by Stuart M. Tave in a review of Josephine Bauer's *The London Magazine*, *MP*, LII (Nov., 1954), 139–41.

49. Quoted by L. A. Brewer, *My Leigh Hunt Library: The Holograph Letters* (Iowa City, Iowa, 1938), p. 155.

50. *Hydriotaphia* was reviewed in Art. VII of Vol. I, part 1, pp. 83 ff. (1820); a MS volume of Browne's letters to his son was treated in Art. X of Vol. I, part 1, pp. 1 ff. of the same year.

51. W. J. Graham, *English Literary Periodicals* (New York, 1930), p. 286.

52. C. T. Winchester, "Leigh Hunt," *A Group of English Essayists of the Early Nineteenth Century* (New York, 1910), p. 246.

53. W. J. Graham states (op. cit., p. 51) that the "monthly numbers of the *Spy* [1698–1700] are full of well-drawn sketches of London life."

54. Those entitled "Edax on Appetite," "On the Inconveniences Resulting From Being Hanged," "Hospita on the Immoderate Indulgence of the Pleasures of the Palate," "On Burial Societies and the Character of an Undertaker," "A Bachelor's Complaint of the Behaviour of Married People," "On the Danger of Confounding Moral with Personal Deformity," "On the Ambiguities Arising from Proper Names," and "On the Custom of Hissing at Theatres."

55. Now in the permanent custody of the Berg Collection of the N.Y. Public Library. For further analysis of this review and a discussion explaining why it was not published, see George L. Barnett, "An Unpublished Review by Charles Lamb," *MLQ*, XVII (Dec., 1956), 352–56.

56. *Letters*, II, 300.

57. Ibid., I, 43–44.

58. Jules Derocquigny, *Charles Lamb: sa vie et ses œuvres* (Lille, 1904), p. 394.

Chapter II

1. A. D. McKillop, "Charles Lamb Sees London," *Rice Institute Pamphlet*, XXII (Apr., 1935), 124.

2. B. I. Evans, "Charles Lamb," *Nineteenth Century*, CXVI (Dec., 1934), 681.

3. H. A. Roberts, *The Records of the Amicable Society of Blues* (quoted in *TLS*, July 3, 1924, p. 417).

4. *Letters*, I, 293.

5. Ibid., p. 303 note.

6. Ibid., p. 211.

7. Ibid., II, 405–6.

8. B. W. Procter, *An Autobiographical Fragment and Biographical Notes* (Boston, 1877), pp. 79–80.

9. "Recollections of Charles Lamb," *The Athenaeum* (Jan. 24, 1835), p. 72.

10. Ibid.

11. *Letters*, II, 373.

12. Ibid., p. 97 (undated by Lucas but postmarked Mar. 30, 1810; the original is in the Henry W. and Albert A. Berg Collection of the New York Public Library).

13. Ibid., p. 218.

14. *Charles Lamb: His Life Recorded by His Contemporaries* (London, 1934), p. 114, note 1.

15. *Letters*, II, 226.

16. *Works*, II, 337.

17. *The Novello-Cowden Clarke Collection* (The Brotherton Library of the University of Leeds [Leeds, 1955]), p. 7.

18. *Clara Novello's Reminiscences Compiled by her daughter Contessa Valeria Gigliucci with a Memoir by Arthur D. Coleridge* (London, 1910), p. 33.

19. *Letters*, II, 374.

20. Ibid., pp. 74–75; I have followed the punctuation and wording of the original letter here, which Lucas alters.

21. Ibid., p. 392.

22. Ibid., I, 178.

23. Ibid., pp. 31, 257.

24. Ibid., p. 118.

25. Bryan W. Procter, *Charles Lamb: A Memoir* (London, 1866), p. 18.

26. Op. cit., p. 122.

27. *Letters*, II, 373.

28. These items are reproduced by permission from the originals in The Henry E. Huntington Library, San Marino, California. Since the content of the first letter is almost identical with that of Lucas' No. 377 (II, 293), which is printed as "undated," we may conjecture that the date for the letter is the same.

29. Op. cit., pp. 141–43.

30. Ibid., pp. 146–47.

31. Benjamin R. Haydon, *Correspondence and Table-Talk* (London, 1876), II, 339.

32. This item is reproduced by permission of the Trustees of the Pierpont Morgan Library. It was taken from the album of Fanny Burney (Mme. D'Arblay), the novelist, who was the aunt of John Payne's wife. Fanny Burney later helped to support her nephew, Payne's brother-in-law Martin, who was one of Lamb's closest friends.

33. George Ticknor, *Life and Letters* (Boston, 1876), I, 294.

34. *Thomas Hood and Charles Lamb,* ed. Walter Jerrold (Lon-

don, 1930), pp. 113–14. Clare's own account of Lamb, probably
based on a visit to Colebrook July 6, 1824, is less than enthusiastic;
he describes Lamb's fondness for snuff and labels his talk repetitious
(*Sketches in the Life of John Clare*, ed. Edmund Blunden [London,
1931], pp. 112–13).

35. Procter, *Charles Lamb: A Memoir*, p. 11.

36. Thomas Powell, *The Living Authors of England* (New York,
1849), pp. 238–39.

37. *Charles Lamb: A Memoir*, pp. 143–44.

38. P. G. Patmore, "Charles Lamb," *My Friends and Acquaintance* (London, 1854) I, 91–92.

39. S. Y. [Sally: Sarah Flower Adams], "An Evening with Charles
Lamb and Coleridge," *The Monthly Repository*, n.s. IX (1835),
162–68.

40. Ibid.

41. *Memoirs, Journal, and Correspondence of Thomas Moore*, ed.
John Russell (Boston, 1853), VI, 85 (Diary for Oct. 5, 1829).

42. "Recollections of Charles Lamb," *The Collected Writings of
Thomas De Quincey*, ed. David Masson (Edinburgh, 1889–97), III,
81. Comments on Lamb's conversation are to be found in the following places: Hazlitt, "Elia and Geoffrey Crayon," *The Spirit of the
Age* (1825); Procter, *Charles Lamb: A Memoir*, pp. 16, 142; Patmore,
op. cit., pp. 21–24; Mrs. Mary Balmanno, "Lamb and Hood," *Pen
and Pencil* (New York, 1858) pp. 136–37; and the Rev. J. F. Russell
in *The Guardian*, May 6, 1874.

43. *Unpublished Letters of Samuel Taylor Coleridge*, ed. Earl
Leslie Griggs (New Haven, 1933), II, 190; on December 21 of the
same year, Crabb Robinson wrote of Coleridge: "He denies Hazlitt,
however, originality, and ascribes to Lamb the best ideas in Hazlitt's
article" (*Henry Crabb Robinson on Books and Their Writers*, ed.
Edith J. Morley [London, 1938], I, 200).

44. W. P. Albrecht comes to the same conclusion when noting that
Hazlitt's observation in "On Wit and Humour" "seems to be the idea
that Lamb, perhaps two years later, developed in his essay 'On the
Artificial Comedy of the Last Century.'" "Hazlitt's Preference for
Tragedy," *PMLA*, LXXI (Dec., 1956), 1047, note 26.

45. P. P. Howe, *The Life of William Hazlitt* (London, 1947),
p. 280, where the phrase "the first days of 1821" is used to introduce
the letter, which bears no date. The date—April 12, 1820—given by
W. C. Hazlitt in *Four Generations of a Literary Family* is obviously

wrong, as E. V. Lucas supposed (*Works*, II, 330); Hazlitt's phrase "young master" is from Lamb's essay.

46. *The Letters of Charles Lamb, with a Sketch of His Life*, ed. Thomas Noon Talfourd (London, 1849), p. 207.

47. *Thomas Hood and Charles Lamb*, ed. Walter Jerrold, p. 127.

48. *Henry Crabb Robinson on Books and Their Writers*, I, 364.

49. Ibid., p. 301.

50. [?John Mitford], "The Letters of Charles Lamb," *The Gentleman's Magazine*, n.s. IX (May, 1838), 464.

51. "Notes of an Interview with the Late Charles Lamb," signed "T. W.," *Eliza Cook's Journal*, III (May 18, 1850), 36.

52. *Letters*, I, 132.

53. Blunden made this suggestion in *Charles Lamb: His Life Recorded by His Contemporaries*, p. 146 note.

54. *The Genesis of Shakespeare Idolatry, 1766–1799* (Chapel Hill, N. C., 1931), p. 231.

55. Text of 1818, when the notes were reprinted as "Characters of Dramatic Writers, Contemporary with Shakespeare" in Lamb's *Works*.

56. *Letters*, III, 32.

57. Ibid., II, 299.

58. Ibid., p. 385.

59. Ibid., p. 462.

Chapter III

1. See *Letters*, II, 376, 379, 418, 460.

2. Ibid., p. 440.

3. Ibid., III, 21.

4. Ibid., p. 259.

5. Ibid., p. 37.

6. His letter of October 24, 1831, refers to a letter from Moxon, "which, rarely as I keep letters, shall be preserved." Moxon's letter of January 27, 1835 (quoted in *The Letters of Charles Lamb*, ed. H. H. Harper, I, 65), comments: "nor did he ever preserve, with two exceptions, a single letter." This statement is in error, for we know he kept Manning's letters, and in a letter to John Bates Didbin, of September 5, 1827, he threatened to "rummage out some of your old pleasant letters." His letters of December 10, 1796, and June 13, 1797, to Coleridge prove that he preserved Coleridge's letters like

treasures, which on one occasion he lent to Manning (*Letters*, I, 235). Yet after Coleridge's death in 1834 he replied to requests for the loan of Coleridge's letters by saying that he had none (*Letters*, III, 416, 417–18).

7. *Letters*, III, 37.

8. Dorothy Odell treated the more obvious similarities in "The Relation of the Letters of Charles Lamb to the Essays of Elia" (unpublished master's thesis, University of Chicago, 1929).

9. See George L. Barnett, "Dating Lamb's Contributions to the *Table Book*," *PMLA*, LX (June, 1945), 602–5.

10. The three-volume work was published in November, 1829, with the date "1830."

11. *Letters*, III, 233.

12. *Memoirs, Journal, and Correspondence of Thomas Moore*, ed. John Russell (Boston, 1853), IV, 51.

13. *Letters*, I, 420–21.

14. Ibid., II, 450–51.

15. Ibid., p. 447.

16. Ibid., pp. 288–89.

17. The letter to Dodwell and Chambers was sold at Sotheby & Co., London, on July 16, 1957, to Mr. Robert H. Taylor of Yonkers, New York, for £460. It is described and a portion of the text transcribed in their sale catalogue for July 15 and 16, 1957, where this item is No. 500. It is discussed by C. R. Woodring, "Lamb Takes a Holiday," *Harvard Library Bulletin*, XIV (spring, 1960), 258–59.

18. *Letters*, I, 241.

19. Ibid., p. 245.

20. Ibid., pp. 223–24, 251.

21. Ibid., pp. 385–86.

22. Ibid., II, 317–18.

23. Ibid., p. 90.

24. Ibid., I, 367; the wording in the Lucas edition differs slightly from the original, which is here followed.

25. See Mary and Charles Lamb to Sarah Stoddart, *Letters*, I, 373; Lamb to Robert Lloyd, ibid., p. 365; Lamb to Manning, ibid., II, 25–26, 182.

26. *The Letters of Thomas Manning to Charles Lamb*, pp. 100–101. Manning remained at Canton until 1810; in December, 1811, he became the first Englishman to visit Lhasa, Tibet.

27. *Letters*, II, 184.

28. Ibid., pp. 209–10.

29. Ibid., p. 467.

30. Ibid., III, 4.

31. Ibid., II, 356.

32. Ibid., III, 1.

33. The relationship of these letters to the essay is discussed by George Williamson, "The Equation of the Essay," *Sewanee Review,* XXXV (1927), 73–77.

34. *Letters,* II, 332.

35. Ibid., p. 432.

36. Ibid., p. 419; dated March 5, 1824, by Mrs. G. A. Anderson, "On the Dating of Lamb's Letters," *London Mercury,* XVIII (Aug., 1928), 391–94.

37. *Letters,* II, 275, where Lucas dates it May 16, 1820; however, examination of the original, now at the Folger Shakespeare Library, reveals that this date is pencilled in by an unknown hand. It is undated by Lamb, and the postmark, "MY 16," does not contain the year. J. P. Collier printed it under the date "May 16, 1821" in *An Old Man's Diary* (London, 1871), IV, Dec. 9, 1833.

38. *Letters,* I, 161.

39. Ibid., II, 246.

40. Ibid., p. 75; I have followed the original punctuation, which Lucas alters, with a consequent change in meaning.

41. Ibid., p. 187.

42. Ibid., pp. 284–85.

43. Ibid., III, 264.

44. Ibid., II, 126–27.

45. Ibid., I, 259.

46. Ibid., III, 97–98.

47. It was printed in part in Moxon's *Reflector* at the end of 1832, when that periodical ceased. Printed in *The Last Essays of Elia* as "Barrenness of the Imaginative Faculty in the Production of Modern Art."

48. *Letters,* III, 22–23.

49. Ibid., II, 395.

50. An analysis of the manuscript revisions in this essay was made by J. Milton French, "A Chip from Elia's Workshop," *SP,* XXXVII (Jan., 1940), 88–99.

51. *Letters,* II, 212.

52. Ibid., p. 218.

53. Ibid., pp. 74, 88.

54. Ibid., p. 68 (erroneously dated by Lucas "29th March, 1809").

55. Ibid., p. 196.

56. Ibid., p. 133.

57. Ibid., p. 167.

58. Ibid., p. 84.

59. Ibid., I, 376.

60. Ibid., II, 428, where Lucas dates it "P.M. 26th June 1824"; however, while the Manuscript Division of the N.Y. Public Library owns a portion of a letter with this postmark, it contains only the address: "Mesr Taylor & Hessey, Booksellers, Fleetstreet. Mr. Hessey" and does not fit a separate piece of paper, also in the N.Y. Public Library, containing the text substantially as printed by Lucas (there is a difference in the chain lines of the papers amounting to close to four centimeters). The original text contains the word "Tuesd."; Tuesday fell on the twenty-second of June in 1824, not the "26th." There is no evidence for a pencilled note on the reverse of the original letter, "Mar. 29, 25." We have here two pieces of different letters, and the dating of the one printed by Lucas (II, 428) must depend upon further evidence than the postmark on the address portion of the other letter.

61. Ibid., I, 376–77.

62. Ibid., II, 26.

63. Ibid., I, 334.

64. Ibid., p. 205.

65. Reported by Mary Shelley in a letter of September 9, 1823, to Hunt. *Letters of Mary W. Shelley,* ed. H. H. Harper (Boston, 1918), pp. 126–27.

66. Letters, II, 48.

67. The text and a discussion of this manuscript letter, now in the Manuscript Division of the N.Y. Public Library, were given by George L. Barnett, "Charles Lamb to John Britton: An Unpublished Letter," *MLQ,* XIII (Dec., 1952) 353–55.

68. Letters, II, 170.

69. Ibid., I, 177.

70. *Memoirs,* VI, 249–50.

71. *Letters,* I, 73.

72. Ibid., II, 49.

73. Ibid., p. 159.

74. Ibid., p. 155.

75. Ibid., p. 315.
76. Ibid., I, 129.
77. Ibid., II, 148.
78. Ibid., III, 121, 144, 200–201.
79. Ibid., I, 94.
80. Ibid., II, 460; I, 330–31; II, 179.
81. Ibid., I, 101.
82. Ibid., II, 91.
83. Ibid., III, 141.
84. *Works*, I, 533.
85. *Letters*, II, 191.
86. *Works*, II, 459.
87. *Letters*, II, 392–93, 434; III, 49–50.
88. *Works*, I, 441.
89. Josephine Bauer, *The London Magazine 1820–29* (Copenhagen, 1953), p. 156.
90. *Works*, I, 445.
91. Ibid., p. 405.
92. *Letters*, II, 224–26; I, 316–17; II, 7–8.

Chapter IV

1. "Recollections of Charles Lamb," *Collected Writings*, III, 39.
2. The Rev. J. H. Twichell, "Concerning Charles Lamb," *Scribner's Magazine*, XI (Mar., 1876), 725.
3. R. H. Mottram, *Traders' Dream, the Romance of the East India Company* (New York & London, 1939), p. 291.
4. William Foster, *The East India House: Its History and Associations* (London, 1924), p. 182.
5. *Letters*, II, 170.
6. Ibid., p. 191.
7. Ibid., p. 319.
8. Op. cit., p. 235.
9. Ibid., p. 176.
10. Ibid., p. 210, where Strachey's *Recollections of T. L. Peacock* is quoted.
11. Ibid., p. 235.
12. Algernon Black, "Charles Lamb," *Macmillan's Magazine*, XXXIX (Mar., 1879), 431–32.
13. This manuscript was sold by Sotheby and Co., London, on

July 16, 1957, for £340. It is now owned by Harvard University. It is described and a portion of the text transcribed in the Sotheby sale catalogue for July 15 and 16, 1957, where it is item No. 501. The text is printed by C. R. Woodring, "Lamb Takes a Holiday," *Harvard Library Bulletin*, XIV (spring, 1960), 260–62.

14. The cross, in the first line, as Woodring suggests in "Lamb Takes a Holiday" (p. 255), "may even be one of his cheerful blasphemies, designating himself by a symbol for the Lamb of God (compare *Letters*, II, 90)." In any case, the pun on the "remaining vowels," "U" and "I," seems to have been anticipated by the designation of himself with the cross. The letter is now in the Henry W. and Albert A. Berg Collection of the New York Public Library.

15. *Letters*, II, 230.

16. Ibid., p. 352.

17. Ibid., p. 191.

18. Ibid., p. 231.

19. Foster, *The East India House*, p. 214.

20. *Letters*, I, 93–94.

21. Beckles Willson, *Ledger and Sword* (London, New York, & Bombay, 1903), II, 432.

22. "Charles Lamb," *Collected Writings*, V, 226–27.

23. *Letters*, II, 363–64.

24. Ibid., p. 393.

25. Ibid., p. 338.

26. Ibid., p. 352.

27. Ibid., I, 94.

28. Ibid., p. 313.

29. John R. Barker, "Some Early Correspondence of Sarah Stoddart and the Lambs," *HLQ*, XXIV (Nov., 1960), 65.

30. Ibid., p. 66.

31. *Letters*, II, 213–16; Lucas gives October [1817] as a partially conjectural date, but the original, now in the Berg Collection of the N.Y. Public Library, is clearly dated 1816 by Lamb and bears the postmark [18]16.

32. Ibid., I, 291.

33. The Whatman-Balston paper made for the East India Company bears the latter's device in the watermark. The basis of the statement that certain essays were written on India House paper is, in most cases, examination of the original MSS and, in the others, examination of photostats and facsimiles, supported by the state-

ments of J. Milton French in the case of "Grace before Meat," in "A Chip from Elia's Workshop," *SP*, XXXVII (Jan., 1940), 88–99, and of A. Edward Newton in the case of "Dream-Children," *End Papers* (Boston, 1933), p. 9. A year after his retirement Lamb seems still to have a source of India House paper: "You may know my letters by the paper and the folding. For the former, I live on scraps obtained in charity from an old friend whose stationery is a permanent perquisite . . . . I surprise most of my friends by writing to them on ruled paper, as if I had not got past pothooks and hangers. All the time I was at the E. I. H. I never mended a pen; I now cut 'em to the stumps, marring rather than mending the primitive quill. I cannot bear to pay for articles I used to get for nothing" (*Letters*, III, 37).

34. *Letters*, I, 293.
35. Ibid., p. 362.
36. Ibid., p. 379.
37. Ibid., II, 306.
38. Ibid., p. 320.
39. Ibid., pp. 373–74.
40. Ibid., p. 385.
41. Ibid., p. 415.
42. Ibid., p. 426.
43. Ibid., p. 437.
44. Ibid., p. 449.
45. Ibid., p. 323 (the wording in the Lucas edition differs considerably from the original, which is here followed).
46. Ibid., p. 456.
47. Ibid., III, 19.
48. Ibid., p. 47.
49. Ibid., p. 57.
50. Ibid., p. 325.
51. *Charles Lamb: A Memoir*, p. 128.
52. *Letters*, II, 10. Another letter by Mary to Sarah Stoddart (July 21, 1802), recently discovered, likewise confirms Lamb's protest, previously quoted, to Godwin that he "sometimes cannot put the thoughts of a common letter into sane prose": "Charles received a letter from your brother the same day I did yours, and like me neglected to answer it 'till yesterday, when after writing and burning a dozen sheets of paper (which perhaps you do not know is his usual habit) he sent your brother a little short nothing-at-all-about letter of six lines . . . ." John R. Barker, "Some Early Correspondence of

Sarah Stoddart and the Lambs," *HLQ, XXIV* (Nov., 1960), 65-66.

53. *Letters,* I, 424.

54. Ibid., II, 141.

Chapter V

1. The letter is one to Coleridge, postmarked September 27, 1796 (*Letters,* I, 39) sold by Parke-Bernet, October 18-19, 1955 (see *TLS,* Dec. 23, 1955). The manuscript essay was purchased by the Pierpont Morgan Library; it came from the Furness Collection (sales catalogue of Jan. 16, 1930) and was sold through Rosenbach. At Sotheby & Co., on October 27, 1959, the manuscripts of "My First Play," "The Praise of Chimney-Sweepers," and Part I of "Barrenness of the Imaginative Faculty . . ." sold for £1300, £1900, and £1700 respectively.

2. William Macdonald, *The Works of Charles Lamb* (New York & London, 1903-4).

3. "Charles Lamb at His Desk," *The Gentleman's Magazine,* n.s. VI (Feb., 1871), 287.

4. *Letters,* I, 314.

5. Ibid., pp. 205-6; this letter is in The Henry E. Huntington Library.

6. J. Milton French, "A Chip from Elia's Workshop."

7. The titles of these essays, together with the date and place of publication and the location of the manuscript, follow:

"A Quaker's Meeting"—*The London Magazine,* April, 1821—the Victoria and Albert Museum (fragment only).

"Mackery End in Hertfordshire"—*The London Magazine,* July, 1821— V. & A. Museum.

"Imperfect Sympathies" (postmarked July 18)—*The London Magazine,* Aug., 1821—The Carl H. Pforzheimer Library.

"The Old Benchers of the Inner Temple"—*The London Magazine,* Sept., 1821—the Henry W. and Albert A. Berg Collection, New York Public Library.

"Grace before Meat" (postmarked Oct. 1, 1821)—*The London Magazine,* Nov., 1821—Harvard University Library.

"A Dissertation upon Roast Pig"—*The London Magazine,* Sept., 1822 —the Pierpont Morgan Library.

"Poor Relations"—*The London Magazine,* May, 1823—V. & A. Museum.

"The Child Angel"—*The London Magazine,* June, 1823—V. & A. Museum.

"Letter to an Old Gentleman Whose Education Has Been Neglected" —*The London Magazine,* Jan., 1825—Harvard Univ. Library.

"Remarkable Correspondent" (postmarked May 2, 1825), signed "The Twenty Ninth of February"—*The Every-Day Book,* May 1, 1825—the University of Texas.

"Dog Days" (postmarked July 16, 1825)—*The Every-Day Book,* July 14, 1825—The Henry E. Huntington Library.

"The Humble Petition of an Unfortunate Day" (postmarked Aug. 22, 1825)—*The Every-Day Book,* Aug. 12, 1825—The Henry E. Huntington Library.

"In Re Squirrels" (postmarked Oct. 24, 1825)—*The Every-Day Book,* Oct. 17, 1825—The Henry E. Huntington Library.

"That Verbal Allusions are Not Wit . . ."—*The New Monthly Magazine,* Jan., 1826—Berg Collection, N.Y. Public Library.

"That the Poor Copy the Vices of the Rich"—*The New Monthly Magazine,* Jan., 1826—The Henry E. Huntington Library.

"That the Worst Puns Are the Best"—*The New Monthly Magazine,* Jan., 1826—Berg Collection, N.Y. Public Library.

"An Appearance of the Season"—*The Every-Day Book,* Jan. 28, 1826 —The Henry E. Huntington Library.

"The Months"—*The Every-Day Book,* April 16, 1826—the Scribner Lamb Collection, Princeton University Library.

"Maid Marion" (postmarked June 27, 1827)—*The Table Book,* July 7, 1827—The Henry E. Huntington Library.

"Mrs. Gilpin's Riding to Edmonton" (postmarked July 17, 1827)— *The Table Book,* July 21, 1827—The Henry E. Huntington Library.

"The Defeat of Time"—*The Table Book,* Sept. 15, 1827—The Henry E. Huntington Library.

"Munden the Comedian" (postmarked Feb. 9, 1832)—*The Athenaeum,* Feb. 11, 1832—Berg Collection, N.Y. Public Library.

"Barrenness of the Imaginative Faculty in the Productions of Modern Art" (Part 2 of four installments, collected in *Last Essays of Elia* under this title; printed in *Athenaeum* as "On the Total Defect of the Quality of Imagination Observable in the Works of Modern British Artists")— *The Athenaeum,* Jan. 19, 1833—V. & A. Museum.

In addition to the manuscripts listed above, that of "Dream-Children" (*The London Magazine,* Jan., 1822) is described and facsimiled in the A. E. Newton sale catalogue, Part II (May 15, 1941), pp. 187–89. The sale catalogue of Sotheby & Co. for October 26 and 27, 1959, describes partially the following manuscript essays:

"My First Play"—*The London Magazine,* Dec., 1821.

"The Praise of Chimney-Sweepers"—*The London Magazine*, May, 1822.

"Barrenness of the Imaginative Faculty in the Productions of Modern Art" (Part 1 of four installments)—*The Athenaeum*, Jan. 12, 1833.

"The Tombs in the Abbey" (first paragraph only, revised from the antepenultimate paragraph of "Letter of Elia to Robert Southey, Esquire" —*The London Magazine*, Oct., 1823)—*The Last Essays of Elia*.

"That Handsome Is That Handsome Does" (second and final page only)—*The New Monthly Magazine*, March, 1826.

"That Home is Home Though It Is Never So Homely" (first page only)— *The New Monthly Magazine*, March, 1826.

8. For another example of lengthy copying, see George L. Barnett, "First American Review of Charles Lamb," *PMLA*, LXI (June, 1946), 597–600.

9. John M. Turnbull, "An Elian Make-Weight," *N&Q*, CXCIV (Jan. 22, 1949), 35–36, demonstrated that this fragment was a substitute for perhaps a whole page of the original draft.

10. "Holding the original against a strong light, one may see that the first title was not 'Dream-Children' but 'My Children.' Then Lamb, with unerring taste, realized that a bachelor should only have 'Dream-Children,' and changed the title of his essay accordingly." A. Edward Newton, *End Papers*, pp. 9–10. Another instance of title revision is evident on the verso of the MS of the first paragraph of "The Tombs in the Abbey; in a Letter to R—— S——, Esq.," where the cancelled first draft reads "Westminster Abbey. From a Letter to Robert Southey, Esq." See Bernard Quaritch sales catalogue No. 807 (1960), p. 28.

11. *Letters*, III, 37; see also ibid., p. 21.

12. *The Life, Letters, and Writings of Charles Lamb* (London, 1875), VI, 246.

13. W. C. Hazlitt, *Mary and Charles Lamb: Poems, Letters, and Remains* . . . (London, 1874), pp. 266–67.

14. This item (HM13297) is reproduced by permission of The Henry E. Huntington Library, San Marino, California.

15. *Letters*, II, 375.

16. This item is reproduced by permission of the Widener Collection, Harvard Univ. Library. The text and a facsimile reproduction were included by Carl R. Woodring in "Charles Lamb in the Harvard Library," *Harvard Library Bulletin*, X (spring and autumn, 1956), 208–39, 367–401.

17. J. Milton French in his analysis of "Grace before Meat" (op. cit., p. 96) called attention to the "subtle distinction, which he followed through this draft, between 'grace' and 'Grace,' denoting respectively the condition of soul and the ceremony, but which was discarded (by the publishers?) in the printed version . . . ."

18. *Letters,* III, 132.

19. Op. cit., p. 91.

20. Words printed in pointed brackets, as here, were later insertions.

21. "Mrs. Coe did not remember anything about Mr. Lamb's taste in food, except that he was fond of turnips." E. V. Lucas, *Life,* p. 573.

22. *Letters,* III, 36.

23. Ibid., II, 149.

24. G. A. Bonnard, "Lamb's 'Samuel Salt' and Mrs. Milman's 'Mr. St——te,' " *Review of English Studies,* XIII (Jan., 1937), 80–84.

25. Sotheby & Co. sales catalogue for October 26 and 27, 1959, p. 82.

26. For an explanation of the apparent discrepancy between the statement concerning the revision of this title and that concerning the similar title "On the Total Defect of the faculty . . ." (*supra*), see Lucas' notes, *Works,* II, 439, 446.

27. *Letters,* I, 132, where it is given the conjectural date "[29th October 1798]."

Chapter VI

1. *A History of the Royal Foundation of Christ's Hospital* (London, 1834), pp. 182–83. The Rev. Arthur William Trollope became Head Master with the death of the Rev. James Boyer in 1814 and held the position until 1826.

2. E. H. Pearce, *Annals of Christ's Hospital* (London, 1908), p. 96.

3. "The Classical Culture of Charles Lamb," *The Classical Weekly,* XVIII (Oct. 6, 1924), 1–3.

4. *Letters,* II, 77.

5. Ibid., p. 121.

6. Ibid., I, 187.

7. Ibid., p. 314.

8. Ibid., pp. 185, 192; II, 159–60, 216; III, 86, 110, 122.

9. Ibid., II, 151.

10. *Biographia Literaria*, Ch. I.

11. *Letters*, I, 55–56.

12. *A General Introduction to Charles Lamb together with a Special Study of His Relation to Robert Burton* (Leipzig, 1903), p. 47.

13. J. S. Iseman, *A Perfect Sympathy: Charles Lamb and Sir Thomas Browne* (Cambridge, Mass., 1937), pp. 42, 45.

14. *Anatomy of Melancholy*, Part 2, Sect. 2, Memb. 6, Subsection 2 (p. 243 of the 1624 edition).

15. *Letters*, II, 413.

16. "Charles Lamb," *Collected Writings*, V, 217.

17. A. C. Ward, *The Frolic and the Gentle* (London, 1934), pp. 191–92.

18. *Letters*, II, 447.

19. Ibid., III, 84.

20. Ibid., p. 37.

21. Ibid., II, 219.

22. Ibid., p. 305. See also the cancelled comment on his epistolary style, previously noted, in a letter to Coleridge (ibid., I, 205).

23. Ibid., II, 317–18.

24. Hazlitt, "On Persons One Would Wish to Have Seen."

25. "Sanity of True Genius," *Works*, II, 187–89.

26. Charles I. Patterson's statement that Lamb "went on to praise Sir Walter Scott for vanquishing these 'innutritious phantoms' and giving readers something more substantial" is based only on the reference to "a happier genius" in the passage just quoted ("Charles Lamb's Insight into the Nature of the Novel," *PMLA*, LXVII [June, 1952], 377).

27. Patterson examines Lamb's criticism of fiction and concludes that "he understood much of the nature of the novel, saw deeply into its possibilities, and could penetrate to its central technical problems" (ibid., p. 382).

28. *Letters*, III, 151. The MSS are now at The Henry E. Huntington Library.

29. This letter, undated, without address or signature, is transcribed from a copy made by Mary Cowden Clarke, in the Novello-Cowden Clarke Collection of the Brotherton Library of the University of Leeds, by whose permission it is here reproduced. It

obviously antedates the publication of Clarke's *Tales* of 1833 and postdates Lamb's letter to Clarke on the same subject, asking "where is the Prioress's Tale" (Lucas No. 900), which is incorrectly transcribed and too dogmatically dated "P.M. 14th April 1832." The original of No. 900 (The Henry W. and Albert A. Berg Collection, New York Public Library) shows that this is the postmark for a letter addressed *to* Lamb, who apparently wrote his note on a blank portion of Clarke's letter to him. Lamb did not address his letter and there is no other postmark. More precisely, then, No. 900 was written sometime after April 14, 1832. The allusion to "mirth" in the letter here transcribed suggests the Christmas season of 1832 as a possible date. Both letters were authenticated by Clarke: "Charles Lamb's writing C. C. C."

30. See *Letters*, II, 278, 426, 437.

31. Hazlitt, "On Persons One Would Wish to Have Seen."

32. *Letters*, II, 410; Lucas gives 1823 as the date, but, though Lamb's writing of the last digit is indefinite ("India-House, 9 Dec 2[?]"), the postmark is definitely December 10, [1]822. This item is now in the Lilly Library of Indiana University, inserted in Lamb's black-letter Chaucer, referred to in this letter; I am indebted to the Lilly Library for permission to examine and quote from it. For further comments by Lamb on *Faust*, see his letter to Coleridge of August 26, 1814, and Robinson's *Diary* for August 25, 1811.

33. A. G. van Kranendonk, "Notes on the Style of the Essays of Elia," *English Studies*, XIV (Feb., 1932), 5.

34. "Lamb and Milton," *SP*, XXXI (Jan., 1934), 92.

35. "Lamb and Spenser," *SP*, XXX (Apr., 1933), 207.

36. "Lamb and Spenser Again, *SP*, XXX (July, 1933), 534.

37. *The Best Letters of William Cowper*, ed. A. B. McMahan (Chicago, 1893), pp. 96–97.

38. *Letters*, III, 105.

39. "The Wedding," *Works*, II, 239–43.

40. *The Autobiography and Memoirs of Benjamin Robert Haydon* . . . , ed. Tom Taylor (New York, 1926), I, 269–71 (Dec. 28, 1817).

41. "The Wedding," *Works*, II, 239–43.

42. "The Wife of Abraham Lincoln," *Wives* (New York & London, 1925), p. 21.

43. *Letters*, I, 180.

44. Iseman (*A Perfect Sympathy*, pp. 20–23) found a parallel between a passage on bells in "New Year's Eve" and two passages in

Religio Medici and another between a passage in "On the Melancholy of Tailors" and phrases in *The Garden of Cyrus*, the *Letter to a Friend*, and *Vulgar Errors*.

45. Ibid., pp. 24–25.

46. Ibid., p. 58.

47. "Sir Thomas Browne," *Appreciations* (New York, 1911), p. 124.

48. See Iseman, op. cit., pp. 47–48 and 147 note.

49. *Mary and Charles Lamb*, p. 153 note.

50. Louise Griswold, "The Diction of Charles Lamb," *Quarterly Journal of the University of North Dakota*, XVII (Apr., 1927), 234–35.

51. *Sir Thomas Browne*, English Men of Letters Series (New York, 1905), p. 193.

52. Iseman, op. cit., p. 26.

53. "A la base du style de Lamb, il y a l'attrait que le mot exerce sur son esprit . . . . Le style de Lamb est donc un style de mots. La phrase ne vient pas d'un bloc, si l'on peut dire, mais elle s'agrège autour d'un mot . . . . Le mot arrête attention . . . . Le mot, arrivant dans l'esprit de Lamb chargé de toutes les associations qu'il comporte, se fait sentir sur toute la phrase et sur les phrases qui suivent." *Charles Lamb*, pp. 368–69.

54. *Letters*, II, 91.

55. Ibid., p. 41.

56. Ibid., p. 387.

57. Charles and Mary Cowden Clarke, *Recollections of Writers* (New York, 1878), p. 55.

58. E. V. Lucas has traced most of the quotations in his notes to the essays in *Works;* subsequent Elians have identified other borrowings.

59. *Letters*, II, 400.

60. Ibid., pp. 369–70.

61. Thomas Powell, *The Living Authors of England*, pp. 230–31.

62. The three lines quoted in "The Ass" were copied in a letter of May 16, 1820, to Collier; the phrase from Drayton in "The Good Clerk" was used in a letter of September 19, 1814, to Wordsworth; the motto for "The Superannuated Man," attributed to O'Keefe, was incorporated in a letter of August 9, 1815, to Wordsworth; and the phrase "cherishers of my infancy" in *Rosamund Gray*, which has never been traced, is used in a letter of February 13, 1797, to Coleridge, in reference to Aunt Hetty. The quotation from Vanbrugh's

"Relapse" in "Detached Thoughts" was again used in "Reminiscence of Sir Jeffery Dunstan," and part of it is found in a letter of November 25, 1819, to Dorothy Wordsworth; Fuller's description of Negroes as "images of God cut in ebony" is found in the "Specimens from the Writings of Fuller" and in "Imperfect Sympathies"; the quotation from Robert Howard's "Vestal Virgin" in "The Superannuated Man" is also found in "Serious Fragments," at the end of the *Extracts from the Garrick Plays.*

63. Line 262.

64. "Charles Lamb," *Collected Writings,* V, 237.

65. *Letters,* I, 117.

66. Unless otherwise noted, the quotations discussed are those in the essays.

67. *Eunuchus,* II, iii, 6: "These daily forms annoy me."

68. *Letters,* I, 30; II, 319.

69. The quotation from *Tristia* was used in a letter of November 25, 1819, to Dorothy Wordsworth; one of those from Juvenal was used in a letter of November 30, 1829, to James Gillman.

70. Two quotations from Psalms are found in a letter of January 10, 1797, to Coleridge, and in one to Sir Anthony Carlisle that is undated (*Letters,* III, 286).

71. Lines 502, 514-17, 536-37, 541-43 (twice), 567-69; the others are lines 391, 768, 294-96 (twice).

72. Lines 164, 628, 672-73, 708-11, 964-65.

73. Lines 445-58, 466-67, 470-71, 471-72, 478-79, 484-93; the other three are lines 17, 51-52, 588-90.

74. Lines 268-71, 278-79; the others are lines 181, 338-40, 1013-15.

75. X, lines 279, 507-9 & 521-26, 524, 699; VI, lines 578-80, 767-68; XI, line 244.

76. VII, line 23; VIII, line 454; IX, line 445; XII, line 644.

77. II, lines 7, 264-78, 277-78, 340-47, 455-56; IV, lines 400, 425.

78. *Comus,* lines 151-53, 175-77, 221-22, 263-64, 398, 980-83; *Il Penseroso,* lines 28-30, 39, 49-50, 83-84; *Lycidas,* lines 50-51, 124, 153-55; *Samson Agonistes,* line 1695. There are also two quotations from the "Hymn on the Morning of Christ's Nativity"; a reference to, and a quotation from, the "Tractate on Education"; and quotations from two or three minor pieces.

79. "I repeat, to this day, no verses to myself more frequently or

with kindlier emotion, than those of Spenser, where he speaks of this spot. 'there when they came, whereas those bricky towers . . . etc.' " "The Old Benchers of the Inner Temple." The earlier use was in "A Town Residence."

80. Lines 359–60 of Book II of Armstrong's *The Art of Preserving Health* (1744) are used in "Newspapers Thirty-Five Years Ago"; Lucas gave the wrong Christian name: "Mr. W. J. Craig ran these lines to earth in the Scottish poet, William Armstrong's *The Art* . . . ." (*Works*, II, 442).

81. The mention of Cresseid begging in "A Complaint of the Decay of Beggars" may have come from Henryson's *Testament of Cresseid*, but Lamb could have had in mind *Twelfth Night*, III, i, 62.

82. This is attributed to Brooke in Ward's *English Poets* chiefly on Lamb's authority: "from internal testimony I believe to be Lord Brooke's" ("Some Sonnets of Sir Philip Sidney"). See also Lamb's letter of May 16, 1820, to Collier. It has variously been attributed to Sir Edward Dyer and to Raleigh.

83. *Letters*, II, 157.

84. Ibid., p. 299.

85. Ariel's song, mentioned in "Rejoicings upon the New Year's Coming of Age," was often applied by Lamb to his feelings on coming home on the coachman's back after indulging too freely in his host's hospitality. See the letter of May, 1809, to Robinson and the undated ones to Dr. J. Vale Asbury (*Letters*, III, 265) and to H. F. Cary (*Letters*, III, 406).

86. The unmarked phrase "My sight dazzles," in his "Reflections in the Pillory," may be a recollection of "Cover her face: mine eyes dazzle: she died young."

87. "He was his 'flapper,' " in "The Old Benchers," may allude to the practice of keeping Laputans awake in *Gulliver's Travels* by striking them with air-filled bladders.

88. *Letters*, III, 89.

89. Jan. 27, 1835 (quoted in *The Letters of Charles Lamb*, ed. H. H. Harper, I, 63).

90. *Letters*, III, 77.

91. *Letters of the Wordsworth Family*, ed. William Knight (Boston & London, 1907), II, 76.

92. *Table Talk*, Aug. 6, 1832.

A Selected Bibliography

EDITIONS

Fitzgerald, Percy (ed.). *The Life, Letters, and Writings of Charles Lamb.* 6 vols. London: Constable, 1875.

Harper, H. H. (ed.). *The Letters of Charles Lamb.* 5 vols. Boston: Boston Bibliophile Society, 1905.

Hutchinson, Thomas (ed.). *The Works of Charles Lamb.* 2 vols. London: Oxford University Press, 1908.

Lucas, E. V. (ed.). *The Works of Charles and Mary Lamb.* 7 vols. London: Methuen, 1903–5.

——— (ed.). *The Letters of Charles Lamb: To Which Are Added Those of His Sister Mary Lamb.* 3 vols. London: Dent & Methuen, 1935.

Macdonald, William (ed.). *The Works of Charles Lamb.* 12 vols. New York: Dutton and London: Dent, 1903–4.

BIOGRAPHY AND CRITICISM

Ainger, Alfred. *Charles Lamb.* English Men of Letters Series. London & New York: Harper & Brothers, 1882.

Barnett, George L. and Stuart M. Tave. "Charles Lamb," in *The English Romantic Poets and Essayists: A Review of Research and Criticism,* ed. Carolyn W. Houtchens and Lawrence H. Houtchens. New York: The Modern Language Association of America, 1957.

Blunden, Edmund. *Charles Lamb and His Contemporaries.* Cambridge: Cambridge University Press; New York: Macmillan, 1933.

Blunden, Edmund (comp.). *Charles Lamb: His Life Recorded by His Contemporaries.* London: Hogarth Press, 1934.

Derocquigny, Jules. *Charles Lamb: sa vie et ses œuvres.* Lille, 1904.

Hine, R. L. *Charles Lamb and His Hertfordshire.* New York: Macmillan, 1949.

Johnson, Edith. *Lamb Always Elia.* London: Methuen, 1935.

Lucas, E. V. *The Life of Charles Lamb,* 2 vols. London: Methuen, 1905; rev., 1921.

Ross, E. C. *The Ordeal of Bridget Elia.* Norman, Okla.: University of Oklahoma Press, 1940.

INDEX

Acrostic: on Harriet Isola, 14–15

Addison: Lamb on, 22, 42–44; essays of, 23, 24, 26, 35; contrast with Lamb, 32

Agriculture: ignorance of, 10

Albion, The: association with, 15

Albums: protest against, 97

Allen, Robert: at Christ's, 49

Allsop, Thomas: unpublished letters to, 59

"Amicus Redivivus": factual basis of, 50–52

Ampersand: and expansion of, 154

Anecdotes: from letters, 98

Anti-Jacobin, The, 28

"Appearance of the Season, An": MS compared with printed texts, 144–46

Armstrong, John: quotation from, 223

Ascham, Roger: letters of, 77

Ashmole, Elias: quotation from, 228

Asparagus: Lamb on, 53

"Ass, The": source of idea, 89

Ayrton, William: friendship with, 54, 61

"Bachelor's Complaint, A": reprinting of, 40

Bacon, Francis: contrast with Montaigne, 21; quotation from, 228

Baldwin, Robert: and the *London*, 30

"Barbara S——": Addisonian tendency, 41; based on Fanny Kelly, 49

Barnfield, Richard: quotation from, 224

"Barrenness of the Imaginative Faculty": MSS of, 176, 261n1; change in title, 264n26

Barton, Bernard: letters to, 10, 13, 31, 52, 54, 116; and the *London*, 31; letter to compared with essay 81–82; advice to, 115–16

Battle, Mrs.: reality of, 47, 61

Beaumont, Francis: quotation from, 224

Bee, The: no longer read, 4; characteristics of, 24; review of, 25

Beggar: in "Dissertation," 153–54

Betham, Matilda: letter to, 98

Bible: quotations from, 222

Bickerstaff, Isaac. *See* Steele

Blackford, Martha. *See* Stoddart, Lady Isabella

Blackwood's Magazine: essays in, 27; Lamb on, 29

273